ELIGIOUS PLURALISM

and the

NIGERIAN STATE

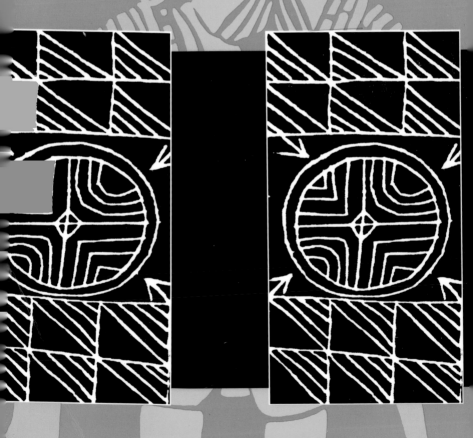

Simeon O. Ilesanmi

Religious Pluralism and
the Nigerian State

This series of publications on Africa, Latin America, and Southeast Asia is designed to present significant research, translation, and opinion to area specialists and to a wide community of persons interested in world affairs. The editor seeks manuscripts of quality on any subject and can generally make a decision regarding publication within three months of receipt of the original work. Production methods generally permit a work to appear within one year of acceptance. The editor works closely with authors to produce a high quality book. The series appears in a paperback format and is distributed worldwide. For more information, contact the executive editor at Ohio University Press, Scott Quadrangle, University Terrace, Athens, Ohio 45701.

Executive editor: Gillian Berchowitz
AREA CONSULTANTS
Africa: Diane Ciekawy
Latin America: Thomas Walker
Southeast Asia: James L. Cobban

The Monographs in International Studies series is published for the Center for International Studies by the Ohio University Press. The views expressed in individual monographs are those of the authors and should not be considered to represent the policies or beliefs of the Center for International Studies, the Ohio Univeristy Press, or Ohio University.

Religious Pluralism and the Nigerian State

Simeon O. Ilesanmi

Ohio University Center for International Studies
Monographs in International Studies
Africa Series, No. 66
Athens

Published in association with
Religions of Africa
a series of the
African Association for the Study of Religions

© 1997 by the
Center for International Studies
Ohio University
Printed in the United States of America
All rights reserved
03 02 01 00 99 98 97   5 4 3 2 1

The books in the Center for International Studies Monograph Series
are printed on acid-free paper ∞

Library of Congress Cataloging-in-Publication Data

Ilesanmi, Simeon O., 1963-
    Religious pluralism and the Nigerian state / by Simeon O.
Ilesanmi.
        p.   cm. — (Monographs in international studies. Africa
series ; no. 66)
    Includes bibliographical references and index.
    ISBN 0-89680-194-2 (pbk. : alk. paper)
    1. Religious pluralism—Nigeria.   2. Religion and state—Nigeria.
3. Nigeria—Politics and government—1960-   4. Nigeria—Religion.
I. Title.   II. Series.
BL2470.N5I37   1996
291.1'72'09669—dc20
                                                        96-33643
                                                        CIP

Religions of Africa is edited by Jacob K. Olupona and David Westerlund. The series covers all forms of religion found in Africa. Works on religions of African origin in other parts of the world may also be included. Special attempts are made to encourage African scholars to contribute to the series. The series is published by several publishers. It is open not only to scholars of religion but also other academics who write on African religions. For further information, please contact Professor Jacob K. Olupona, African-American and African Studies Program, University of California, Davis, CA 95616, USA or Associate Professor David Westerlund, History of Religions, Faculty of Theology, University of Uppsala, Box 1604, S-75146, Sweden.

The African Association for the Study of Religions, which is affiliated to the International Association for the History of Religions, was formed in Harare, Zimbabwe, in 1992. It aims to promote the academic study of African religions; and it is open to all scholars in African studies, whether resident in Africa or elsewhere. For more information, please contact the secretary, Dr. Abdulkader Tayob, Department of Religious Studies, University of Cape Town, Private Bag Rondebosch 7700, Cape Town, South Africa.

Religious Pluralism and the Nigerian State is the second volume in the Religions of Africa series.
ISSN number 1026-9355

For Bola and Adeolu

Contents

Foreword

With great skill, elegance, and mastery of the literature, Dr. Simeon O. Ilesanmi has moved the study of religion in contemporary Nigeria to its highest peak. Religion in Nigeria is as diverse as its people, with millions of people subscribing to varieties of Islam, Christianity, and local religions. This diversity is both a source of strength and weakness. There is strength in the choices that individuals make, and in the beauties of religious self-presentations. However, one weakness has become obvious: pluralism endangers political stability.

What dominates Dr. Ilesanmi's study is the elaboration of pluralism in Nigerian politics, with a focus on its troubles and how they can be overcome. The study offers a brilliant combination of ideas from theology, political science, sociology, history, religious studies, and philosophy. The book owes its success to the competence of Dr. Ilesanmi to use these ideas to explain the Nigerian situation in a way that is unique, engaging, learned, and stimulating. The appreciation of the theoretical works on pluralism offers yet another direction, one which makes the book both dense and analytical. This book is an effective reminder of the complex nature of religion, something that is lost in most contemporary accounts of Nigeria. It achieves a level of sympathetic and nuanced criticism of religion itself.

Why do Nigerian Muslims and Christians fight? How do religious leaders define the state and power? How can the Nigerian state achieve stability in the face of competing worldviews? How can different ethnic groups agree on issues of law and philosophy so that they can live in one united country? These are some of the profound questions that Dr. Ilesanmi helps to address. His answers and criticisms are wisely organized around the theme of pluralism, a concept which outlines a problem and at the same time explains and defines the solution. He succeeds as well in presenting an interpretive examination of the impact of religion on the state, in interrogating the past, and in reworking beliefs about present identities. He affirms that pluralism is an acceptable feature, rather than an obstacle to a modern state.

Each chapter illuminates a dimension of the major theme in a way that engages and provokes the reader in a personal fashion. The book offers more than its title promises—it is not just about Nigeria, but also a critical examination of theories about state and religion. The argument on pluralism is carefully constructed, well written, and grounded in theoretical and empirical evidence. In general, Dr. Ilesanmi's style is lucid and vivid, and the presentation is very persuasive.

This important book, destined to stand the test of time, is provocative, engaging, and ambitious. Here is one of the finest works on the creation and re-creation of religious meanings in Nigeria, the relevance of applied ethics, the nature of religious representation, and the difficulty of constructing identities. It is the best study to date on the ethics of pluralism and self-fashioning with respect to religions in Nigeria. Dr. Ilesanmi's tolerance for pluralism has given us a superb book, one that moves Nigeria to the center stage of theoretical discourse.

All students of African religions owe the author a debt of gratitude for a marvelous work that provides generous and wide vision, uncommon learning, original insights, wisdom, information, and challenges.

Toyin Falola
University of Texas at Austin

Acknowledgments

I am pleased to take this opportunity to express my gratitude to those many people who have helped to make the present volume possible. Most of the research that went into the writing of this book was undertaken while I was a graduate student at Southern Methodist University. For their constant support and excellent supervision during those years, and for their continuing friendship since, I am particularly grateful to members of my dissertation committee: Professors Joseph L. Allen, Frederick S. Carney, and Dennis Cordell. But like most graduate students, my intellectual journey began considerably before the writing of my dissertation, and it has been influenced by a large community of teachers on three different continents. It was Professor Jacob K. Olupona who first taught me that the study of religion is about the study of society and of the values that underpin it, and that these values are usually articulated by and reflected in the patterns and dynamics of power relations within the society. At the time when choosing religion as a major was the least popular thing to do at the University of Ife, Olupona saved me from a morass of intellectual confusion. His candor, gentleness, zest, and subtle guidance made my work more productive, certainly, but above all an enjoyable and relaxed adventure. But if Olupona laid the foundation for my socio-scientific understanding of religion, it was Joseph Allen who enabled me to see the issue of religion and politics as a moral quandary. To him more than any other individual I owe my present ethical understanding of the complex relations between religious convictions and socio-political realities. His moral support at those times of self-doubt that every young scholar must surely experience has been invaluable. Professors William F. May, Charles M. Wood, Schubert M. Ogden, David Martin, William S. Babcock, Steven Sverdlik, and Theodore Walker have all exemplified for me the ideal of humanistic thought and expression to which this book inadequately aspires, and instructed me in the mode of ethical and interdisciplinary inquiry which this book inadequately represents.

A financial grant from the Methodist Church, Overseas Division, United Kingdom, in conjunction with the British Foreign Office and the Churches Commission on Overseas Students, enabled me to spend a year of research at the School of Oriental and African Studies, University of London. I am grateful to Miss Susan F. Barr, Secretary of the MCOD scholarship program, and to Professors John Peel, Donal Cruise O'Brien, Louis Brenner, and Richard Jeffries, who directed my studies at SOAS.

In revising the dissertation for publication, I have benefited immensely from the stimulating and unsparing criticisms and insights of several individuals. Professors Segun Gbadegesin and Toyin Falola, the first people outside the walls of Southern Methodist University to read the project, gave me the confidence to believe that the idea was not limited to a doctoral rite of passage, and I will never forget their exceptional kindness. I also wish to record my gratitude to Professors Lamin Sanneh, Bruce Grelle, Sumner B. Twiss, Femi Taiwo, and Mary Ellen Chijioke for their constructive criticisms and comparative insights. One is, of course, responsible for what one makes of one's inheritance. The mistakes are mine.

Wake Forest University and, in particular, my department, have, over the past three years, provided a tolerant forum for me to advance, in more or less coherent form, many of the arguments and concepts here. I have learned much from comments offered by my colleagues Win-Chiat Lee and Alton Pollard, and have enjoyed the generous moral and collegial support of Provost David Brown, Dean Paul Escott, Professors Thomas Mullen, Samuel T. Gladding, Fred Horton, Ralph Wood, Charles Talbert, John Collins, Stephen Boyd, Kenneth Hoglund, and Ulrike Wiethaus. My graduate student, Christia J. Hayes, who labored over the index, is a truly remarkable woman who has become a steadfast friend. It is my sacred honor to count all these Wake Forest members as lifelong companions of my heart. In comparison with their love, beauty, and humility, their considerable help with the book pales in importance.

The transformation of a rather less wieldy manuscript into a more concise book has been facilitated by the professionally competent and sympathetic support of Ohio University Press. The comments of its two anonymous reviewers have prodded me to make certain corrections and clarifications of substance, while the sustained editorial work of Gillian Berchowitz has much enhanced the book's readability. Most recently, I have become acquainted with Professor David Westerlund of Uppsala University in Sweden. He not only suggested the idea that the book be included in the African Association for the Study of Religions series, but his critical readings have also helped to shape this study in its final stages.

The occasional tedium of writing has always been turned to joy by the boundless love with which I have been surrounded by members of my family. My uncle, Archbishop Timothy A. Akinnigbagbe, now rests in the bosom of God; I can do no more than cherish his memory and his unparalleled contributions to my personal, as well as intellectual, development. Equally deserving of my deepest gratitude are my aunt, Mrs. Abigail O. Akinnigbabge; my father, Chief Abraham Ilesanmi; my mother, Mrs. Abigail Ilesanmi; my parents-in-law, Bishop and Mrs. Ayo Ladigbolu; my uncle and his wife, Mr. and Mrs. Ayo Oni; my brothers, Mr. Banjo Akinnigbagbe and Mr. Ayodele Ilesanmi; and my cousin, Dr. Ayodele Ojo, for the constancy of their love and support since I began my academic voyage in the United States. Niran Olayinka, Niyi Oladipo, Paschal Uwakwe, and Akintunde Akinade are dear and loyal friends whose individual contributions to my life cannot be rendered in words.

Finally, I express my appreciation to my wife, Adebola, and daughter, Adeolu, who labored alongside me, sharing encounters with trying obstacles as well as experiencing moments of discovery, while offering the emotional strength that makes a scholarly project such as this worthwhile. I dedicate this book to both of them as an expression of our shared hope in the continuing manyness and oneness of our family.

Abbreviations

AFRC	Armed Forces Ruling Council
AG	Action Group
BYM	Bornu Youth Movement
CAN	Christian Association of Nigeria
CCN	Christian Council of Nigeria
CDC	Constitution Drafting Committee
CMS	Church Missionary Society
KPP	Kano People's Party
MAMSER	[Directorate for Public Enlightenment and Social Mobilization]
NAS	Native Authority System
NCNC	National Council of Nigerian Citizens
NEPU	Northern [Nigerian] Elements Progressive Union
NML	National Muslim League
NPC	Northern People's Congress
NSCIA	Nigerian Supreme Council for Islamic Affairs
OIC	Organization of Islamic Conference
SAP	Structural Adjustment Program
SCM	Student Christian Movement of Nigeria
SIM	Sudan Interior Mission
SMC	Supreme Military Council
SUM	Sudan United Mission
UMBC	United Middle Belt Congress
UMP	United Muslim Party
UPN	United Party of Nigeria

Introduction

> . . . Whatever we may say about liberality
> and equality, as long as you identify one cul-
> ture, one race, one religion as your key con-
> cept for defining the public agenda, you may
> be magnanimous, you may be humane, you
> may be tolerant, but those who are outside
> that faith can never feel that they are equal.
>
> —*Francis Deng,* "Let's Define Arab and Afri-
> can in Terms That Will Shed Light on the
> Common Ground"

In the last decade of the twentieth century, the widespread
collapse of communism has been hailed as ushering in a unique
opportunity for the politics of liberal democracy to establish
itself as the unchallenged global ideological orthodoxy. However, the striking resurgence, on a near global scale, of ethnic
conflicts and the politics of religious affirmation serve as cautionary reminders of the divisive potential of identities in states
characterized by cultural, religious, and linguistic diversity. Unlike in the modern West, where religion has been a minimal or
even missing dimension of statecraft, in other societies religious considerations are inseparably and symbiotically linked
to politics. Many of these plural societies are having to address
with renewed urgency the dilemma of how to reconcile, on the
one hand, the compulsions for national integration and, on the
other, the tolerance of differences that is imperative for the
building and preservation of viable states.

In this book, I undertake a socio-ethical study of this dilemma as it has manifested itself in Nigeria. More specifically,
I address the ethical problems involved in the competition between the creation of a powerful sense of identity based on religion and the sustenance of a pluralist and democratic Nigerian

state. The crisis of religion and the state is relatively modern in Nigerian political history. To an extent, precolonial Nigeria was monolithic, in that the sacred and the secular were not artificially bifurcated. Every adventure of life, as well as all instruments of governance and survival, were clothed in religious ritual, language, and symbolism.[1] But colonialism introduced a dimension of ambiguity to public life in Nigeria.

By drawing peoples of different faith traditions into one geographical orbit, colonialism accentuated and broadened the provincialized pluralism that was already present in Nigerian society. Missionary Christianity, which conceded to the state the uninhibited right to define political questions, was brought into conjunction with an all-encompassing and integralist Islamic faith within the same territorial framework. Each of these world religions has often claimed to be the main bastion of civilization and has perceived the other to be religiously inferior and a danger to the integrity and unity of the state. Moreover, the initial coincidence of region, religion, and ethnicity led to the emergence of distinctive social histories and disparate sacred geographies within a single polity.

The conjunction of two major proselytizing religions in the country, their rival claims to superiority, and the erstwhile political regionalization of missionary activities have blended together to make the nature and structure of Nigerian diversity more complex. But this is only one aspect of the colonialist impact on Nigerian life. Another contribution, and by far the more controversial, was the philosophy that undergirded the colonialist conception of the state. As a political ideology, colonialism was a child of the Enlightenment. Central to this ideology was the concept of progress, understood as a movement away from all forms of cultural conditioning.

On the attainment of independence in 1960, the political elite conceived of the Nigerian state as a significant center of value to which all loyalties must be channeled. Two distinct antinomic and contradictory strategies were adopted to steer the course of the envisioned absolutist Nigerian state. At one extreme were those who thought that particularist visions of life should be bracketed out of the civilizing process. Religious values in particular came to be disparaged by the state elite, including influential elements of the intelligentsia, as an expression of primordial sentiment and communal attachment that would quietly "wither away" with increased exposure to modernizing influence. Nationalist politicians and the contemporary ruling class in the country have held out the illusion that politics must be liberated from the encumbrance of religious atavism if the state is to catch up with the rest of the world. Not only is a distinctive religious socialization frowned upon, but public morality is also bereft of specific historic density and is reduced to what is believed to be minimum acceptable functional necessities, or approved political wisdom. In addition to the nationalist ideology of the fifties and sixties and the offensive of secularism, Austin Ahanotu also suggests such factors as "the transition from an oligarchic feudal state to a more democratic one, the emergence of a 'middle class' with its own secular values, . . . modernization, and revenues from petroleum"[2] to account for this ironic marginalization of religion.

Running concurrent with this perceptible project of demythologizing the state was a contrasting pattern of religious relativization palpably demonstrated by the ease with which the ruling class has habitually infected religious motivation with tactical rewards. This second crystallized articulation of religion entails a systemic remapping of the country by the politicians along confessional identities. Nigeria thus presents a spectacle in which religion is ambivalently involved in politics: a reality that refutes the generalized secularist assertion that only the "unenlightened" classes are attracted to the religious domain. Actually, the inflexible contradiction inherent in the modern Nigerian state is in part a consequence of a gyrated class patronage of religious influence.

This is the multilayered context in which to understand Nigeria's pluralist dilemma, a dilemma that has often expressed itself in recent years in terms of religious passion and civil tumult. First, there is a cultural scramble between Islam and Christianity for hegemony, a totalizing ambition to monopolize all the legitimizing structures of private and public life. Expressions of hegemonic tendencies among organized religions are, of course, not new; what is striking in the Nigerian case is the aggressive, and sometimes destabilizing, manner in which these tendencies impinge themselves upon public consciousness. The impact of this trend is most clearly seen in the upsurge of scholarly works aimed at demonstrating the cathartic efficacy of the concept of hegemony for an understanding of the factors and forces central to Nigerian politics, economy, and society. In his study of religious politics among the Yoruba Nigerians, for example, David Laitin observes the divergent patterns of hegemonic construction by the political elite, who use either coercion or negotiation, to institutionalize a pattern of their activity in the state and to ensure an idealization of their "schema into a dominant symbolic framework that reigns as common sense."[3] Other scholars go beyond the local provenance of ethno-religious politics to explain the multilevel operations of power within the country's social practices. According to Adigun Agbaje, the operative levels of power are not limited to the political elite; they include the press, the intelligentsia, professional associations, labor unions, and most notably, the religious institutions. Thus, for him, hegemony is a "social system of intra-cleavage and cross-cleavage relations in which power is secured and contested not only through direct and undisguised coercion but also via the agency of a broad popular consensus arrived at from the interplay of the dual claim of consent and dissent and achieved through and within political, economic, non-institutional, and moral means and levels of society."4

Whether at a micro-ethnic or macro-country level, it is abundantly clear that diverse social and cultural groups in Nigeria are involved in the construction, assertion, and counterassertion of hegemonic projects. The complex nature of this enterprise has tended to eclipse the second aspect of the Nigerian pluralist dilemma, which is the cultural imposition of Christianity and Islam over the residue of the indigenous religions. Finally, there is a competition between theological perspectives generally and the henotheism of state worship.

Recent scholarly efforts to explore the basic theoretical grounding for an understanding of the relation of religion and political life in Nigeria have failed to clarify the pluralistic context of this interaction, as well as the hegemonic pretensions of the state to regiment life on the basis of its own sociodicies. The issue has usually been posed as one of tension between private and public life or between the spiritual realm and the secular realm. There are some social and political theorists who see the recent high-profile involvement of Nigerian communities of faith in sociopolitical issues as an indicator of their recalcitrance to imbibe secularist prescriptions, which are understood as guaranteed pillars of modern civilization. Moreover, there are others who view such involvement as nothing but a manipulative strategy of the politicians to foster their selfish ambitions.

While not seriously challenging the factual assertions accompanying these explanations, it is the thesis of this book that their fundamental premise is significantly flawed. What is presupposed in most of these analyses is a dichotomy of life in which religion is assigned a private role while the state is defined coextensively with the public. Unfortunately, such positions have inadvertently continued to reinforce the polarizing potential of dogmatic proclivities of certain religious authori-

ties toward public issues. Properly understood, religion itself is
a constant reminder of the unity of public and private life, but
also of the boundary between them. Although religion and
politics are different realms, they nevertheless need each other.
The validity and the distinctive character of each contributes to
a healthy society. Religious imagination affirms the public-
private distinction, and also the unity that lies beneath that distinction.[5]

To be sure, the confusion over the appropriate way in which
religious convictions should be related to matters of great social and political import extends beyond the academic community. Religious persons themselves are not univocal on this
fundamental issue, and the Nigerian experience is not an iso-
lated case. There are, for example, disagreements between
Protestants and Catholics in Northern Ireland; the Muslims,
Druze, and Christians in Lebanon; Christian Armenians and
Azerbaijani Muslims; Hindu Tamils and Buddhist Singhalese
in Sri Lanka; Muslims, and Orthodox and Catholic Christians
in the former Yugoslavia; Sikhs and Hindus in India. How
then might the discourse on religion and the Nigerian state be
enriched?

As a work in applied ethics, this book will explore certain
normative models, motives, paradigms, and themes which
might guide our reflection about many of the basic features of
religious and civil life in Nigeria. I will attempt to clarify the
complex connections among religion, politics, and the Nigerian state. Efforts at clarification will be subordinate, however,
to a normative concern. I hope to show in this work that one
prerequisite to any enduring civic amity in Nigeria is a public
philosophy—that is, a set of principles, vibrant enough to motivate the general participation of all religious and nonreligious groups, despite their differences, in the oneness of the
nation. Moreover, I will argue that such a public philosophy, if
found, need not hinder the maintenance by each group of its

own distinctive identity. This basic concern is congruent with the objective of moral reflection. The task of ethics, it has been argued, is to supply a type of *corrective* vision: "Ethics relies heavily on the distinction between what is and what ought to be. Such corrective vision, however, challenges not so much the world the descriptive sciences see as the world distorted through the bias of institutional structures or through the prism of human imperfection and vice."[6]

The analytical task of the book will be marked by a polymethodic focus. I shall combine historical, theological, philosophical, political, and sociological approaches to the normative question of how Nigeria's varied groups can be united by a common agreement about laws and rights and a common desire for mutual, not just selfish, advantage. This interdisciplinary approach is dictated by the nature of the problem to be examined and the variety of existing perspectives from which it has been usually studied. There is the need to provide a synthetic conceptual framework for assessing extant works on the relationship between religion and the Nigerian state. More significantly, such a framework has the added value of guiding further reflections on how to reduce the strains created by the interaction between these two institutions.

In developing my constructive and normative arguments, I have drawn especially upon the works of John Courtney Murray, Ibn Khaldūn, Lamin Sanneh, Crawford Young, John Peel, Michael J. Perry, and Robin W. Lovin. It is the focus of these thinkers on the theme of pluralism that makes their approaches relevant to a study of Nigerian society. Their frameworks avoid the error of those who prematurely blame religion for the crisis of public life, as well as the theocratic perspective of those who seek to clothe the state with their particularist and narrowly conceived religious ideology. For these thinkers, the pluralist dilemma introduced by the presence of many religions cannot be resolved without asking broader questions of political culture, questions which have to do with the web of beliefs that people have about their political system, the mechanisms they develop to sustain that system, and the characteristic patterns of political interaction among them.

The central question of the book is, then, not one to be answered merely in a descriptive way. It has a normative import which is in fact lexically prior to descriptive analysis. In my deployment of these theoretical resources in the study of Nigeria's pluralist dilemma, I pose two different normative questions. First, what kind of *political framework* would more fully encourage just relationships between the state and the varied religious constituencies? Second, what kind of *political and religious attitudes* would most encourage a sense of mutual acceptance within which the differing particularistic religious allegiances can find both their freedom and their limits?

I intend to answer these questions in a way that shows pluralism to be an acceptable feature of religious and political life, and not an obstacle to be overcome. Toward this end, two criteria are stipulated for measuring the adequacy of any precepts on how to relate religion to the state. The first is the extent to which a particular mode of religious engagement with sociopolitical issues avoids the evil of *religious imperialism;* and the second is the extent to which the policy of the state toward religion reflects an appreciation for and a conscious effort to promote the moral-political virtues of justice, liberty, and equality. The first criterion is especially important for our overall understanding of the religious terrain. It is inspired by the method of historical research developed and refined during the nineteenth century, and which has had considerable influence on the study of religion. In contrast to the old dogmatic and authoritarian method of theology, Ernst Troeltsch argues that historical research presupposes "the interaction of all phenomena in the history of civilization."[7] The significance of this assertion is that all historical matters, including religion, are taken to emerge out of, and to be conditioned by, other historical events. This new historical consciousness has a twofold effect on our view of religion. It not only relativizes one's own tradition, thereby preventing imperialistic religious projects but it also opens up the possibility of appreciating the worth of alternative religious traditions as they are investigated within their own historical contexts.

In addition to the theoretical sources referred to above, I also made extensive use of Nigerian churches' synodal and conference statements, communiqués, pastoral letters, and other documents from both the religious and nonreligious circles (e.g., newspapers and magazines) dealing with the question of religion and public life in a pluralistic context. Although I did not administer any formal questionnaire, I interviewed a wide spectrum of Nigerian citizens—religious authorities, students, members of professional associations, politicians, and a few past and present state officials for the purpose of broadening my awareness of the range and substance of views that Nigerians have about the relationship of religion, politics, and the state.

If justification is required for the undertaking of this study, it can be argued that the crisis of the proper relation of the state to diverse religious allegiances has been the single most important issue in Nigeria's post-civil war history. This crisis has indeed become the plumb line for testing the capacity, or lack of it, of Nigeria as a nation-state to flourish or to founder. The country's contextual plurality creates many uncertainties about the normative ideas and ideals that should provide direction in judgment, decision, and conduct. While the number of debates and symposia on how best to resolve the crisis has multiplied in recent years, religious participants as well as state managers still find themselves confused about how to work out a harmonious relationship between two of their most important institutions. Extant scholarly works on this problem have hardly been helpful because of their inexcusable neglect of its ethical dimensions. Scholars of both religion and politics shy away from raising normative questions for fear of being branded sentimentalists or subjectivists. But by seeking to remain value neutral, they inadvertently impose the norm of normlessness on a space that can hardly sustain itself without a vision. Urgently needed, then, is a way to proceed in reflection that will help us to overcome the prevalent antinomy of intellectual biases.

The task of such moral reflection, as already indicated, is to turn a type of corrective lens upon issues and affairs in our social environment. A Nigerian religious ethicist, from his or her own particular perspective, has opportunity to engage in reflection that seeks to clarify the problematic herein identified, to construct a normative theory of political and religious life, and to critically evaluate the proposals and approaches that are put forward to ameliorate problems impeding that life. Essentially, I argue in this book that in order for Nigeria's diverse religious and nonreligious population to establish and maintain a civil amity, *it is both unnecessary and undesirable to strip the state of religious values, or conversely to make it the guardian of holy shrines; what is called for instead is to endow it with robust civility wherein "citizens of all religious faiths, or none, engage one another in continuing democratic discourse."*[8]

Since the issue of religion and the state has been and is so variously conceptualized, it is necessary to begin by clarifying the problem. Thus in chapter 1, I define the key concepts that are germane to the entire work. Then I turn to the literature on religion, politics, and the state in Nigeria to create a typology of theoretical stances in order to clarify how and why the discourse on religion and state in Nigeria is still in need of further inquiry. The chapter concludes with a comparative survey of classical texts in the history of religion and political philosophy as a way of announcing the lines of argument to be taken in subsequent chapters.

Chapter 2 introduces the concept of "dialogic politics" to present the ideas of my principal theoretical guides. The term is used in two different senses in this chapter. First, it designates a type of political community that is desirable for a religiously pluralistic political society. Second, it denotes a type of political method that is conducive to bringing about, and sustaining, such a political community. Correspondingly, dialogic politics also has two main objectives. First, it seeks to discern a common political ground in a plural society with major perspectival differences. Second, dialogic politics proposes a democratic framework marked by accountability, public conversation, mutual respect, and the spirit of humility, as one promising way of confronting the challenges of pluralism and the attendant fragmentation of moral meaning in public life.

Besides theoretical views on the problem of religion and the Nigerian state, there is the need to inquire about the modes in which these two institutions have interacted historically. I address this concern in chapters 3 and 4. Chapter 3 covers the colonial period up to the end of Nigeria's First Republic, which ended in 1966. I endeavor to show how concerns for order, power, domination, freedom, and social justice shaped the patterns of interaction between religion and the political realm during that period. A special feature of that era was the regional basis of political participation, which hindered the development of a coherent national policy on the issue of religion and the state.

Chapter 4 examines the attempts since the early 1970s to rectify the problem identified in Chapter 3. An aspect of the post-civil war reconstruction involved a conscious attempt on the part of the Nigerian elite to develop a public philosophy which would provide an overarching perspective on the general problem of faith and civil life. Several elements of this emerging public philosophy are identified, as are also the problems that beset it: notably the ambiguity that still characterizes the discourse on religion and the state.

Chapter 5 presents an overview of the main thesis of the book and identifies its implications for religious and political life in Nigeria. The chapter also highlights some major problems that might impede the practical application of my thesis to a pluralistic society like Nigeria. The conclusion underscores the significance of my approach as a resource in the formulation of a normative theory of religion and the state, not only in Nigeria but in other societies as well.

Given the currents of thought in many so-called Third-World countries today, where the trend is in favor of asserting cultural and territorial particularity, a study of this nature risks being misconstrued as one further vestige of neocolonialist sentiment. I must point out, however, that throughout this study, the intent is not to impose alien concepts upon Nigerian reality. Rather, my theoretical and practical ambition is to explore the possibility of critically abstracting certain ethical insights from the sociocultural and political contexts in which they were originally proposed and to employ them for cross-cultural analysis. My hope is that this study will represent one constructive religious ethical response to the malaise of institutional decay, social unrest, and political instability that continue to undermine the legitimacy of Nigeria as a nation-state.

Notes

1. E. Bolaji Idowu, *African Traditional Religion: A Definition* (London: SCM, 1973), 84.

2. Austin Ahanotu, "Muslims and Christians in Nigeria: A Contemporary Political Discourse," in *Religion, State and Society in Con-*

temporary Africa: Nigeria, Sudan, South Africa, Zaire and Mozambique, ed. Austin M. Ahanotu (New York: Peter Lang, 1992), 12.

3. David Laitin, *Hegemony and Culture: Politics and Religious Change among the Yoruba* (Chicago: University of Chicago Press, 1986), 19.

4. Adigun A. B. Agbaje, *The Nigerian Press, Hegemony, and the Social Construction of Legitimacy 1960–1983* (Lewiston: Edwin Mellen Press, 1992), 18–19.

5. Douglas Sturm, "On the Reconstruction of Public Life in America: An Agenda," chap. in *Community and Alienation: Essays on Process Thought and Public Life* (Notre Dame, Ind.: University of Notre Dame Press, 1988), 10–30.

6. William F. May, *The Physician's Covenant: Images of the Healer in Medical Ethics* (Philadelphia: Westminster Press, 1983), 13–14.

7. Ernst Troeltsch, *Religion in History,* trans. James Luther Adams and Walter F. Bense (Minneapolis: Fortress Press, 1991), 13.

8. Michael J. Perry, *Love and Power: The Role of Religion and Morality in American Politics* (New York: Oxford University Press, 1991), 45.

NIGERIA , 1976–1986 (19 States)

NIGERIA, 1991 (30 States)

Chapter 1

Theoretical Perspectives on Religion, Politics, and the State: The Nigerian Example

THE TITLE OF THIS chapter indicates its manifold purposes. The intention is, first, to clarify the issue of religion and the state by exploring a few definitions of the three working concepts central to the entire work, namely, pluralism, religion, and the state. Following this is a critical review of the existing theories of religion and the state in Nigeria. My agenda in this second part is to sift, shift, and realign these theories so as to reveal their progressive, as well as their inhibitive potential. Finally, I examine certain influential theories of religion and the state in the Islamic juristic tradition and in social and political philosophy. Here I inquire into the possibility of finding resources within these disciplines for initiating a fruitful political dialogue among people of diverse religions.

Concepts, Definitions, and Classifications

None of the three operative concepts in this study has lent itself to easy analysis and definition. Each has remained a very ambiguous, ubiquitous, and contentious term. Besides the individual thinker's interests, it has been observed that there are other factors such as "ideology, paradigm, culture, or context" which may influence the way in which a term is used or defined."[1] I hope the following analysis will enable the reader to discern salient issues that are theoretically and morally relevant to socio-ethical inquiry.

Pluralism

Ordinarily, *pluralism* is used as a synonym for diversity.[2] To some thinkers, however, it is a cherished theme in philosophical investigations. According to Rupert Breitling, pluralism is "an abstract principle of 'several' and 'many' contrasted with similar numerical principles of 'monism' and 'dualism.'"[3] So conceived, pluralism may designate a philosophical doctrine emphasizing the diversity of existence. William James emphasizes this philosophical thrust of pluralism when he claims that there are epistemological and existential warrants "for the legitimacy of the notion of some: each part of the world is in some ways connected, in some other ways not connected with its other parts, and the ways can be discriminated."[4]

Generally speaking, analysts use the concept of pluralism in three distinctive senses: sociological, political and normative.[5] A sociological use refers to how a society is constituted, whether in terms of its belief systems and moral visions or in terms of the various subunits or associations existing in that society. This kind of use could also refer to features with which people typically identify themselves, such as race, gender, ethnicity, and class. A sociological definition of pluralism is merely descriptive; it does not make value judgments about what is thereby described. It acknowledges diversity "as a fact that is worth noting."[6] Michael Perry provides an illustrative definition of this kind of use by designating a pluralistic society as that in which there are, among its members, "competing beliefs or convictions about the good or fitting way for human beings . . . to live their lives."[7]

Political pluralist theories focus on the distribution of political power. When used in the context of public affairs and political thought, pluralism refers to "specific institutional arrangements for distributing and sharing governmental power, to the doctrinal defense of these arrangements, and to an approach for gaining understanding of political behavior."[8] Like its sociological counterpart, a political pluralist theory is also descriptive. Neither of them proceeds from the analysis of society to an ideal vision of the future, nor from the analysis of human nature to an understanding of political life.

By contrast, normative pluralist theories are directional. Proponents of these are more interested in commending plurality as a good state of affairs than in a mere description of its features. Normative pluralist theories have two theoretical components, namely, anthropological and cognitive. An anthropological normative theory of pluralism "recognizes that whatever the nature and extent of their commonality, human beings generally differ from one another in important respects . . . and that therefore the way of life that is good for some of them may well not be good for all of them, and may even be bad for some (others) of them."[9]

Cognitive normative pluralist theory is concerned with the value we place on pluralism as a sociological and empirical fact. There are theorists who see pluralism as an evil to be conquered or overcome, and define a plural society as a bad type of society, defective primarily because of its lack of a social will or unity. In a series of studies on colonialism in southeast Asia, J. S. Furnivall rendered a plural society in purely political and administrative terms, and argued that in such a society, there is no social will, hence it is held together by an alien economic system and by force. He believed that democracy is impossible

3

in this type of society because democracy demands that the government be responsible to the people, and where there is no social will, there is no people.[10] Perry rejects that position, and proposes instead a positive understanding of pluralism, "according to which a morally (or religiously) pluralistic context can often be a much more fertile source of deepening moral insight than can a morally monistic context."[11]

I shall employ these different interpretations of pluralism in this work. As the work progresses, however, it will be evident that I argue for an appreciation of pluralism, especially of religious pluralism, with which this work is mainly concerned, as a positive element of life.

Religion and Religious Pluralism

Of my three operational concepts, religion is the most controversial, cheapened, misused, and misunderstood. Some definitions of religion appear to be nothing more than an ideological castigation or indictment of religion. Kent Greenawalt's observation in this regard is both cautionary and instructive. "A good many professors and other intellectuals," he says, "display a hostility or skeptical indifference to religion that often amounts to a thinly disguised contempt for belief in any reality beyond that discoverable by scientific inquiry or ordinary human experience."[12]

My purpose here is not to rehearse the definitions of religion that people have offered, or to identify schools of thought that may have correctly presented the truths of religion. E. Bolaji Idowu has shown in his study the near impossibility of providing a universally acceptable definition of religion. He reported the exploit of Professor Leuba, who collected forty-eight definitions of religion from forty-eight experts, added two of his own, and yet felt dissatisfied with all fifty.[13] I shall be using *religion* only referentially in this work "both in its

4

personalized sense of religiousness and in its institutionalized sense of denominations whose teachings and worship foster such religiousness."[14] Religion is part of, and interacts with, other elements of a society's culture, that is, the artificial social environment imposed on the natural environment, including language, habits, ideas, beliefs, customs, social organization, inherited artifacts, technical processes, and especially, values.[15]

Accordingly, *religious pluralism* will be used to refer to the presence of diverse "beliefs" and "communities" that are religious; that is, to the two prominent dimensions of the religious enterprise: the evaluative and the organizational. For a religiously pluralistic political community is one in which there is "the coexistence . . . of groups who hold divergent and incompatible views with regard to religious questions—those ultimate questions that concern the nature and destiny of man within a universe that stands under the reign of God."[16]

Granting the validity of these interpretations, we may ask: How should religious beliefs be related to the politics of a state with a deep-rooted pluralistic base structure? How should religious persons relate their beliefs to issues that are of public significance—issues that fall outside the exclusive jurisdiction of their particular religious communities and that have a great bearing on the lives and interests of other persons and other religious or nonreligious communities? What role should the state give to religious considerations—beliefs and communities—in its conduct of public affairs?

State

The general notion of the state, according to Pat Williams, "is varied, complex and controversial."[17] In its modern shape and form, the idea of the state began with Machiavelli in the sixteenth century, but it was not until 1648 that the doctrine of statehood became axiomatic for defining a political and administrative unit. The lapidary formula of the historic Peace of Westphalia (*cuius regio eius religio,* "whose the region, his the religion"; that is, the religion of a region would be determined by the religion of the ruler) established a basis for the subsequent apotheosis of the state. Against this backdrop, we have come to understand the doctrine in both descriptive and normative senses.

A state can be conceived of as "a geographically delimited segment of human society united by common obedience to a single sovereign."[18] Thus, to qualify as a state such an entity must be an association of people; these people must be politically organized, that is, they must be capable of acting collectively; and the entity must be located within a definite territory. This minimalist definition sums up a near canonical way of conceptualizing the state, in that we readily assume "territoriality and sovereignty" to be its "major universal properties."[19]

But conjoined to the notion of the state is that of "nation," itself commonly used to refer to the inhabitants of a state. So closely linked have the two concepts become that we readily regard the nation-state as the *ideal* unit of international politics. However, the concepts to which "state" and "nation" refer are different and should be distinguished. Even though 1648 marks the beginning of the modern state, states then were in at least one way very different from states today. States were then considered the property of the ruler; they could be bought, sold, traded, or used as security for loans. The compound expression *nation-state* was "a recent and novel development . . . which appeared on the scene at the time of the French Revolution, strongly influenced by the intellectual currents of that time," notably "the demise of the absolute state, the spread of the doctrine of popular sovereignty, and the crystallization of organized civil societies activated by a steadily enlarging franchise."[20] In effect, the idea of the "nation" added "emotional content to the purely juridical concept of citizenship."[21]

The assimilation of nation doctrine by states was a matter of practical necessity. The Euro-American societies saw nationhood as a means of generating a national identity, and in the Afro-Asiatic colonized world the doctrine "demonstrated its utility as anti-imperial weapon."[22] This integrative and transformative power of the national idea underlies the meaning we have come to associate with a nation, as denoting a human group bound together by common solidarity—a group whose members place loyalty to the group as a whole over any conflicting loyalties. J. S. Mill accents this affective bond inherent in national sentiments: "a portion of mankind may be said to constitute Nationality if they are united among themselves by common sympathies, which do not exist between them and any others—which make them cooperate with each other more willingly than with other people, desire to be under the same government, and desire that it should be government by themselves, or a portion of themselves, exclusively."[23]

Some Christian ethicists are, however, reluctant to endorse an unbridled proselytization of nationalist sentiments, for in their views such outlooks are often fed by illusions of power and grandeur. The idealistic pretensions of nation-states to invest themselves with transcendent moral sanctions and a quasi-religious sanctity are unquestionably evident today in the manner in which many authoritarian governments defiantly solidify the status quo, suppress dissent, rationalize economic interests, obstruct international cooperation, launch aggressive conquests, or wage total war. Because nations are nothing more than a collection of the self-interests of all the individuals contained within them, Reinhold Niebuhr asserts that neither nations nor their governments are morally innocent. Both are capable of self-deception, a persistent and perceptibly twofold evil in human society. One aspect of that self-deception is that the very loyalty and altruism of the individual citizen, which give her moral satisfaction as a person, tend to support her nation's most characteristic sins, its prideful ambition, its greed, and its will to power. As Niebuhr puts it, "patriotism transmutes individual unselfishness into national egoism." The second aspect is the tendency of nations to clothe the national will with idealistic pretensions. Thus, for Niebuhr, "the most significant moral characteristic of a nation is hypocrisy," and that hypocrisy is "the tribute which morality pays to immorality."[24]

Another problem with the definitions being explored here is their assumption that state and nation ought to absorb each other to the point that each state would come to represent one and only one nation. This vision has remained an *ideal* that hardly corresponds to any empirical reality. Not only are some states multinational, some nationalities are also spread over several states. Both of these features are strikingly present in modern African states that were created arbitrarily by Western imperial powers and that have only rarely the slightest historical pedigree or cultural coherence. The cultural contradictions inherent in the emergent African nation-states are certainly not unrelated to the present social and political disarray on the continent.

Moreover, the foregoing definitions of nation-states emphasize the political ability of the state to govern as well as the obligation and loyalty of the citizens to the state. Their main weakness, however, consists in the implicit endorsement of a monopolistic relationship between the state and its citizens. Without a theory of the state that accents not only the state's right to govern, but also it's responsibility to be just, citizens would be stripped of the moral resources needed to assess the quality of their government's performance. Properly understood, the relationship between the state and its citizenry is bipolar and dialogical. The state needs the support and loyalty of the civil society in order to remain a legitimate framework and the authoritative arena for conceptualizing identity and conflict. At the same, it has the responsibility to foster for its citizens a life more prosperous, just, and equitable.

That the state exists not just to govern, but also to be checked, points up a line of inquiry that is not merely descriptive but also normative. Jacques Maritain, a French Roman Catholic moral philosopher, posits two theories that are germane to an understanding of the moral nature of the state and its concomitant obligation. First, there is "an instrumentalist theory," which Maritain regarded as the foundation for "the genuinely political notion of state."[25] According to this theory, the state is "only that part of the body politic especially concerned with the maintenance of law, the promotion of the common welfare and public order, and the administration of public affairs. The state is a part which specializes in the interests of the whole."[26]

This interpretation differs considerably from the liberal political theories associated with John Locke, as well as from those totalizing and monolithic conceptions of life that provide the underlying rationale for many autocratic regimes. From the standpoint of social-contract theory, the state has no purpose beyond protecting the self-defined aims of the individuals who create it. Any suggestion of the need to forge a common ground or purpose that transcends the egoistic desire to maintain a neutral or an amoral state is considered to be a facile romanticism born out of nostalgia to revert to an exotic innocence— that is, an archaic return to a situation that is no longer existent or feasible.

The second theory of the state identified by Maritain promotes a "substantialist" or "absolutist" vision of political life. This theory, with all its seductions of totalizing thinking, regards the state as "a subject of right, i.e., a moral person, and consequently a whole; as a result it is either superimposed on the body politic or made to absorb the body politic entirely, and it enjoys supreme power by virtue of its own natural, inalienable right and for its own final sake."[27] Maritain rejected this theory because of its failure to recognize the many levels of interaction and associational life through which human life is enriched and relationships deepened. He insisted that any adequate definition of the state must enable us to discern the public relevance of the ethical notions of freedom and social justice;[28] for "the true dignity of the state comes not from power and prestige, but from the exercise of justice."[29] This is so because, as Niebuhr pointed out, human beings have two dimensions of existence, of which the state must be cognizant. First is their "spiritual stature and . . . social character," and second is "the uniqueness and variety of life."[30] For both of these aspects of life to flourish, it is necessary to prevent the state from destroying the vitality and freedom of component elements in the civil society in the name of order, and to ensure that there is neither domination of one life by another nor the enslavement of the weak by the strong.

I will use the above definitions of pluralism, religion, and the state as a prismatic basis for assessing certain theories of religion and state in Nigeria.

Theoretical Perspectives on Religion, Politics, and the State in Nigeria

In an illuminating commentary on the question of religion and politics, broadly construed, Mark A. Noll identifies three distinct levels at which judgments about the interaction of these two realms can be made. First is the level involving "the exercise of authority between the institutions of government and the structures of religion."[31] The second level, which focuses on "more mundane political behavior" is basically an attempt to explain the persistence of religion as a political influence in itself, as opposed to merely appearing as a dependent variable or surrogate for some other modern factor. The third level deals with "the fundamental ordering of society" or the "cultural balance of trade." The analytical focus at this level is on those "'rhetorical worlds' that bridge the domains of religion and politics—that is, . . . those deeply rooted assumptions that shape a community's perception of its role in both the eternal economy of God and the political economy of a nation."[32] Here, according to Noll, "the issue is not so much who controls whom, or who voted for whom, but the broader matter of how expectations, and symbols of a society's beliefs, practices, and communal values relate to the activities, expectations, and symbols of a society's public life."[33]

Noll's paradigms provide a valuable insight on how we might interpret the Nigerian data, although my aim in this section is not to explicate those data strictly on the basis of his typology. Rather, I plan to conduct an audit of what I take to be the assets and the liabilities of extant theories of religion and the state in Nigeria. Two dominant perspectives on religious politics are discernible in the current debate, namely, the privatization and the manipulation theses. Against the background of my theoretical balance sheet, I suggest another approach to understanding the dynamics of state-religion interactions in Nigeria. The hegemonic state thesis lays the foundation for the constructive project I undertake in this book. Here I argue that robust civility in both the religious and public spheres cannot be sufficiently present in Nigeria until citizens are first wrenched free of blind obedience to the self-defined ominicompetent state. The history of the postcolonial Nigerian state is a catalog of crimes against its citizens.

The Privatization Thesis

Some scholars and observers of Nigerian political and religious events have theorized that the continued failure of the country to establish and institutionalize itself as a nation-state is largely due to the unbridled rivalry among its religious segments. One Nigerian journalist bemoaned the way in which "Nigeria has become a hapless hostage to religion and its skilful manipulators."[34] A Roman Catholic priest also perceived in the activities of Islam and Christianity, the two religions that are "straddled across the Nigerian polity," the aim "to take over the architectural design and construction of the Nigerian polity."[35] In short, this school of thought establishes, through a diachronic analysis, a link between interfaith antagonism and political instability in Nigeria.

In a recent review of the post-1980s history of Nigeria, John O. Hunwick concludes that the period has been characterized by "an atmosphere of distrust."[36] The country has witnessed an increased "polarization of public opinion around widely differing philosophies of government and law."[37] More importantly, from this period emerges two conflicting dynamics within Nigeria. First is the resurgence of the *zamanin siyasa* (political party activities, 1979–1983), derived from a concert of efforts to civilianize and democratize Nigerian politics. The second aspect of these dynamics is that of Nigerians unwilling to ground this civilizing and democratizing vision upon more inclusive objectives. Since Nigeria was granted independence in 1960, Hunwick appositely remarks, "there have been no parties of any significance based on clear-cut political ideologies."[38] Contrariwise, interfaith intolerance, fanatical confessionalism, and homicidal religiosity have inserted themselves as permanent features of political interaction, thus establishing Nigeria's checkered political history as anything but predictable.

In effect, laudable and ambitious political projects on a national scale have been continually suppressed, understandably to the frustration of many, by uncivil religious parochialism— sometimes even under the disguise of ethnoconsciousness. According to an astute student of Nigerian affairs, A. H. M. Kirk-Greene, the seemingly customary crisis of Nigeria since Lord Lugard amalgamated the two protectorates of the south and north in 1914 has been an "inherent tug-of-war between the claims of belonging to the nation and the claim of local loyalty attaching to recognized diversity."[39]

Of particular relevance here is the claim that confessional loyalties in the country have actually degenerated into spiritual arrogance. This judgment is buttressed by the observable posture of some religious adherents whose only term of dialogue is a crusade or jihad. The prevailing pattern of religious behavior in Nigeria is, it is argued, the systemic transmutation of religion into "a weapon for revolutionary struggle, the creation of personal empires, the building of utopias and the pursuit of retrograde right-wing political objectives."[40] Another observer even goes as far as accusing "religious entrepreneurs" of theological duplicity, the abominable sin of supplanting the true God with humanly created gods. In a tone that reeks with crude patriotism, Don Ohadike asserts that Nigerian religious adherents are indisputably "obsessed with illusion" and live a life of atavistic escapism. He warns his fellow citizens of the "need to realize that any society that draws its entire inspiration from religion, whether traditional or universalistic, lives in the past. Such a society progresses in a cyclical fashion, living under the same old economic, legal, and political systems, and, in concrete terms, achieves nothing."[41]

Thus in the political calculations of Don Ohadike and the like, the presence of religion in politics constitutes an illicit courtship. For by the very nature of the case, the true God has no business with politics or economics; these are mundane zones that could defile God's pure nature. Not unlike the Old

Testament prophets, proponents of the privatization thesis posit that a secular compromise of divine purity would have both immediate and eschatological repercussions. Regardless of its merit, the following diatribe against religion by Sowande expresses this sentiment more forcefully:

> all religions reek with the blood of human carnage, not because God is blood-thirsty but because in the primordial irony, man created a god limited by man's own weaknesses; lust for a political base, economic dominance. . . . By way of generalization, the God of the "Christians" or the Allah of the "Muslims" in Nigeria who now seek for political constituencies are the God or Allah they created.[42]

Although there appears to be no consensus within this school of thought as to why religions in Nigeria have been so obtrusive upon and subversive of national unity, these views represent the official position of the government. From the latter's perspective, the problem originates from the nature of the two organized religions in Nigeria, which have always shown the "negative tendency" to "create competing social orders" and define themselves as "the most basic community," thus challenging "the national community of Nigeria" and delaying its integration.[43]

These interpretations are hardly convincing. If anything, they replay the characteristic insouciance with which a significant number of the Nigerian intelligentsia have always treated religion. In the subsequent chapters, I shall discuss more fully the "pure secularist position" that has ideologically embodied this intellectualist critique of religion. Suffice it here to say that the ultimate goal of many proponents of the privatization thesis is to banish religion from society because it represents for them a kind of mystical irrationality, something that citizens of a modern state would do better to avoid. Not only is this position inherently contradictory, it also offends the phenomenological integrity of religion as a cultural fount from which the faithful derive profound existential meaning. The position tends to encourage a superficial interpretation of religious values in politics. Religious persons seeking changes in the public realm are unjustifiably presented as extremists, menacing voices of a resurrected past, obstacles to modernity; and religious ideas expressed in public are myopically seen as flashes of political insanity—spasmodic symptoms of civic maladjustment—against the routine conduct of public affairs.

Contrary to the underlying assumptions of this school, I would like to argue that the presence of religion and religious people in public affairs is nothing new, and there is nothing improper in their desire to contribute to the building of society by seeking to appropriate the social visions of their religious traditions. The questions that must be asked—but which were overlooked by this school due to its deep immersion in naive rationalism and secularism—are, in what manner and to what end are religious social visions appropriated? "Appropriation of one's tradition," Nicholas Wolterstorff insightfully explains, "implies neither uncritical acceptance nor total rejection; it entails a discriminating adaptation of its features to one's own situation."[44] Especially within the constraints of pluralism, the proper ethical role of religious persons and institutions must be gauged, according to David Hollenbach, in terms of their ability to "realize their potentials as positive forces of justice and human dignity while avoiding moralistic oversimplification of public debates."[45] An important question to raise in this regard is whether a particular religious community's method of political engagement that is currently pervasive encourages dialogue or precipitates violence. I will return to this issue in the next chapter.

Another inadequate aspect of the privatization thesis is its view of human nature. Its proponents are correct insofar as they recognize the possibility of human corruption of the religious essence. Equally true, however, is the shallowness of the explanation they offer for what they recognize to be the dark side of human nature, which for them constitutes the totality of the human condition. In effect, their methodological and normative prescriptions for averting religious crises in Nigeria are disappointingly inadequate.

Reinhold Niebuhr argues in his magisterial work on the phenomenology of selfhood that a balanced view of human nature must be cognizant of its two-sided possibilities: on the one hand, its inclination to moral and spiritual corruptions, and, on the other hand, its capacity for creativity, justice, and self-transcendence.[46] More significantly, he offers a thorough-going theological-ethical account of the persistence of moral and spiritual corruption in human life. For Niebuhr, the critical fact with which any philosophical or theological anthropology must first reckon is the situation of humans at the juncture between necessity and freedom, between nature and spirit. The psychological consequence of this paradoxical involvement in finitude and freedom is that people are anxious creatures, and this anxiety is understood by Niebuhr as the essential problematic of selfhood. It is the precondition and the source of human temptation, since it invites people either to seek some form of self-indulgence as an escape from the anguish of freedom or to deny the contingent character of their existence by making the claim of absoluteness for what is in fact only finite and conditioned.[47] The world, says Niebuhr, "is a tragic world, troubled not by finiteness so much as by 'false eternals' and false absolutes, and expressing the pride of these false absolutes even in the highest reaches of its spirituality."[48]

The political import of Niebuhr's thesis for the assessment of human interests, religious and nonreligious, is the humble recognition that human beings are capable of distorting their real interests, of interpreting mere preferences as basic needs.

Even more disturbing about human life is the fact that in our articulation and defense of these interests, we are likely to be, as we so often are, noninclusive. We tend to determine collective happiness by highly circumscribed and selfish rules of conduct.

That these corruptions have occurred in the major world religions is sufficiently clear from the depth of hostility that many people feel toward religion today. However, to say that human beings are universally and pathologically sinners is not to say that they are totally depraved. They are just as much sinners as they are saints. Indeed, as Niebuhr also says, "Total depravity is an impossibility, since man can be a sinner only because he is a child of God. He can do evil only because he has freedom; and freedom is the mark of his divine sonship."[49]

Human beings are thus curiously divided and internally contradictory creatures. They are simultaneously children of God, possessing absolute worth and dignity, and rebellious ingrates, deserving only of brutal chastisement. When they truly acknowledge their own finitude and dependence, and the full transcendence of their Creator, they are the most creative of creatures. Yet when they pretend to be their own creators, turning away from their true source and ground in prideful rebellion, they are the most destructive of creatures. Hence, their creativity and their destructiveness are curiously mixed, providing the spectacle of a human creativity that is inevitably destructive and a human destructiveness that is inevitably, in part, creative.

The primary point here is that the moral discontinuity inherent in human beings follows them wherever they go, whether into politics or family life, into religion or atheism. For while religious, as well as nonreligious, insights can support public life, they can also disrupt it. Proponents of the privatization thesis ignore this entrenched contradiction in all human aspirations—moral, religious, and political. Moreover, the pessimism that prompts and justifies their intellectualist critique of religion is not applied, as it should be, to the state or government of Nigeria. It is this lopsided reading of the situation that has led some other scholars to search for alternative ways of explaining the ambiguous interface of religion and politics in Nigeria.

The Manipulation Thesis

The second dominant explanation of the interface of religion and politics in Nigeria is the manipulation thesis. The thesis, as lucidly summarized by Jibrin Ibrahim, posits that "political actors often amplify differences and provoke confessional conflicts as part of a wider strategy for the acquisition of political power and/or enhancing the political assets of groups involved in the process of power brokerage."[50] A good number of studies on the politics of plural societies have espoused this view. In his work on the political behavior of the Hausa-Muslim migrants in Ibadan, the defunct western Nigerian regional capital, Cohen declared as his aim the investigation of "the manner and the process by which cultural norms, values, myths, and symbols are manipulated in the informal articulation of political interests."[51] The avant-garde of this thesis today are the radical elements within the Nigerian intelligentsia, the so-called progressive thinkers.

The contextual background out of which the debate over the manipulation and politicization of religion arose was the transformation of Nigeria's economic base from agriculture to petroleum, a process which led to the centralization of the country's financial resources. The petro-dollar economy exacerbated all forms of struggle for political power and consequently for economic resources. Religion, commonly regarded as an effective weapon for social mobilization, came to play an important role in what Nigerians call the distribution of the national cake.

In a pathbreaking study on this theme, Bala Usman constituted the series of religious crises that Nigeria has been experiencing in the last two decades within the manipulation hermeneutic. According to him, these events are not symptomatic of theological maladies; rather, they stem directly from the actions of the intermediary bourgeoisie, who manipulate religion as a ploy to obscure their exploitation of the masses.[52]

While this interpretation may offer a profound social analysis of and historical judgment upon political practices in Nigeria, it encourages a priori philosophical rejection of religious life. Popular religious movements are seen within this purview as lacking theological validity since they merely offer themselves as sacred canopies for economic and political interests. In consonance with the privatization thesis, this interpretation also concludes that secular sensibilities are the only prerequisites for progressive outlooks, and that religious beliefs can at best function as a sign of political reaction.

The manipulation thesis may be better evaluated if seen within a wider intellectual tradition. One way of appreciating the thesis is to see it as a modern formulation of crude Marxism, which conceives of religion as the opium of the people and in which religious masses are viewed as passive and ignorant objects upon which monolithic religious institutions impose fantasies of otherworldly fulfillment. So conceived, the thesis reveals more about its proponents' prejudices than the nature of religion. In fact, much of what is trumpeted today as a Marxist theory of religion cannot be associated with Karl Marx. For Marx, religion is a profound human response to, and protest against, intolerable conditions. He sees religion as an opiate not because it is a mere political pacification imposed from above but rather "a historically circumscribed existential and experiential assertion of being (or somebodiness) by dehumanized historical agents under unexamined socioeconomic conditions."[53] Marx was disenchanted with particular forms of religious life, the accommodationist ones, which are shot through with existential emptiness because these forms usually overlook the socioeconomic conditions responsible for people's material wretchedness, and thereby delimit human powers and efforts to transform these conditions. His point is not simply that religion is, because of its preoccupation with cosmic vision, ontological pronouncements on human nature, and personal morality, an impotent and inadequate form of protest, but also that without a probing and illuminating social and historical analysis of the present even the best-intentioned religionists and moralists will impede fundamental social and historical change.

The importance of seeing the link between what is experienced politically and economically (what I will refer to as *situational context* in chapter 2) on the one hand, and religious expressions, on the other, has been underscored by other proponents of the manipulation thesis. In particular, the question is being raised about the relationship between an existing "policy environment" and the extent of manipulation. Which segments of the ruling class—military or civilian—are more likely to manipulate cultural resources? Nigerian students of politics diverge on this. Agbaje argues that it has been principally under military rule that attempts to change the vocabulary of public discourse or policy and constitutional provisions have occurred. According to him, "the tendency to engage in the politics of religion or to protect or challenge particular conceptions of the relationship between state and religion has been more visible under military regimes than during republics characterized by party politics."[54] He cites the example of the "lack of religious parity in the deployment of strategic personnel in military regimes."[55] His own diagnosis concludes that it is the specific logic of military regimes, or the absence "of a vigorous network of democratic institutions" that has heightened religion-state tensions in Nigeria. In order to contain Nigeria's diverse interests, Agbaje calls for supporting a policy environment that is capable of producing and sustaining democratic institutions, which will in turn perform a "mediating role" and produce a "mellowing influence . . . on those seeking political power or who wish to maintain themselves in power through the ballot box."[56]

Agbaje's trust in the potentiality of democracy to mitigate the egoism of diverse interest groups is, with a necessary caveat, justifiable when viewed in relation to certain theological and philosophical understandings of human nature and of the ends of political life. Maritain represents one important tradition in this regard. He argues that democracy is "the only way of bringing about a moral rationalization of politics"—that is, of recognizing

> the essentially human ends of political life and of its deepest springs: justice, law, and mutual friendship; [of making all the] structures and organs of body politic serve the common good, the dignity of the human person, and the sense of fraternal love . . . [and of basing] political activity not on childish greed, jealousy, selfishness, pride and guile, claims to prestige and domination transformed into sacred rules of the most serious game, but instead on a grown-up awareness of the innermost needs of mankind's life, of the real requirements of peace and love, and of the moral and spiritual energies of man.[57]

Not every Nigerian, however, would want to apportion all the blame to the military class. In a study focused on "civilian politics" during Nigeria's second republic (1979-83), Segun Gbadegesin argued that the "politicization of society" that occurred at various levels and in different dimensions—economy, education, ethnicity, law, religion, and the press—was a peculiar strategy of the politicians "in their quest for power and in their use of power when they acquired it." The Nigerian politicians have always regarded "politicization, in the form of manipulation of institutions and policies for partisan and individual interests . . . as a perfectly rational means."[58]

Gbadegesin blames Nigeria's woes on the leadership spectrum as a whole—military and civilian—accusing both of using "the political sector as a ladder to personal wealth," and of engaging in a kind of "market politics" where "the stakes" always dictate "the means." Politics and administration, in the perception of both forms of leadership, were always "identified with business, judging success in it by the amount of wealth an actor was able to make." For Gbadegesin, it is not the ordinary religious citizens who are uncivil, rather it is the leadership which lacks what he calls "civic virtue." He observes, appropriately it would seem, that Nigerian leaders did not hesitate to jettison morality "if it stood in the way of good business."[59]

There is something about the manipulation thesis that seems to command almost intuitive assent. In part, at least, it exposes the other aspect of human corruption that predominates in Nigeria; and in this case, it is not the religious corruption of politics, but the political corruption of religion. It underscores the connections and political networks of dominant groups who use religion for their political ends. But the thesis also contains a paradoxical mix. Christian Coulon considers the thesis a theoretical failure for ignoring the very important question, why do people allow themselves to be manipulated? Coulon appeals to the cultural integrity and essence of religion qua religion to support his case: "[T]he religious arena constitutes an ideological space with its symbols, morality, aesthetics, historical references and codes of action in which dominant and non-dominant classes and groups engage in 'cultural negotiation.' It is therefore an arena that has meaning to a wide group of actors."[60]

Several other notable students of Nigerian culture and society have criticized the skewed focus of the manipulation thesis. Having found both the "thick cultural world" of Clifford Geertz and the utilitarian political theory of Jeremy Bentham inadequate, Laitin argues that people are not simply "utility maximizers" who "manipulate their cultural identities in order to enhance their power and wealth." He suggests that not only do people regard their cultural (and religious) tradition(s) as "ideological guidelines for collective action," it is also the case that the political leaders who constitute the "privileged loci of symbolic production" are well aware of this Janus-faced nature of culture. It is only in consequence of such recognition that the political entrepreneurs can be effective in deploying cultural properties to establish an ideological hegemony—that is, to engage their citizens in a web of symbolic and material sanctions that have the potential of binding them securely to the political system.[61] J. D. Y. Peel is particularly critical of this thesis because it tends to reduce social and political history to "a mere 'mythical charter' conjoined solely out of contemporary interests."[62] For Lamin Sanneh, the theory is inadequte because it encourages a reductionist view of religion: "It is as if in our concern to describe the sunlight, we concentrated on the shadows, using that derivative relationship as the justification for a reductionist approach."[63]

It would certainly be simplistic to deny the reality of religious interests when expressed within the context of politics. To see religion as simply a pawn in the hand of the politicians, whose interests alone are real, is to underplay the heroism of religious martyrdom, which has occurred out of burning desires to "reform" Nigeria's political life. At the same time, the character of politics in Nigeria cannot but lead us to see some wisdom in the manipulation thesis. The unsettled nature of the case should prompt us to search for appropriate ethical criteria that might help to contribute to the emergence of what has been called "a corrective vision" or "a binding ingredient" for Nigeria.[64] Ibrahim is probably right in his depiction of the ambivalent character of Nigeria's politico-religious arena. In his judgment, while it may be true that "there is more to religious space than manipulation by dominant groups, there is a certain specificity of cyclical politico-religious conflicts that arise at periods of political transition in which the hidden hands of man become discernible."[65]

With no intention to make any premature conclusive claim, I suggest that an "enlightened civic consciousness" is needed across the board in Nigeria. Three elements of this consciousness are worthy of special note. First is "civic virtue," which "exists among some aggregate of persons if each person involved in making collective decisions (hence in a democratic system, all citizens) acts steadily on the conscious intention of achieving the good of all the persons in the aggregate." The second element is "a general acceptance of political conflict as an inevitable and entirely appropriate aspect of political life." And the third element of an enlightened civic orientation is "a deep concern for ways of strengthening civic virtue by achieving a greater convergence of interests and a corresponding reduction of conflicts."[66] To bring these conditions about, all the constituencies involved in the current conflict—religious people, professional politicians, and state officials—need to engage in a process of reenvisioning a new Nigerian state in which all could find both their freedom and their limits. The blame and the solution must be collectively shared. But there is a third theory of religion and state in Nigeria, which I will now examine.

The Hegemonic State Thesis

Proponents of the hegemonic state thesis conceive the issue of religion and politics in Nigeria as a complex of juridical and cultural crises. They assert that the Nigerian state, as embodied in the government, is its own undoing. In particular, that the state has inflated its prestige and functional role, a fact abundantly revealed by its unbridled ambition to control, suppress, and if allowed, obliterate religion and other societal elements. The Nigerian polity, as it is presently constituted, gravitates toward what one student of the country's politics identifies as a "statist orientation," and in effect, has become "swollen."[67]

This orientation is premised upon two inadequate assumptions that many African people, according to Sanneh, already hold. First is the belief that "the state is a rational institution and . . . as such it sets the bounds necessary for rational conduct in society." Second is the ascription of "exclusive authority" to the state, "which justifies rules of ethics and morality that obtain their coherence from the rational state."[68] In effect, the state has transformed itself into a quasi-religious agency, making decisions in arguably religious areas, and in pursuit of these epiphenomenal religious functions it produces its own sociodicies—that is, normative conceptions of life-in-society, which "are at least potential rivals of the theodicies of religious groups."[69] And as Roland Robertson rightly said, "it is the autonomous production of these [by the state] which is the target of those who militantly decry the salience of 'secular humanism.'"[70]

The natural consequence of this is a basic contradiction in the state-society relationship in Nigeria, a contradiction that could have profound implications for the future of Nigeria's political institutions. For, while "pluralism is vigorously established and increasingly assertive in the country's ethnic structure, associational life, and information order . . . , the state elite, including influential elements of the intelligentsia, continue to push the expansion of state control."[71]

Regarding the state-religion relationship in Nigeria, this contradiction is vividly revealed in the confusion over the appropriate meaning of the concept of the secular state. Although in none of the Federal Constitutions has this concept ever been explicitly used, it has generally been taken as the meaning of the constitutional provision for a functional separation of religion and state. However, the political class has taken this secular outlook as the basis for promoting an omnicompetent state, a state that "arrogates to itself not only the power to restrain and arbitrate but also to prescribe faith of a certain kind and conformity of a certain pattern."[72]

Thus, religious protests or interfaith rivalry for political recognition in Nigeria are not simply the by-products of retrograde behavior of the religious people or of their failure to imbibe the irenic tenets of their religious doctrines. To understand these events, we must focus our analysis upon "the pattern that emerges from state action, the extent to which such a pattern exhibits balance and fairness (rather than 'neutrality') and the unravelling of the dynamics that make the state and its managers behave the way they do."[73]

Nigeria is presently in a twilight zone of moral paradox, a situation that presents a deep crisis of legitimacy. At the core of this crisis is the Kulturkampf, the collision of heterogenous religious cultures and the culture or ethos of state omnipotence. Significantly, the heightened form of this crisis is the increasing "nakedness" of Nigeria's public square (*public square* understood as "a space for conversation, contention, and compromise among moral actors") as a result of what Coulon describes as "state fetishism"—that is, "its totalitarian and teleological ambitions." Excluding particularist religious and moral beliefs from public discourse is precisely what it means to render the public square naked. However, such nakedness is a condition that cannot remain interminably. The state knows it must remain legitimate and meaningful in the perception of its incurably religious citizens, so it is often driven to promulgate its own perverse forms of religion, sometimes euphemistically dubbed civil religion. According to Richard John Neuhaus, "the public square will not and cannot remain naked. If it is not clothed with the 'meanings' borne of religion, new 'meanings' will be imposed by virtue of the ambitions of the modern state."[74]

The Nigerian version of the political orthodoxy with which the state has sought to replace religion and combat its vestigial dangers is national integration—a goal certainly desirable for the country, but one that has been wrongly pursued. In its particular incarnation in Nigeria, integrative enterprise has imposed upon the state "a radical arbitrary posture for which a suitable motto might be, 'if the state loses the confidence of the people, it shall dissolve the people and elect another.'"[75] Perhaps no other experience demonstrates the absolutist character of the Nigerian state more than the singular fact that it has been ruled by the military dictators in all but eight of its thirty-five years since independence. More recently, the Nigerian state has manifested a systemic brutalization and violation of people's lives and operates its insolent machineries with a senseless and savage force. Citizenship and religious pluralism are the natural victims of this extensive entrenchment of demagoguery in a nation considered to be the hope of Africa about two decades ago. The combustible nature of current religious expressions in Nigeria is an understandable response to an institution perceived to be lacking in any moral credit. In fact, these expressions constitute genuine efforts "to overcome the ontological chasm" that presently exists in Nigeria's public square, and "to transform the symbolic and institutional frameworks of collective life."[76]

The Nigerian Dilemma

What bearing do these three different kinds of assessment— the call for a domestication of religious beliefs, the selfishness of the elite class who manipulate religious idioms, and the monolithic preference of the ruling class—have on our understanding of the predicament faced by Nigeria? First, it is clear from the positions reviewed above that Nigeria is a country with a poorly developed political culture, in that "its political structures have not been institutionalized or only weakly institutionalized, and dominant political rules, 'the rules of the game,' have not been sufficiently internalized."[77] In an essay revealing the depth of the Nigerians' frustration with their state managers, a London-based Nigerian journalist, Eddie Iroh, describes himself as "a product of a political culture based more on the bullet than the ballot; politics where checkbooks buy more votes than issues and policies can, [and where] no means is too mean in the quest for political power."[78]

The issue is, however, more complex than Iroh has presented it. A more adequate assessment would require a comparative historical and cultural perspective. The vicious circle of institutional decay in Nigeria has been said to be typical of all "transitional societies."[79] In his 1983 inaugural lecture at the University of Ibadan, Peter Ekeh argued that, due to new historical conditions introduced by colonialism, what now exists in Africa is a multiplicity of public spheres rather than a single and morally unified public sphere. Unlike the Western world, where a common morality informs both the public and the private realms, the African situation is different. There is, on the one hand, a primordial public that operates on societal morality and is therefore bound to the private realm. And, on the other hand, there is a civic realm tied to the modern state that is amoral and devoid of any claims to morality. The individual finds himself straddled between these two publics, and the public law he obeys might not always be that of the state. Reacting to the position of the well-known Ibadan history school, which contends that colonialism was a small episode in African history with little significance for contemporary reality,[80] Ekeh responds that colonialism was not an episode but a historical epoch that integrated Africa into the modern world system and designed its present space-time boundaries. He contends that "the moral and social order which formally encased the pre-colonial indigenous institutions is burst by the social forces of colonialism and they seek new anchors in the changed milieux of colonialism."[81]

Perhaps even more revealing about the features of these colonially fabricated nations or transitional societies is that they were composed of peoples with no historic antecedents or sanction. For most of these nations, their shared historic memory is limited to the common experience of a single colonial ruler and the collective struggle to secure independence. The dual imperative that Nigeria in particular has faced in its post-independence existence has been precisely "how to define a new cultural identity linked to the dimensions of the polity and related to commonalities among the polity's populace, while eschewing identification of the state with any one of the cultural segments within it, which would immediately threaten the identity of other collectivities."[82]

Whether the Nigerian state has successfully balanced this dual imperative is a matter of historical judgment, now copiously illustrated by the three different perspectives analyzed above. My immediate concern in this book is how the country can proceed in heeding the imperative. The imperative is ethical in nature, embodying the two dimensions that constitute pluralism, namely, agreement and disagreement, or dissension and consensus. To the extent that any society seeks to be "a rational process, some set of principles must motivate the general participation of all religious groups, despite their dissensions, in the oneness of [that] community. On the other hand, these common principles must not hinder the maintenance by each group of its own different identity."[83]

Given this formulation of the pluralist dilemma, the saliency of the two main questions I wish to pursue in the next chapter becomes clear. The first is about the kind of political framework that would more fully encourage just relationships between the state and the different religious bodies, as well as among the different religious bodies; and the second deals with the kind of political attitudes that would most encourage a sense of mutual acceptance within which the diverse religious allegiances can find both their freedom and their limits.

There are abundant resources in social and political theories, as well as in the intellectual histories of the two world religions in Nigeria—Islam and Christianity—that may guide us on how to answer these questions. Specifically, certain methodological and substantive prescriptions have been suggested that offer a great deal of promise. Of course, there are some proposals that may foil our constructive efforts, but even such must be proven to be inadequate before we reject them.

Proposals, Solutions, and Approaches

The objective audiences addressed by some of the proposed solutions to be examined below are religion and the state, and both the evaluative and the organizational dimensions of the former are presupposed. These proposals were designed to settle two kinds of issues. The first is how religious resources (or ideas) might be retrieved for public application, and the second revolves around the kinds of policies a state might adopt regarding the religious question. By way of generalization, it is the social theorists and historians who have largely addressed the religious audience, while political theorists focus on the state or the "political audience." I shall examine these two approaches in turn.

The Religious Audience: The Formal Approach versus the Historical Approach

Some sociologists are of the opinion that one way of determining the relative conjunction and disjunction of religion and the state is to address "the general issue of the ways in which and degrees to which different world views, more often than not embodied in religiocultural traditions, express the relationship between worldly and supra- or extra-worldly spheres and the worldly manifestations or vehicles of those spheres."[84]

This view derives from the assumption that there is only one way of relating religion to society. As such, scholars who adopt this approach are mostly interested in postulating and defending a "formal" understanding of religion. The problem with this approach, however, is that it reduces the multifarious and ever-changing particulars of a religion to iron-cast "ideal types" or "constructs." As I will show in chapter 2, this approach is analogous to a theory of religious liberty that Murray characterizes as "classicism."

By way of illustration, scholars who adopt this approach present Islam as a religion that aims to engage in the regulation of the mundane social world and not to proclaim a kingdom in dramatic contrast to it.[85] As a cultural system, Islam is understood as having historically promoted "an organic connection with society, in the sense of more or less equating the religion . . . with the society or civilization in which it is objectively located."[86] The theological basis for this Islamic political stance is, other scholars contend, the religion's doctrine of the divine origin of government:

> In Islam there is no doctrine of the temporal end which alone belongs to the state and the eternal end which belongs to, and is the prerogative of the Church. . . . The state is "given," and it is not limited by the existence of an association claiming to be its equal or superior, to which it can leave the preaching of morality and the finding of sanctions for its truth. It has itself to repress evil and show the way to righteousness.[87]

Christian social ethicists generally believe that normative reflection focuses, in part, on "how individuals should respond to social institutions and processes" and "how given social contexts shape and direct moral selfhood and moral action."[88] Of particular importance are three interrelated sets of considerations, helpfully identified by Frederick S. Carney as deontological, teleological, and axiological, which point up the interactive roles of the individual, the state and the law. Deontology asks questions of obligation or duty such as, What ought to be done? Teleological concerns respond to such questions as, What kind of person or society is most appropriate to be? Axiological ethical theory asks, Which objects or states of affairs are important, and which are more important than others?[89] The classical position in Islam on these issues is that "the law (*sharīʿa*) precedes the state, which exists for the sole purpose of maintaining and enforcing the law." The sharīʿa "regulates, in theory, all aspects of public and private life and commercial and business affairs and forms the basis of political theory." With respect to the functional relationship between the individual and the state, Ann K. S. Lambton shows that neither the conception of the individual nor of rights is prominent in Islam: "Islam does not in fact recognize the legal personality of the individual in which his rights are secured to him and vested in him by law."[90]

A good number of experts on Islam and Muslim scholars have challenged the kind of classicist position represented by Lambton. They regard her interpretation as an anachronistic error of reading a medieval solution into problems that are shaped by a different set of sociohistorical factors. Such an interpretation, according to Roger Garaudy, is like "reading the Qurʾan with the eyes of the dead, as though being a Muslim meant living like a tenth-century Arab subject to the Abbassides and according to their laws."[91]

Christianity as a religion has equally been cast in this rigidly classicist fashion. Martin regards it as a religion that only "leans towards interiority and an open texture rather than to

exterior observance and a closed system of legal requirements."[92] Christianity is for him not a blueprint for a complete social organization, but a dramatic contrast between the
kingdom of God and the kingdom of this world. In like manner, medieval Catholicism is said to have promoted a view of
the Corpus Christianum, such that while church and state
were, in principle, distinct societies, they were united in one
commonwealth; the distinction between them was to be seen
chiefly in "their separate hierarchies (pope and emperor, etc)
with their different functions and in the systems of law they
administer."[93]

The "formal approach" is not only impossibly restrictive for
a study of religiously heterogeneous and culturally complex societies, it is an approach that overlooks the historical dimensions, the nonstatic character, and the diffuse manifestations of
political philosophies within those religious traditions. Religious traditions "are rarely isomorphic"; on the contrary, they
"pick up different baggage in different eras and different areas,"
and their adherents "are not limited in their repertoires for action by a single system of symbols."[94] Nowhere is this complex
character of religion more perceptible than in Nigeria, where
Islam and Christianity have each splintered into countless denominations. This fragmentation of the religious terrain is not
simply a consequence of an insatiable human craving for the
exotic; it is engendered by the structure of religion itself. Each
denomination, sect, or brotherhood is an organizational embodiment of the doctrines that emanate from one or more of
the strands of which every religion, as a complex social reality,
is constituted. These strands, according to Laitin, include "the
original books and founding ideology, the various traditions of
the priests, and the contemporary developments of the religion elsewhere in the world."[95] In the remainder of this section, I shall limit myself to examining works in Islamic political history that offer a critique of the "formal" approach; and

in chapter 2, I will explore samples of Christian ethical critique of the same position.

To resolve the crisis of religion in a pluralist state, Abdullahi Ahmed An-Naʾim, a Sudanese legal scholar, emphasizes the importance of appreciating the impact of historical context on the interpretation of a religion's sources. With respect to his religion, Islam, he argues that "throughout its history the understanding and implementation of Islam was influenced by the social and political realities of Muslim communities, [by which he means] the practical impact of human understanding of its scriptural sources in the particular historical context." Essentially, then, "in the same way that early Muslims interpreted the Qurʾān and other sources in their context, contemporary Muslims must do the same at the present time."[96]

In his own study of some contemporary West African countries where Islam is a major religious presence, Louis Brenner documents the variety of political options, characterized in a binary fashion as political involvement and political withdrawal, that Muslim ideologies offered groups from different social strata organized around the promotion of Islam. Through a careful analysis of the maraboutic lineage structures in Mauritania and the Senegal River valley, the pedagogical network of Sufi brotherhoods as a model of reformed social organization, and the religious education policy of the *madrasa* movement in Mali, Brenner demonstrates an articulation of "representational dichotomies which distinguish between political power and Islam."[97]

The socio-ethical implications of these analyses for political strategy are far-reaching. The standard classicist prescriptions, now being "advocated by many Muslims, as well as scholars of Islam, that because of its fundamentally theocratic nature, the fullest realization of Islam can only be found in the seizing of political power and the establishment of theocratic polities" are, in light of historical evidence, not the only political position allowed in Islam. A more accurate reading of Islamic political history and institutions reveals that "many social and political options . . . were available within the context of Muslim discourse."[98]

The sociohistorical hermeneutics of Islamic political theory offered by Ibn Khaldūn, a distinguished medieval Muslim historian, provides an excellent resource for appreciating these diverse social and political stances available in Islam. In *al-Muqaddima*, the introductory volume of his monumental work, *Kitāb al-ibar* (A Universal History), he sets out a theory of the state and religion that makes a dialectical affirmation of a functional separation between the two and of their mutual ethical interdependence.[99] His primary interest was to discover the principles of political organization, to find out how the state functions. For this task, his points of reference are two: first, the *sharī'a* of Islam, the constitution of a theocracy founded by the Prophet Muhammad, the lawgiver; and, second, the emerging insight derived from contemporary events, especially from his dispassionate study of the Islamic empires of his day—for example, the collapse of Islamic political unity, and the history of the Almoravids and Almohads, with their variety of political entities and cultural levels.

The evolution of *mulk* (nation-state), according to Ibn Khaldūn, must be seen as part of the emerging *madanīya* or *'umrān* (civilization), an inevitable consequence of the unfolding transition from *badāwa* (rural life, characterized by food gathering and cattle raising) to **ha*dāra* (settled, organized urban life, in the sense of the Greek *polis*). The increasing widening of the social scale, and the progressive enlargement of the range of social, economic, and political relations required a new modus vivendi. The expulsion of people from their tribal brotherhoods into the universal brotherhood of an urban world of strangers forces upon them the task to contrive new "ways of living" (*'a*sabīya,* a common bond or a binding ingredient) with unknown others without transforming them into either brothers or enemies. In short, urbanization requires urbanity and civilization requires civility.[100]

It is in this context that Ibn Khaldūn argues that *siyāsa diniya* (government based on the divinely revealed law—*Sharī'a*) will be inadequate because it will fail the test of *'a*sabīya* that is appropriate to the ordering or governance of a complex state. In the earlier Islamic political history, the type of state embodied in this government was *khilāfa* (a state whose nature and purpose was the combination of religious conviction and political power). In his discussion of the individual believer's loyalty, Ibn Khaldūn upholds the preeminence of Islam: "Islam, in the form of the *khilāfa*, is the choicest fruit of a God-guided and God-centred human association. It is the ideal, the best way to the fulfillment of man's destiny, to the attainment of happiness in this world and in the world to come."[101] But in light of the new levels of human civilization, a continued application of the *khilāfa* polity would be archaic and anachronistic.[102] Thus, *siyāsa 'aqlīya* (government based on a law established by human reason), no less than *siyāsa diniya,* is the natural result of human life which requires *ijtimā* (association or assembly) and organization. Ibn Khaldūn opined that "this association is necessary for mankind, otherwise their existence and God's will to make the world habitable with them would not be perfect."[103] He based his theory of the functional separation of religion and the state on this sociohistorical fact. He grounds this separation on two fundamental differences pertaining to both spheres: their origins and ends. Religion and religious association(s) have their origin in God and are meant to guide individuals toward the fulfillment of their destiny, a destiny that is coextensive with and yet transcends this world. Ibn Khaldūn admonished his fellow Muslims to remember that the prophetic lawgiver pays due attention to human nature and destiny in his law and condemns only excess:

Know that the whole world . . . is for the law-giver [the Prophet Muhammad] but a way to the hereafter. . . . His (the lawgiver's) intention is not to forbid or blame man's deeds . . . or to destroy the forces altogether which produce them, but rather to change their direction towards the aims of truth as far as possible, so that all intentions become right and the direction (of man's desires and plans) a single one (namely, to Allah and the hereafter).[104]

Nation-states have their origin in human reason and in the will to power and domination, and their advantages—which Ibn Khaldūn describes variously as providing security, welfare in general, comforts of life such as better and more varied food, more comfortable houses and elegant clothes in the cities—"accrue in this world only."[105]

From this socioanthropological and historical approach, Ibn Khaldūn was led to reject any explicit and direct ideological mixing of religion and politics. The *imām* (the religious leader) must distance himself from the *malik* (king, temporal ruler), lest he "wreaks havoc on the moral foundations of religion."[106] Ibn Khaldūn insisted on the inevitable "gap between the ideal demands of the ideal Sharīʿa and political reality."[107] Empirical reality must be recognized for what it is rather than predicating it on the ideal realm. To sacralize actions taken in response to historical pressure is an act of theological misjudgment, for "political contingency provides a dubious base for theological consistency."[108]

I must emphasize that Ibn Khaldūn did not, however, affirm that the evolution of nation-states, with their complex organizational demands, necessarily leads to a repudiation of religion. His point is that, under the current condition of human existence, in which new insight has emerged, especially in reference to political life, religion and state can no longer be mutually absorbed but must seek indirect ways of influencing each other. Religion needs the power state because "human civilization certainly needs political government by which its affairs are arranged in proper order."[109] Religion likewise supports the life of the state by sublimating humanity's baser nature through the explication of values that encourage public decorum without inviting doctrinal indifferentism: "For where otherwise rivalry and discord might threaten to disrupt the ʿAsabiya, religion unites all hearts, replaces the desire for the vanity of the world with its rejection and turns men to God, seeking right and truth in unison."[110]

It is pertinent to mention here, by way of digression, that the celebrated views of Alexis de Tocqueville on the place of religion in American politics centers on this theory of the indirect impact of religion on politics. Tocqueville observed that "religion in America takes no direct part in the government of society, but it must nevertheless be regarded as the foremost of the political institutions of that country; for if it does not impart a taste for freedom, it facilitates the use of free institutions."[111] In short, the political power of religion in America depends on the indirect transmission of its values. Tocqueville advisedly remarked that when religious sects are directly involved with public affairs, their transcendent concerns are linked to material wants and partisan dynamics. So linked, religions and their values are subject to the volatility of political change and the valuation of interests. To attempt to act directly, religions must become interest groups, whose claims will be treated like those of others; they will be measured and honored according to political and not moral criteria.[112]

The dominance of religion as a political institution that Tocqueville asserts is manifested in a religion's impact on the mores of the community as parish or congregation. The member, as adherent, adopts these moral values and principles; and, as citizen, the member carries them into the public realm, applying them to social and political issues. In this way, religion provides a coherent moral framework that guides citizen-adherents in their public role. Tocqueville explains that every principle of the moral world is fixed and determinate, although the political won. Thus the human mind is never left to wander across a boundless field; and, whatever may be its pretensions, it is checked from time to time by barriers which it cannot surmount. Before it can perpetrate innovation, certain primal and immutable principles are laid down, and the boldest conceptions of human device are subjected to certain forms which retard and stop their completion.[113]

Tocqueville states one additional, and telling, reality which religion must recognize, and which I shall later develop more fully under Niebuhr's theological anthropology: that the power of religious morals is, particularly within an egalitarian society, insufficient to overcome directly and comprehensively social interests and opinions that are passionately and widely held. Religion must therefore act obliquely, selectively, and realistically.[114] Despite such limitations, Tocqueville insists that there is still important work for religion to perform, for while it may "not succeed in curing men of the love of riches; [it] may persuade men to enrich themselves by none but honest means."[115]

Returning to the work of Ibn Khaldūn, associational life also plays a key role. Rosenthal says that Ibn Khaldūn's "new science of history" represents "a medieval witness to the premature birth of modern scientific inquiry into the realm of the human *group,* transcending the bounds of Islam."[116] Of course, Ibn Khaldūn was realistic enough to note that there are, just as there have always been, autocratic states in which all the resources of the land, religious and nonreligious, as well as the different avenues producing them, are organized around the comfort of the *malik* (temporal ruler or government). He did not endorse this situation as normative. According to him, "exaggerated severity harms and mostly ruins the *mulk* (state)." Human associations are formed and organized around diverse interests—economic, cultural, religious, and educational—and they are all "necessary for man" and all constitute "the meaning of civilization."[117] Religious communities are part of society's pluralist structures; the state cannot swallow them up, and neither should they seek to dominate the state.

Ibn Khaldūn's contributions to Islamic political theory are potential resources for comparative religious and ethical analysis. His approach supports the claims (to be examined in the next chapter) of some Christian ethicists that "the unity of religion is not a prerequisite for political unity," and that persons "subscribing to diverse religious or non-religious creeds [can] share in and work for the same political or temporal common good."[118] At several points in this study, I shall be establishing other theoretical confluences of Christian, Islamic, and secular thinkers' methodologies to demonstrate how Nigerians too might possibly disentangle themselves from the web of intransigent dogmatism and theological authoritarianism. But now we need to look at some of the proposals from political philosophy.

The Political Audience

Two different models of pluralism mark the reflections of the political philosophers and theorists who have specifically addressed the issue of how the state ought to conduct itself in relation to the diverse associations and groups to which its citizens belong. There are pessimists who consider independent associations as cancerous to the health of the state and would like to see their suppression, if not their elimination. The optimists argue that these associations actually serve the state well because they provide intermediary services that the state, due to its highly bureaucratized and anonymous character, could not offer. The state should therefore regard them as "an inevitable and necessary part of politics."[119]

A classic example of the pessimistic thinkers was Thomas

Hobbes. In his *Leviathan,* Hobbes posits a theory of the absolute political community, which is founded on illimitable sovereignty and the boundless obedience of individual to sovereign. Basing his argument on the allegedly natural atomization of the state of nature and, within this, the allegedly solitary character of the individual, who lives in a condition characterized by incessant fear, war, and abject insecurity, he sees order as the greatest challenge facing the political community. To achieve and maintain order, Hobbes offers an intellectual justification for the extermination of all possible social, religious, or cultural limits on the sovereign.

The political ruler is, for Hobbes, the commonwealth embodied; law is not in any way dependent on the social institutions of a people, but it is the command of the ruler. According to his definition, "Law is to every Subject, those Rules which the Commonwealth hath Commanded him, by Word, Writing, or other sufficient Sign of the Will, to make use of, for the Distinction of Right and Wrong."[120] He finds no place for associations and groups within this monolithic state, for he considers them to be breeding areas of dissension and of conflict with the requirements of the unitary state—not reinforcements of order and justice. He compares associations within the state, "which are as it were many lesser Commonwealths in the bowels of a greater," to "wormes in the entrayles of a naturall man."[121]

But of all associations, he fears the religious ones most. By reason of their tenacious hold on humans' spiritual allegiances, they will always be divisive forces within the commonwealth unless they are made strictly subordinate to the political power. Hobbes found it unthinkable that an autonomous spiritual authority should exist, for that would be tantamount to setting up "Supremacy against the Soveraignty, Canons against Lawes, and a Ghostly Authority against the Civill . . . [for] seeing the Ghostly Power challengeth the Right to declare what is

Sinne it challengeth by consequence to declare what is Law, (Sinne being nothing but the transgression of the Law)."[122]

Hobbes consequently calls for the direct involvement of the state in people's religious lives. Justifying this, he defines a church as "a company of men professing Christian Religion, united in the person of one Soveraign, at whose command they ought to assemble, and without whose authority they ought not to assemble."[123] He concludes his discourse on the relation of religion and state with a seeming theory of a benevolent state. In part, he accepts the existence of any religion, irrespective of its dogma, provided it places itself unquestioningly under the state; and, conversely, he opposes any religion that does not so place itself.

J. N. Figgis and Harold Laski, both British political theorists of the Whig tradition, were reputed for their rejection of theories that tended to ignore the important role played by groups in the political process and in the life of the community, theories that conceived of politics largely in terms of the individual versus the state.[124] There are to be found between the state and the individual, they argued, numerous associations and groups of various kinds. These groups absorb much of the life of the individual, and have an existence that does not derive from the state.

The keystone of their arguments is that the various mediating associations found in society—cultural, religious, economic, civic, and other—not only exist, but ought to exist, in a healthy state. The proper question to ask then in any political situation is not, "How much uniformity can we impose?" but "How much diversity can we allow and encourage without threatening the unity of the state?"[125] A monistic state that aims at achieving a coerced unity at the expense of the various organic manifestations of life is adjudged to be "both administratively incomplete and ethically inadequate."[126]

The main task of the state, as interpreted by Figgis and

Laski, is to regulate and control the activities of groups in such a way that they are able to achieve those ends for which they exist. The state exists "to control and limit within the bounds of justice, the activities of all minor associations whatsoever."[127] This relational norm rests on the belief that liberty is the most important political value, and that it is best preserved by power being dispersed. While Figgis and Laski recognize that a degree of order and peace in a country is necessary for individual freedom to be effective, they argue that it should be the object of the state to ensure a maximum of individual freedom in any given set of circumstances.[128]

But groups also have an obligation to the commonwealth. They must not force the government to intervene in the life of the people in order to realize some substantive purpose. They should be concerned simply with obtaining freedom to live in a manner they prefer, while recognizing the rights of other groups to a similar freedom. "Every state," says Figgis, "is a synthesis of living wills. Harmony must be a matter of balance and judgment."[129]

While Figgis and Laski offer a comforting alternative to Hobbes's theory of state absolutism, their approach is inadequate for two reasons. First, not every social theorist would agree that the state has no positive role to play besides being a neutral umpire among contending interests. In the tradition of Aristotle and Aquinas, Maritain suggests that "political society . . . is the most perfect of temporal societies" whose normative task involves fostering justice and promoting friendship among its solidary groups.[130] Although realistically no state ever fully performs this normative task, it is nevertheless true that we do not regard the state as merely existing without a substantive moral responsibility. Ironically, most dictatorial regimes are undergirded by the belief that the state cannot and ought not remain a merely neutral entity. Without accepting the agenda of a dictator, we are challenged by his conception of the state, and indeed counseled to channel the energies and resources of the state toward positive ends.

The second flaw in the positions of Figgis and Laski is their tendency to personalize groups and depersonalize individuals. Within their theory, groups absorb so much of the human person that individuality pales into insignificance. The obvious danger is the possibility of weakening any active defense of human rights. By drawing a curtain on the human face, individuals are disarmed of the ideological weapon with which to resist the hegemonic oligarchy of groups. Jean-François Bayart warns of the serious danger of holding groups inviolate in their sometimes not unjustified bid to resist with a combative spirituality the authoritarianism of the state. He rightly notes that "the challenge to the state's monopoly of power may contain within itself the elaboration of a new monopoly. One actor may be able to capture the political support of his allies and translate it into the management of his own interests."[131]

These theoretical defects notwithstanding, the arguments that independent associations or groups have a right to exist without any fear of molestation or harassment by the state are not trivial. Theoretically, such arguments can be defended on the basis of the anthropological fact of sociality. In defending this intrinsic sociality of the human status, Robert A. Dahl asserts, and with justification, that "concrete human experiences provide a narrow base for creating strong identification and attachments that extend much outside the small, specific, and idiosyncratic cluster of human beings with whom each of us is most intimately associated during the important occasions of our lives."[132]

Moreover, institutional respect for social pluralism is a moral and political necessity. Groups help to provide the avenue needed for resisting what has been described as a "policeystaat ('a well policed state')."[133] Far more fundamental are the political gains that accrue to the state when it recognizes the immorality of repressing those features of culture around which people organize their lives and by which they enrich their endeavors. For it is incontrovertible that "states have not operated in a vacuum and it is ultimately their action in relation to civil society which determines their complexion and the fate of their policies. . . . Successful states devise modus operandi which adapt to and respond to civil society: political accountability. Unsuccessful states either dissolve, absorbed piecemeal by civil society, or they turn to absolutism, tyranny, in opposition to civil society."[134]

Conclusion

I have surveyed in this chapter a number of ways of looking at the problem of religious pluralism and the state. My inquiry has been guided by my two programmatic questions, which have to do with appropriate political institutions and religious attitudes that are indispensable to the emergence and sustenance of civic amity in a pluralistic society. My analysis is critical of certain theories and stances for their mistaken notions of politics and religious beliefs and history. In addition, I utilized a tactic of internal critique by drawing upon some samples of Islamic political theories and practices to suggest the possibility for fruitful political dialogue among people of diverse convictions.

Coupled with the optimistic thrust of my analysis is a note of critical realism which recognizes the formidable obstacles —social, human, and cultural—to dialogic and deliberative participation among people of different and, often conflicting, persuasions. Still, cultural pluralism need not lead to fatal and socially fractured existence. There is a strong moral imperative for every society, especially a religiously pluralistic one, to exercise "civic virtue" and "political intelligence" in the conduct of its public life. Only then can there be that minimum agree-ment through which it can both "enlarge" its dialogue and "re-duce" its "warfare."[135] All of this presupposes that the pluralist dilemma be understood from the start as a fundamental moral problem, the discussion of which must be raised to the level of basic ethical principles. It is this theological-ethical nature of the problem that I discuss in the next chapter.

Notes

1. Larry Diamond, Juan J. Linz, and Seymour M. Lipset, introduc-tion ("Comparing Experiences with Democracy") to *Politics in De-veloping Countries* (Boulder: Lynne Rienner, 1990), 6.

2. Richard Mouw and Sander Griffioen, *Pluralisms and Horizons: An Essay in Christian Public Philosophy* (Grand Rapids, Mich.: Eerdmans, 1993), 13-15.

3. Rupert Breitling, "The Concept of Pluralism," in *Three Faces of Pluralism: Political, Ethnic and Religious,* ed. Stanislaw Ehrlich and Graham Wootton (Westmead, England: Gower, 1980), 15.

4. William James, *Essays in Radical Empiricism and a Pluralistic Universe,* vol. 2 (New York: Longmans, Green, 1958), 79.

5. See David Nicholls, *Three Varieties of Pluralism* (London: Macmillan, 1974) and Leo Kuper and M. G. Smith, eds., *Pluralism in Africa* (Berkeley: University of California Press, 1971).

6. Mouw and Griffioen, *Pluralisms and Horizons,* 15.

7. Michael J. Perry, *Love and Power: The Role of Religion and Morality in American Politics* (New York: Oxford University Press, 1991), 6.

8. *International Encyclopedia of the Social Sciences,* s.v. "Plural-ism," by Henry S. Kariel.

9. Perry, *Love and Power,* 6.

10. See J. S. Furnivall, *Colonial Policy and Practice: A Compara-tive Study of Burma and Netherlands India* (Cambridge: Cambridge University Press, 1948), 290-305. For a similar thesis, see M. G. Smith, "Institutional and Political Conditions of Pluralism," in *Pluralism in*

Africa, ed. Leo Kuper and M. G. Smith (Berkeley: University of California Press, 1971), 27–65.

11. Perry, *Love and Power,* 6.

12. Kent Greenawalt, *Religious Convictions and Political Culture* (New York: Oxford University Press, 1988), 6.

13. E. Bolaji Idowu, *God in Nigerian Belief* (Lagos: Federal Ministry of Information, 1963).

14. Christopher F. Mooney, *Boundaries Dimly Perceived: Law, Religion, and the Common Good* (Notre Dame, Ind.: University of Notre Dame Press, 1990), 2.

15. This was the interpretation offered in H. Richard Niebuhr, *Christ and Culture* (New York: Harper and Row, 1951), 32–39.

16. John Courtney Murray, *We Hold These Truths: Catholic Reflections on the American Proposition* (New York: Sheed and Ward, 1960; New York: Image Books, 1964), 9; all subsequent citations refer to the latter edition.

17. Patricia A. Williams, "The State, Religion and Politics in Nigeria" (Ph. D. thesis, University of Ibadan, Nigeria, 1988), 115.

18. *International Encyclopedia of the Social Sciences,* s.v. "The concept of state," by Frederick M. Walkins.

19. Crawford Young, *The Politics of Cultural Pluralism* (Madison: University of Wisconsin Press, 1976), 67.

20. Crawford Young, "The Dialectics of Cultural Pluralism: Concept and Reality," in *The Rising Tide of Cultural Pluralism: The Nation-State at Bay?,* ed. Crawford Young (Madison: University of Wisconsin Press, 1993), 8.

21. Ibid.

22. Ibid.

23. J. S. Mill, *Collected Works of John Stuart Mill,* ed. J. M. Robson, vol. 19, *Considerations on Representative Government* (Toronto: University of Toronto Press, 1977), 16.

24. Reinhold Niebuhr, *Moral Man and Immoral Society: A Study in Ethics and Politics* (New York: Scribner's, 1932; New York: Scribner Library, 1960), 91, 95.

25. Jacques Maritain, *Man and the State* (Chicago: University of Chicago Press, 1951), 13.

26. Ibid., 12.

27. Ibid., 13–14.

28. Ibid., 18.

29. Ibid., 19.

30. Reinhold Niebuhr, *The Children of Light and the Children of Darkness: A Vindication of Democracy and a Critique of Its Traditional Defense* (New York: Scribner's, 1944; New York: Scribner Library, 1960), 3.

31. Mark A. Noll, introduction to *Religion and American Politics from the Colonial Period to the 1980s,* ed. Mark A. Noll (New York: Oxford University Press, 1990), 3.

32. Ibid.

33. Ibid., 4.

34. Dan Agbese, "The Long Shadow," *Newswatch* (Nigeria), 6 May 1991, 6.

35. Rev. Fr. Matthew Hassan Kukah, "Religion and Politics in Northern Nigeria Since 1960" (Ph.D. thesis, University of London, 1989), 1.

36. John O. Hunwick, introduction to *Religion and National Integration in Africa: Islam, Christianity, and Politics in the Sudan and Nigeria,* ed. John O. Hunwick (Evanston, Ill.: Northwestern University Press, 1992), 7.

37. Ibid., xi.

38. Ibid., 6.

39. A. H. M. Kirk-Greene, "Ethnic Engineering and the 'Federal Character' of Nigeria: Boon of Contentment or Base of Contention?," *Ethnic and Racial Studies* 6, 4 (1983): 471.

40. Jibrin Ibrahim, "Some Considerations on Religion and Political Turbulence in Nigeria: Muslims, Christians, 'Pagans,' 'Fundamentalists,' and All That . . ." (paper delivered at the "Social Movements Seminar," Institute of Social Studies, The Hague, 16 October 1989), 16.

41. Don Ohadike, "Muslim-Christian Conflict and Political Instability in Nigeria," in *Religion and National Integration in Africa: Islam, Christianity, and Politics in the Sudan and Nigeria,* ed. John O. Hunwick (Evanston, Ill.: Northwestern University Press, 1992), 109, 120.

42. Bode Sowande, *The Punch* (Nigeria), 30 August 1988.

43. Federal Government of Nigeria, *The Report of the Political Bureau* (Abuja: Directorate for Public Enlightenment and Social Mobilization, 1987), 188.

44. Nicholas Wolterstorff, *Until Justice and Peace Embrace* (Grand Rapids, Mich.: Eerdmans, 1983), ix.

45. David Hollenbach, S.J., foreword to *The Ethics of Discourse: The Social Philosophy of John Courtney Murray,* by J. Leon Hooper (Washington, D.C.: Georgetown University Press, 1986), ix.

46. Reinhold Niebuhr, *The Nature and Destiny of Man: A Christian Interpretation, vol. 1, Human Nature* (New York: Scribner's, 1941), vii–viii.

47. Ibid., 181–83.

48. Reinhold Niebuhr, "Christian Faith and Natural Law," in *Love and Justice: Selections from the Shorter Writings of Reinhold Niebuhr,* ed. D. B. Robertson (Louisville: Westminster/John Knox Press, 1957), 49.

49. Reinhold Niebuhr, *Beyond Tragedy* (New York: Scribner's, 1937), 167.

50. Ibrahim, "Religion and Political Turbulence in Nigeria," 17.

51. Abner Cohen, *Custom and Politics in Urban Africa: A Study of Hausa Migrants in Yoruba Towns* (Manchester: University of Manchester Press, 1969), 5.

52. Y. B. Usman, *The Manipulation of Religion in Nigeria,* 1977–1987 (Kaduna, Nigeria: Vanguard, 1987). For a similar class analysis of religion and politics in Nigeria, see Paul Lubeck, "Islamic Protest under Semi-Industrial Capitalism: 'Yan Tatsine' Explained," *Africa* 55, 4 (1985): 369–89; Jibrin Ibrahim, "The Politics of Religion in Nigeria: The Parameters of the 1987 Crisis in Kaduna State," *Review of African Political Economy* 45/46 (1989): 65–82.

53. Cornel West, *Prophetic Fragments: Illuminations of the Crisis in American Religion and Culture* (Grand Rapids, Mich.: Eerdmans, 1988), 14.

54. Adigun Agbaje, "Travails of the Secular State: Religion, Politics and the Outlook on Nigeria's Third Republic," *Journal of Commonwealth and Comparative Politics* 28, 3 (1990): 302.

55. Ibid., 305.

56. Ibid., 302.

57. Maritain, *Man and the State,* 59.

58. Segun Gbadegesin, introduction to *The Politicization of Society during Nigeria's Second Republic,* 1979–83, ed. Segun Gbadegesin (Lewiston, N.Y.: Edwin Mellen Press, 1991): 9.

59. Ibid.

60. Christian Coulon, "Les itineraires politiques de l'Islam au Nord Nigeria," cited in Ibrahim, "Religion and Political Turbulence in Nigeria," 18.

61. Laitin, *Hegemony and Culture,* 12.

62. J. D. Y. Peel, *Ijeshas and Nigerians: The Incorporation of a Yoruba Kingdom, 1890s–1970s* (Cambridge: Cambridge University Press, 1983), 161.

63. Lamin Sanneh, *West African Christianity: The Religious Impact* (Maryknoll, N.Y.: Orbis Books, 1983), xi.

64. See William F. May, *The Physician's Covenant,* 13; William Ernest Hocking, *The Coming Civilization* (New York: Harper & Row, 1956).

65. Ibrahim, "Religion and Political Turbulence in Nigeria," 21.

66. Robert A. Dahl, *Dilemmas of Pluralist Democracy: Autonomy vs. Control* (New Haven: Yale University Press, 1982), 142, 187–88.

67. Larry Diamond, "Class Formation in the Swollen African State," *Journal of Modern African Studies* 25, 4 (1987): 567–596.

68. Lamin Sanneh, "Religion, Politics, and National Integration: A Comparative African Perspective," in *Religion and National Integration in Africa: Islam, Christianity, and Politics in the Sudan and Nigeria,* ed. John O. Hunwick (Evanston, Ill.: Northwestern University Press, 1992), 154.

69. Roland Robertson, "Considerations from within the American Context on the Significance of Church-State Tension," *Sociological Analysis* 446 (Fall 1981): 201.

70. Ibid.

71. Larry Diamond, "Nigeria: Pluralism, Statism, and the Struggle for Democracy," in *Politics in Developing Countries: Comparing Experiences with Democracy,* ed. Larry Diamond, Juan J. Linz, and Seymour Martin Lipset (Boulder: Lynne Rienner, 1990), 401.

72. Sanneh, "Religion, Politics, and National Integration," 155.

73. Agbaje, "Travails of the Secular State," 290.

74. Richard John Neuhaus, *The Naked Public Square: Religion and Democracy in America,* 2d ed. (Grand Rapids, Mich.: Eerdmans, 1984), ix, 89.

75. Lamin Sanneh, "Religion and Politics: Third World Perspectives on a Comparative Religious Theme," *Daedalus* 120, 3 (1991), 206.

76. Tunde Lawuyi, "Nigeria in the 1980s: Religion and National Integration," in *Religion and Society in Nigeria: Historical and Sociological Perspectives,* ed. Jacob. K. Olupona and Toyin Falola (Ibadan: Spectrum Books, 1991), 230–31.

77. Billy Dudley, *An Introduction to Nigerian Government and Politics* (Bloomington: Indiana University Press, 1982), 76.

78. Eddie Iroh, "Winning at All Costs," *Newswatch* (Nigeria), 30 November 1992, 8.

79. S. Huntington, *Political Order in Changing Societies* (New Haven: Yale University Press, 1968), 215.

80. See J. F. Ade Ajayi's influential essay, "Colonialism: An Episode in African History," in *Colonialism in Africa,* vol. 1, ed. L. H. Gann and P. Duignan (Cambridge: Cambridge University Press, 1969), 497–508.

81. Peter Ekeh, *Colonialism and Social Structure,* Inaugural Lecture Series (Ibadan: University of Ibadan Press, 1983), 11, and his "Colonialism and the Two Publics in Africa: A Theoretical Statement," *Comparative Studies in Society and History* 17, 1 (1975): 104–11. For a critique of Ekeh's dichotomous view of Africa's two publics, see Peel, *Ijeshas and Nigerians,* 16–43; Richard Joseph, *Democracy and Prebendal Politics in Nigeria: The Rise and Fall of the Second Republic* (Cambridge: Cambridge University Press, 1987), 193–98.

82. Young, *Politics of Cultural Pluralism,* 93.

83. Murray, *We Hold These Truths,* 10.

84. Roland Robertson, "Church-State Relations in Comparative Perspective," in *Church-State Relations: Tensions and Transitions,* ed. Thomas Robbins and Roland Robertson (New Brunswick, N.J.: Transaction Books, 1987), 154.

85. See David Martin, "The Secularization Thesis and the Decline of Particular Religions," in *Der Untergang von Religionen,* ed. Hartmut Zinser (Berlin: Dietrich Reimer Verlag, n.d.): 309-19.

86. Robertson, "Church-State Relations in Comparative Perspective," 156.

87. Ann K. S. Lambton, *State and Government in Medieval Islam: An Introduction to the Study of Islamic Political Theory: The Jurists,* London Oriental Series (Oxford: Oxford University Press, 1981), xv.

88. *The Westminster Dictionary of Christian Ethics,* rev. ed., s.v. "Social Ethics," by Joseph L. Allen.

89. Frederick S. Carney, "Some Aspects of Islamic Ethics," *The Journal of Religion* 63, 2 (April 1983): 159-60.

90. Lambton, *State and Government in Medieval Islam,* xv, 2.

91. Roger Garaudy, "Human Rights and Islam: Foundation, Tradition, Violation," in *The Ethics of World Religions and Human Rights,* Concilium, ed. Hans Küng and Jürgen Moltmann (London: SCM Press, 1990), 51.

92. David Martin, "The Limits of Ecumenism" (London School of Economics, mimeographed, n.d.), 3.

93. *The Westminster Dictionary of Christian Ethics,* rev. ed., s.v. "Church and State," by A. R. Vidler.

94. Laitin, *Hegemony and Culture,* 24.

95. Ibid.

96. Abdullahi Ahmed An-Na'im, "Qur'an, Shari'a and Human Rights: Foundations, Deficiencies and Prospects," in *The Ethics of World Religions and Human Rights,* Concilium, ed. Hans Küng and Jürgen Moltmann (London: SCM Press, 1990), 66-67.

97. Louis Brenner, "Representations of Power and Powerlessness among West African Muslims" (paper presented to the Colloque Religion et Histoire en Afrique au Sud du Sahara, Paris, 15-17 May 1991), 6.

98. Ibid., 2, 3.

99. Ibn Khaldūn, *The Muqaddimah: An Introduction to History,* 3 vols., trans. Franz Rosenthal (London: n.p., 1958).

100. Lambton pointed out that Ibn Khaldūn's stormy involvement in the politics of North Africa, his appointment as the chief *qadi* of the Maliki rite in Cairo, and his encounter with the Berbers contrib-

uted to his firsthand experience of the difference between nomadic and settled life and between the town and the country. See Lambton, *State and Government in Medieval Islam,* 152.

101. Erwin I. J. Rosenthal, *Political Thought in Medieval Islam: An Introductory Outline* (Cambridge: Cambridge University Press, 1958; Westport, Conn.: Greenwood Press, 1985), 85–86.

102. Ibn Khaldūn lived in a time of transition, when the medieval order was gradually giving way to a new grouping of political, economic, and spiritual forces. This historical experience may have helped him to formulate his ideas on the inevitable birth, growth, peak, decline, and fall of society and culture in accordance with the unalterable law of causality.

103. Rosenthal, *Political Thought in Medieval Islam,* 86.

104. Ibid., 99.

105. Ibid., 93.

106. Sanneh, "Religion, Politics, and National Integration," 159.

107. Rosenthal, *Political Thought in Medieval Islam,* 99.

108. Sanneh, "Religion, Politics, and National Integration," 159.

109. Rosenthal, *Political Thought in Medieval Islam,* 93.

110. Ibid., 96–97.

111. Alexis de Tocqueville, *Democracy in America* (New York: Schocken Books, 1961), 1:362.

112. Ibid., 1:365–67.

113. Ibid., 1:361.

114. Ibid., 2:30.

115. Ibid.

116. Rosenthal, *Political Thought in Medieval Islam,* 85. The emphasis, which is Rosenthal's, refers to Ibn Khaldūn's appreciation of a more cosmopolitan and universal *humanitas,* that is, the citizens of the state, a concept commonly associated with the Renaissance and the humanism of the West.

117. Ibid., 93.

118. Maritain, *Man and the State,* 160.

119. Nicholls, *Three Varieties of Pluralism,* 23.

120. Thomas Hobbes, *Leviathan,* ed. with introduction, C. B. Macpherson (London: Penguin Books, 1968), 312.

121. Robert Nisbet, *The Social Philosophers: Community and Conflict in Western Thought* (New York: Pocket Books, 1973), 30.

122. Hobbes, *Leviathan*, 371.

123. Ibid., 498.

124. J. N. Figgis, *Churches in the Modern State* (London: Longman, 1913); H. J. Laski, *Authority in the Modern State* (New Haven: Yale University Press, 1919).

125. J. N. Laski, "The Pluralistic State," *Philosophical Review* 28 (1919): 571.

126. Ibid.

127. Figgis, *Churches in the Modern State* (London: Longman, 1913), 258.

128. Ibid., 263.

129. Ibid., 92.

130. Maritain, *Man and the State*, 10.

131. Jean-François Bayart, "Civil Society in Africa," in *Political Domination in Africa: Reflections on the Limits of Power*, ed. Patrick Chabal (Cambridge: Cambridge University Press, 1986), 123.

132. Robert A. Dahl, "Pluralism Revisited," in *Three Faces of Pluralism: Political, Ethnic, and Religious*, ed. Stanislaw Ehrlich and Graham Wootton (Westmead, England: Gower, 1980), 22.

133. Bayart, "Civil Society in Africa," 113.

134. Patrick Chabal, introduction ("Thinking about Politics in Africa") to *Political Domination in Africa*, ed. Patrick Chabal (Cambridge: Cambridge University Press, 1986), 15.

135. Murray, *We Hold These Truths*, 17–35.

Chapter 2

Religious Pluralism, the State, and Dialogic Politics

> As it found place in America the problem of pluralism was unique in the modern world, chiefly because pluralism was the native condition of American society. . . . This fact made possible a new project; but the new project required, as its basis, a new doctrine. This requirement was met by the First Amendment to the Constitution, in itself and in its relation to the whole theory of limited government that the Constitution incorporates.
>
> —John Courtney Murray,
> *We Hold These Truths*

THIS CHAPTER EXAMINES certain modal theological-ethical reconceptualizations of the problematic of religious pluralism in the context of the modern state. For reasons already stated, my principal resources will be the works of John Courtney Murray, Michael Perry, Robin W. Lovin, and to a lesser extent, Reinhold Niebuhr. In their different case studies of the United States, these thinkers offer models, motives, paradigms, and themes for thinking about many of the basic features of religious and civil life in any religiously pluralistic society. They specifically argue that it is possible to be faithful to one's private or communal religious vision and still see purpose and value in the larger society, where some people do not share the roots of that vision. These authors thus offer us significant theoretical models for studying Nigeria's pluralist dilemma. (A model is understood here as "fundamentally a vehicle for explanation [whose] essence derives from the demonstration of certain relationships among things which exist in the real world.")[1] Their methodologies are not altogether the same; however, they agree substantially on three key areas which I shall outline to provide a structure for this chapter.

First, these authors concur that the *political* community is not a given; rather, it comes into being through the conscious efforts of persons and groups occupying the same social space. More significantly, they contend that pluralism deriving from religious particularities need not be a barrier to the formation of the political community. Second, they agree that not all political communities perdure, and that central to the stability and flourishing of any political community is the common subscription of its members to a moral capital, a public consensus, which must be grounded in a comprehensive moral principle, and thus provides authoritative standards for evaluating political institutions and political behavior. Finally, they argue that the necessity of an integrative political-moral consensus must not obscure the equally important requirement of political and civil freedom, without which the citizens and groups of a political community would be unable to maintain their identity.

These prerequisites are considered "ideals" that may not be fully and completely present in any particular society. They are nevertheless crucial for thinking about the most desirable ways to equilibrate the dual imperative of civil unity and religious integrity. Indeed, they more or less underlie the varied political structures found around the world. This is because, like any other human artifacts, political structures are "not only systems of constraint but also fields of opportunity; they work, generally speaking, but they are also there to be worked."[2] And "public life," as Douglas Sturm says, "is not a given. However indomitable its current structures appear, it is a construction. It is a work never fully accomplished. It is an enactment. By what

we are, do, and say, we are engaged in a process of its formation or reformation."[3]

Without a doubt, religious pluralism is a congenital feature
of Nigeria. The veracity of this assertion is well encapsulated
in the comment of a distinguished Nigerian church historian
that "religious pluralism is now a cardinal feature of the status
of religion in Independent Nigeria."[4] What is presently un-
clear is the potential capacity of this feature to respond to a
new political project rooted in a new doctrine.

Constitutional Paradigms of Religion and the State

The question about the proper mode of religion-state relations, whether in pluralistically or uniformly constituted societies, is not one that can, or ought to, be resolved by arbitrary
governmental decisions or purely external power relationships.
Ernst Troeltsch suggests that any regulative policy of the state
regarding its official position on religion must be guided by
"the inner position of society vis-à-vis the religious life generally."[5] David Martin specifies this guiding principle more clearly
as referring to the "objective patterns—or frames—of religion-
society relationships," by which he means the number and variety of religious confessions in a society, on the one hand, and
the degree to which that circumstance is, as a matter of degree,
rigid or flexible, on the other.[6]

Theoretically, one can say that pluralism of religions is one
underlying factor for the tacit endorsement of the principle of
political neutrality in many constitutional definitions of the
place of religion around the world today. The most vivid example of this principle is the religion clauses in the First
Amendment to the United States' Federal Constitution, which
stipulates that "congress shall make no law respecting an es-

tablishment of religion or prohibiting the free exercise thereof.
. . ." Many of the world's national constitutions have either
explicitly expressed a similar intent or declared positions that
are very close to it. In fact, one distinctive feature of modern
states' political arrangements is that national constitutions have
become the "improbable templates on which to gauge and locate religious aspirations and to chart the ways in which religion
enters into political conflict."[7] Moreover, with the exception of
the Islamic world, there has been "a virtual global movement,
in principle, toward the delineation of an inviolable private
niche within which individuals possess inalienable rights, and
against which the state can make few if any claims."[8]

Despite this seemingly explicit global commitment to constitutionalism, the human rights records of some nations have
been morally repugnant. Ideological documents such as constitutions, therefore, despite their binding legalistic tone, are un-
dependable guides to political action. What Osita Eze, Henry
Shue, and others have noted, regarding the international
agreements that nations have signed, is also true for their constitutions: the gap between constitutional word and political
deed has become a chasm.[9] As observed by Richard Joseph,
"many contemporary dictatorships have constitutions which
serve more to camouflage the exercise of power than to guide
and determine it."[10]

Worse still, the constitutional statements themselves fre-
quently teem with qualifying clauses, so that in many cases the
guarantee of rights is far from absolute. For instance, the Nigerian 1979 constitution contains a chapter stating the "fundamental objectives and directive principles of state policy." The
express intent of these objectives and policies was to "cast on
the state definite duties towards its subjects." One of these duties that is relevant to our discussion is that "the Government
of the Federation or of a State shall not adopt any religion as
State Religion."[11] However, in the explanatory note on this

constitutional chapter in the *Draft Constitution,* it is stated that the stipulations contained therein are "nonjusticiable."[12] This declared nonjusticiability of constitutional provisions clearly reveals that Nigeria's Second Republic was doomed to failure ab initio. The use of the term *duties* to refer to nonenforceable objectives is illogical and philosophically nonsensical. John Stuart Mill states that "It is a part of the notion of duty in every one of its forms that a person may rightfully be compelled to fulfill it. Duty is a thing which may be exacted from a person as one exacts a debt. Unless we think that it may be *exacted* from him, we do not call it his duty."[13] Thus, before the state can claim any legitimate rights to citizens' obedience and loyalty, it must demonstrate its preparedness to perform its own obligations or duties. The state, no less than its citizens, needs to be aware of the "moral correlation of rights and duties," in that the acquisition of rights by any individual (except children, the mentally challenged, the senile, and the insane) or institution is contingent upon "the ability and willingness to shoulder duties and responsibilities."[14]

This brief comparative assessment indicates the possibility of multiple interpretations for the notion of constitutional government. The mere presence of a constitution within a nation's political system says very little about the quality of its politics. "Constitution-gazing is a perilously inaccurate way of discovering, much less predicting, a nation's politics."[15] Murray contends that pertinent to an adequate understanding of any political institution is the nature or character of its political culture. Especially in the context of a pluralistic society, "the immediate question is not whether [that society] is really free (although this is equally important) . . . [but whether it] is properly civil."[16]

The central conception here is of "political culture," defined by Sidney Verba as "the system of beliefs about patterns of political interaction and political institutions."[17] These include empirical beliefs about the actual nature of politics in a system, goals and values that people hold for that system, and emotions and feelings they have about it and its various roles. Gabriel A. Almond and Verba have labeled these components as the cognitive, evaluational, and affective elements of political culture.[18] Lucian Pye amends Verba's definition to emphasize the behavioral implications of these beliefs—that they "provide underlying assumptions and rules that govern behavior in the political system"—and to stress as well their systemic or patterned nature, the ways in which they fit together and so "give order and meaning to a political process."[19]

In this light, the late Billy Dudley, a foremost Nigerian political theorist, pointed out that one clue to explaining what appears to be Nigerians' Hobbesian approach to politics is their conception of power (*agbara,* in Yoruba). For most Nigerians, power is not a relation, but a property or a predicate, and as such something to be valued not only for its own sake, but also because its possession is what makes everything else possible. Power is might and might is power; it is as simple as that. Referring specifically to the ruling class, Dudley remarks that "for the political elite, power was an end-in-itself and not a means to the realization of some greater 'good' for the community, and whatever the instrumentalities employed in the pursuit of power, such instrumentalities were legitimate."[20] This belief in the majesty of power shapes many Nigerians' perception of the political arena, and explains why some see the public relevance of religion essentially in terms of its mobilizing potential for the acquisition and retention of power.

Power is, of course, not irrelevant to politics; it is indeed impossible to conceive of politics without a notion of power. "The contest of power is," according to Niebuhr, "the heart of political life."[21] In fact, power has remained central to many standard definitions of politics offered by political scientists. Politics is generally construed as the process by which some individuals and groups acquire power and exercise that power over others. S. E. Finer says that "politics connotes a special case in the exercise of power."[22] Dahl regards it as "any persistent pattern of human relationship that involves to a significant extent power, rule, and authority."[23] Hence, whether construed as an activity for determining "who gets what, when, and how"[24] or as "a game in which individuals or groups of individuals make moves,"[25] it is almost a canon among the political scientists and professional politicians that the art of politics consists in how to maneuver the location of power within a given social context.

There are two main problems with this conception of politics. First, it presupposes a view of human nature that understands human beings as incapable of generating and sustaining any concerns beyond those attaching to the self—whether the self be one's own being or the primary community to which one belongs. Second, it envisions an ideal of politics in which the rules of the game consist mainly in the arbitration of conflicts and negotiation of mutually differentiated interests with less or no regard to how some commonly grounded human good can be generated.

Dialogic Politics

A question I would like to raise here is whether there is a conception of political life in which the lure of power is not the underlying rationale for political participation. Murray and Michael J. Perry offer one promising approach. According to Perry, politics is "in part about the credibility of competing conceptions of human good."[26] Human good, with the means of achieving it, is one of the many desirable teloi of politics; indeed, an indispensable feature of it. This conception of politics gives political life what David Nicholls has called "the moral face."[27] But even more significant is the accent this conception puts not only on the ends, but also the practice, of politics. Ultimately, the common good becomes the ethical criterion for organizing the political life of a religiously pluralistic society.

But the conception is also fraught with some practical difficulties. An obvious one is how to bring about a common political good out of divergent visions of it, especially when they are derived from different authoritative sources. A more serious danger is the likelihood of a state arrogating to itself the absolute prerogative to determine what will count as the common good, a situation to which history amply testifies. Examples of these leviathan states include "a benevolent despotism" and a "bureaucratic parentalism," both of which typically exercise compulsion against people on the ground that such an action promotes the people's good—people are being helped to live the life that they would really like to live. A leviathan state tends to legitimize itself under the pretext that "it is one of the rights of the citizen to be protected against his own weakness."[28]

Anticipating these and similar objections, Murray and Perry deploy the intertwined notions of "public consensus," "public philosophy," "ecumenical politics," and "ecumenical political dialogue" to specify the material contents of the common human good in a pluralistic society as consisting of (a) some substantive truths without which agreement on the good cannot perdure, (b) common agreement to a political method within which every conception of human good can have a hearing, and (c) a common resolve that such a political method is a good to be valued. The implications of this understanding for the political life of a religiously pluralistic society are that valid moral insights could arise outside the conventional religions and that religious communities ought to be attentive to those insights; and, second, that religious arguments can be used in articulating an idea of the human good.

In short, there can be a congruence between religious visions of the good political life and the aspirations of secular persons. The appeal to a religious vision, however, is not simply endorsement of prevailing cultural standards. Rather when religious persons appeal to their convictions, they do so because of the capacity of such convictions to "enrich our sense of the possibilities life offers, extend our concerns to people and places we have heretofore ignored, and transform our sense of what would make us happy by showing us ways of life that our own limited experience could not devise."[29]

Public Consensus or Public Philosophy

Murray uses *consensus* to emphasize that decisions about the basic direction of society are not spontaneous. "No society in history," he writes, "has ever achieved and maintained an identity and a vigor in action unless it has had some substance, unless it has been sustained and directed by some body of substantive truths."[30] Perry too discerns a symbiosis between public consensus and political community. The former supplies the moral language or normative premises for the articulation of political discourse while political community provides the spacial and institutional context for this discourse.[31] Thus, not only the stability but also the meaningfulness and quality of political life are ultimately determined by an acknowledgment of a more fundamental set of truths—the public consensus—which, given the transcendent nature of the truths involved, has come to be called the public philosophy. Public consensus is a moral conception, and its validity and intelligibility rest on a moral theory.

According to Walter Lippmann, public philosophy is "a body

of positive principles which a good citizen cannot deny or ignore."[32] In a similar vein, Murray states that public consensus is "an ensemble of substantive truths, a structure of basic knowledge, an order of elementary affirmations that reflect realities inherent in the order of existence."[33] The functional relevance of the material contents of public consensus is that they constitute the "underlying grounds of political judgment-grounds concerning how the collective life, the life in common, is to be lived—which citizens, *qua* members of a judging community, share, and which serve to unite them in dialogue, notwithstanding their (sometimes radical) disagreements."[34] Citing Cicero's *De Re Publica*, Murray says that a true republic is not just any association of people but is a people *juris consensu et utilitatis communione sociatus*—a people united by a common agreement about laws and rights and a common desire for mutual, not just selfish, advantage. This feature is what distinguishes a true human community from a formless mass of people. "The masses," Murray says, "are amorphous; their principle is external to themselves. A people is a structured moral community, fashioned by a consciously shared consensus; it is capable—both as a collectivity and in its individual members—of protecting its own moral identity and directing its own social life."[35] Similarly, John H. Hallowell argues that government truly based on the consent of the governed "is found . . . only in those nations where there is a community of values and interests, where there is a positive affirmation of certain fundamental values common to the large majority of individuals and groups within the nation."[36]

Within his own parameters of public consensus, Murray challenges pluralistic societies to strive to overcome the anomic cancer of social and moral tepidity. He proposes two directive questions which any such society must answer: "How much pluralism and what kinds of pluralism can a pluralist society stand? And conversely, how much unity and what kind of unity does a pluralist society need in order to be a society at all, effectively organized for action in history. . . ."[37] Putting the questions in this way suggests that a pluralistic society must come to terms with what human beings are, what is good and bad for them, and the basic moral principles and structure of social existence that should govern human life. These are not simply programmatic, but also moral, questions. Thus, the consensual will to an organization of political authority must be informed by, and cannot be divorced from, "the will to a common life in the body politic"—which is to say, "the will to form a state, an order of peace and justice, whose contents are not purely formal or procedural but substantive and material."[38]

What are the epistemological warrants for these substantive truths, and what are their political consequences? Murray argues that the first principle of the public philosophy is that human reason is capable of discovering valid principles about the common good and about the natural moral law. The common good entails, among other things, the state's duty to ensure peace, order, and justice so that citizens can pursue good lives- specifically, lives of moral self-improvement and personal religious salvation. It also means that both government and citizens, in their political behavior, seek the good of society as a whole instead of personal self-interest. In addition to its specific content, the common good serves as a standard both for evaluating new proposals and for dealing with changes in the political environment.[39]

Human reason can also recognize valid principles of natural law. By reflecting on the ends appropriate to human nature, human reason transcends the statutory or positive law of the state and discovers binding moral principles in the nature of things. Cicero called this law "right reason in agreement with nature." It is a universal moral law that binds all people in all places and that may not rightly be altered by human beings. The author of the natural law is God himself, who is the author of nature. Murray spelled out what he considered the four essential principles of natural law which all persons of good will could accept. They are "(1) a religious conviction as to the sovereignty of God over nations as well as over individuals; (2) a right conscience as to the essential demands of the moral law in social life; (3) a religious respect for human dignity in oneself and in others—the dignity with which man is invested inasmuch as he is the image of God; and (4) a religious conviction as to the essential unity of the human race."[40]

These natural law principles place moral limits on the actions of both rulers and citizens, and "fix the boundaries beyond which the Sovereign—the King, the Parliament, the voters— were forbidden to go." In short, they civilize society because a law "above the ruler and the sovereign people, above the whole community of mortals," restricts arbitrary government and dictatorship on the one hand, and popular license and tyranny of the majority on the other.[41] Niebuhr discovers a complementarity between these natural law principles and religious insights derived from revelation, which have strengthened the insights of reason concerning human dignity, humanity's unique nature, human rights and duties, and limit the state's role over citizens.[42]

Public philosophy, however, has a limited scope. While its contents may derive partly from religious insights, it does not require consensus at the level of religious truths nor does it pronounce judgments on the internal ordering of religious doctrines. Public philosophy, according to Murray, "is narrow in its scope, operative on the level of political life, with regard to the rational truths and moral precepts that govern the structure of the constitutional state, specify the substance of the commonweal, and determine the ends of public policy."[43] The potency of public philosophy as a binding agent derives not from its abstract nature but from its rootedness in concrete human situations. To be effective, therefore, public philosophy must exist at two interlocking levels of society. The first is the level of "the people at large," who would be expected to possess the public philosophy "almost intuitively, in the form of a simple faith rather than an articulate philosophy." The second "is the level of the 'clerks,' the intellectuals," who have "to be in conscious possession of the public philosophy as philosophy; for them it would be a personal acquisition and not simply a patrimony."[44]

If public consensus is essentially political in nature, does this mean that every citizen and communal group would always be able to agree on every political issue? If this is the presupposition of public consensus, then it begs the issues arising from the dilemma of a religiously pluralistic society. What therefore is the sort of political life being envisioned by public consensus, as being construed here? How is such a political life possible in a religiously pluralistic society without reducing that society to a monolithic cosmos?

To answer these queries, Perry proposes the idea of "ecumenical politics," whose chief objective is the discernment or achievement, in a religiously and morally pluralistic context, of "a common political ground."[45] Particularistic visions of human good, religious or secular or both, are neither marginalized nor suppressed. This is an idea of politics "in which, not withstanding [a people's] religious/moral pluralism, [they] continually cultivate the bonds of political community—and in which [they] sometimes succeed in strengthening these bonds, even, occasionally, in forging new bonds—through dialogue of a certain kind."[46]

Within these parameters, public philosophy ceases to be merely a prudential social contract for the sole purpose of conducting political a fight among atomistically differentiated citizens. Rather it becomes "a common moral language"[47] that mediates between people who do not share the same religious beliefs. More important, it becomes a creed, constituting "a part of the deeply believed assumptions of a people built into the fabric of a society."[48] An essential feature of a creed is that, besides its being held to be true, it must be "embraced with commitment, celebrated in concert with others, and used as a fundamental guide for action."[49] Public consensus, and the idea of politics it helps to build, is thus ultimately a guide on how religiously diverse citizens "should contend with each other's deepest differences in the public square."[50]

The defining characteristic of this politics is not domination, but deliberation or dialogue. Joseph L. Allen defines political dialogue as "the communication that goes on among members of a community when they deliberate together over the policies of the community."[51] But no such dialogue can achieve tangible and enduring results if it is not based on mutual commitment to the process and an abiding faith in the validity of a common destiny. For genuine political dialogue is grounded in the premise that argument begins not when people have disagreement but rather when they are in agreement on certain principles. Says Murray, "There are laws of argument [dialogue], the observance of which is imperative if discourse is to be civilized. Argument ceases to be civil when it is dominated by passion and prejudice; when its vocabulary becomes solipsist, premised on the theory that my insight is mine alone and cannot be shared; when dialogue gives way to a series of monologues. . . ."[52] In a true dialogue, the participants share a common frame of reference, recognize the importance of the issues being discussed, and exhibit a common concern for the manner in which those issues are resolved. On this, too, Murray further reminds us that

> the whole premise of the public argument, if it is to be civilized and civilizing, is that the consensus is real, that among the people everything is not in doubt, but that there is a core of agreement, accord, concurrence, acquiescence. We hold certain truths; there-

fore we can argue about them. . . . There can be no argument except on the premise, and within a context, of agreement. *Mutatis mutandis*, this is true of scientific, philosophical, and theological argument. It is no less true of political argument.[53]

The exigency of political dialogue rests on a moral anthropological view that there is "a human and not merely local good," a good that is "common to every human being."[54] This view derives from another socioanthropological fact that "there are significant needs common to all human beings," the benefits of which we can discover through joint deliberative efforts.[55] And precisely because this is a consensus that is public based and public related, ecumenical politics affirms the validity, and in fact, the desirability, of "great diversity in preferred ways of life, even among [persons] living at the same place at the same time."[56]

Hence, dissensus is not only anticipated but also accommodated within the notion of public consensus and ecumenical politics. In fact, dissent plays an integrative role within this conception of political life by solidifying, rather than undermining or destroying, the public consensus. "Without some conflict, dialogue would be unnecessary; and yet without some harmony, it would be impossible."[57] The true test of political dialogue is not agreement, but the undeviating commitment to this method as a good way of organizing political life. As Murray argues, "the specifying note of political association is its rational deliberative quality, its dependence for its permanent cohesiveness on argument among men."[58]

When consensus and dissensus are able to coexist and to resist the temptation of mutual extermination, genuine disagreement becomes an accomplishment, and authentic debate a virtuous activity. This happens when all contenders, however much they disagree on relevant issues, do not kill each other over their differences, do not desecrate what the others hold sublime, and do not eschew principled discourse with one another. To be genuinely committed to dialogue as a political method is to be civil.

Civility is a particular mode of behavior that is indispensable to the political life of a religiously pluralistic society. Admittedly, there is a certain risk, an existential ordeal, that is involved in the art of cultivating a civil character. For religious adherents in particular, notably those of the monotheistic strand, there is the theological compulsion to resist any requirement that purports to divest them of any sense of "sacred particularity." But civility defies this religious particularity precisely because it requires that "each sect is to remain the one true and revealed faith for itself and in private, but each must *behave in the public arena as if* its truth were as tentative as an aesthetic opinion or a scientific theory."[59]

Nonetheless, it is this restraining import of civility that makes it a political exigency, for it is the only attitude "which enables transactions to proceed without close acquaintance-ship."[60] From this perspective, then, the essence of civilized living is conversation. This is the thrust of Murray's point when he defines a civil society as a "form of dialogue" which "does not disguise but brings to light the differences of men."[61] According to Mill, a civilized collectivity exists "wherever . . . we find human beings acting together for common purposes in large bodies, and enjoying the pleasures of social intercourse."[62] Central to the life of such a collectivity are "the operation of law, administration of justice, and a systematic employment of the collective strength of society." Accordingly, we "call a people civilized, where the arrangements of society, for protecting the persons and property of its members, are sufficiently perfect to maintain peace, i.e., to induce the bulk of the community to rely for their security mainly upon the social arrangements, and renounce for the most part, and in ordinary circumstances, the vindication of their interests (whether in the way of aggression or defence) by their individual strength or courage."[63]

From this gamut of uses, it is clear that civility, which has to do with how people handle their disputes, means more than politeness or courtesy—although, to be sure, the importance of politeness and courtesy in a religiously pluralistic society should not be underestimated. In contrast to civility, however, "politeness and courtesy come from an acknowledgment of the need for restraint and deference, especially in the face of disagreement and the disagreeable." But restraint and politeness remain empty virtues unless they are exercised for the sake of sustaining and advancing something more vibrant. An emancipatory vision of the good life transforms the negative thrust of restraint into vibrant civility. Thus, as a relational concept, "true civility speaks not merely about limits but about a vision of the *civitas*."[64]

Public Consensus and Political Institutions

While there may be a certain deontic imperativeness about the desirability of a dialogic politics, as opposed to one in which power, expressed most often through violence, is the governing norm, surely the whole notion of conversation or dialogue will be politically absurd if some citizens are arbitrarily excluded from the conversation forum. Thus the political effectiveness and the integrative capacity of the idea of public consensus and ecumenical politics are contingent upon two other criteria, defined by Perry as "situational or contextual prerequisites."[65]

First, there must be present in a political society "conditions in which ecumenical political dialogue, and the sorts of political community it helps to cultivate, may realistically be expected to flourish." These include citizens' "well-being, personal security, educational attainment, and political freedom, including freedom of speech and freedom of religion."[66] Second, there must be "a commitment to the establishment and maintenance of social, economic, political institutions and practices that encourage and facilitate, even nurture, such dialogue as opposed to institutions and practices that discourage, impede, and otherwise frustrate it."[67]

These two prerequisites highlight the crux of Nigeria's dilemma. The widespread suspicions about the nation's political life center on one important question: Do the people have the moral will to initiate, establish, maintain, and defend a form of political life capable of preventing the subordination of political institutions to the interests of one group, whether that group be a secular clique or an ethnic or religious group? What is at stake in every political competition—whether between rival visions of human good or for some political advantage—is, according to Michael Walzer, "the ability of people to dominate others." And, he says further, "domination is always mediated by some set of social goods."[68] For some people, religious symbols are seen as precursors to the attainment of more material good, and political victory is for them a symbolic religious victory. John Hunwick has shown that the dynamics of religious politics in Nigeria reveal this characteristic. What is at stake in the country's politics, according to him, "is the right to retain [for oneself] or impose [upon others] ways of life, patterns of behavior, systems of law, and expressions of culture."[69]

Murray, Niebuhr, and Perry find in democratic institutions the hope of ushering in a political method for ordering the state-society relationship, and adjudicating divergent interests, in such a way that the conditions that produce domination would be considerably reduced. The benefits of a democratic framework, especially for a pluralistic society, cannot be overemphasized. It furnishes a method for expressing the claims and counterclaims of politics, and for arbitrating conflicting social interests, in a nonviolent way.[70] It has also been found to be a good political answer to the problem of accommodating and balancing competing visions of human good because it holds all cultural viewpoints under criticism, and desires to achieve an uncoerced harmony among the various social and cultural vitalities.[71]

More significantly, democracy aims at achieving the social ethical goal of justice, a goal constitutively defined by its three regulative principles of order, freedom, and equality, and its two structures, namely, the organizing center of authority and the equilibrium of power.[72] Both the principles and structures of justice are pertinent to how the place of religion is conceived in a pluralistic society. The concern for order and stability of the nation, which it is the obligation of the central government to ensure, must also be tempered with the normative criteria of freedom and equality. "One perennial justification for democracy," Niebuhr writes, "is that it arms the individual with political and constitutional power to resist the inordinate ambition of rulers, and to check the tendency of the community to achieve order at the price of liberty."[73] Freedom is required to guarantee the integrity and legitimacy of religious practices and expressions, and equality will play out in the way political power and economic opportunities are not made contingent upon religious identifications.

Moreover, a democratic framework makes possible the avoidance of the twin evils of anarchy and tyranny.[74] While liberty has the potential to produce conflicting factions that might threaten civil unity, James Madison argued in *Federalist No. 10* that the method of "curing the mischiefs of faction" was not to remove its causes, but to control its effects through a properly structured and extended republican government.[75] Niebuhr is also instructive on this point. According to him, a healthy democracy "provides for checks and balances upon both the pretensions of men as well as upon their lust for power. . . . [It] never gives all the power to the proponents of any one dogma; it holds all claims to truth under critical review; it balances all social forces, not in an automatic, but in a contrived harmony of power. In this way it distills a modicum of truth from a conflict of error."[76]

This confidence in the capacity of democracy to accommodate and equilibrate interests in a pluralistic and conflicted society presupposes a sanguine political attitude that makes pluralism respectable, and not an obstacle to be overcome. A pluralistic society that seeks solutions to its problems through a democratic framework would be said to be pluralist in outlook; and to be pluralist is "to understand that a morally [and religiously] pluralistic context, with its attendant variety of ways of life, can often be a more fertile source of deepening moral insight—in particular, a more fertile soil for dialogue leading to a deepening moral insight—than can a monistic context."[77] In such a society, diversities not only exist as a matter of fact, but are recognized, accepted, and, most importantly, institutionalized into the structure and functioning of the social order.

Some theorists are, however, not so optimistic about the desirability and the possibility of a democratic framework and the sort of pluralist attitude that is hospitable to it for every plural society. Alvin Rabushka and Kenneth A. Shepsle doubt that it is possible to govern, let alone integrate, communally fragmented political systems, and they believe that the practice of politics along cultural divisions is incompatible with democracy.[78] They contend that scholars who hope for democracy in plural societies are suffering from ideological delusions. They feel that the bias such scholars display for democratic political arrangement has led "to some wishful and as yet unsuccessful attempts to demonstrate that stable democracy can be maintained in the face of cultural diversity."[79] They advise that the best polity a plural society can have is confederation, which they hope will minimize the deleterious effects of pluralism by relegating key issues to lower levels and thus reducing tensions. Cynthia Enloe also considers plural states to be artificial collectivities more often sustained by oppression than by worthwhile goals of political development.[80]

Many studies of third-world politics have virtually followed this approach. The main concern of some of the rulers in these countries, and of the theorists who help to formulate their policies, has been how to strengthen national integration, a goal more often understood as "a coalescence of identities." A process of integration is essentially "a process of depluralizing society" or "a partialization of group identities."[81] This was the objective of Nigerian former military ruler, the late General Aguiyi Ironsi (January-July 1966) when he proposed a unitary system of government.

This approach has been condemned for its insensitivity to the basic composition of the society. According to Omo Omoruyi, unitary political systems in plural societies can only function in an atmosphere of ethnic or racial exclusion, coercion, and inequality. It is merely a facade of structural integration since, in such a system, structural integration cannot be a reflection of societal integration. Structural integration exists where "one group aspires to dominate and actually dominates politics."[82] Theories that buttress this position are problematic because they underestimate the tenacity of cultural distinctions. The adoption of a unitary political system that does not make any concessions to the plural nature of the society in the hope that it will promote cultural homogenization appears to be an inadequate, even a misguided, strategy.

Neither confederation nor cultural homogenization has been considered desirable for Nigeria by any of the post-Ironsi regimes. For a long time federalism has become a political creed and method. Not only has the principle been defended as an adequate antidote for religious and other forms of cultural conflicts, it has also been regarded as a truly liberal pluralist principle.[83] Federalism rests on the conviction that a pluralistic society need not obliterate the social bases of its particularistic identities but must regulate the conflicts arising from their politicization.

While the principle may have reduced some aspects of Nigeria's geopolitical crises through such measures as the creation of states and ethnic balancing in the distribution of key governmental offices, it has been ineffectual in solving the problems of religious politics. There are three reasons for this. First, for most of the country's postindependence era, governance had been operated by military leaders. Their domination of the political space has stultified the integrative capacity of this principle, since they most often disregard the norms governing the principle. To say the least, the application of federalism in the context of military rule is anomalous.

Second, most of the religious crises that have shaken the foundation of the nation clearly fall outside the federalist principle. They have nothing to do with the local and regional autonomy of the religious groups concerned. Rather the issues center on the definition of the Nigerian State, whether it should be defined as secular or multireligious, whether it should be a member of international religious organizations or not, and the very nature of the judicature. What should be the relationship of the *shari'a* (the Muslim law) to the judicial systems? These are issues that belong to what Crawford Young referred to as the "subjective dimension of cultural pluralism,"[84] raising the specific question, not of whether Nigeria should be a country at all, but how or by what principles the country is to be run.

The third reason has to do with the very objective of federalism itself. As a principle for dispersing power among different layers of governmental structure, it was conceived essentially as "a scheme for areal distribution of power. Where cleavages are not wholly territorial, they cannot be captured by this device."[85] In Nigeria, cultural diversity is determined along more than one axis of differentiation. Religion, ethnicity, and region provide interlocking, interacting, but distinctively separate bases for politically relevant identity groups. Religious groups are not regionally compartmentalized, rather they are spread across regional boundaries.

A federalist model is thus too restrictive for addressing Nigeria's religious crises. In what follows, I shall examine more fully another model suggested and defended by Murray, Niebuhr, and Perry. Most of what I have already explored in their thoughts was based on their assessments of the United States' experience, a political experiment that has stood the test of time, despite some understandable vicissitudes. These thinkers identified certain animating principles that guided the formulation of the religion clauses in the First Amendment to the American Constitution. The political community envisioned by these principles is one that is "neither a naked public square where all religion is excluded, nor a sacred public square with any religion established or semi-established," but a "civil public square in which citizens of all religious faiths, or none, engage one another in *continuing democratic discourse*."[86]

The significance of this is not to subscribe to some kind of neocolonialist tendency that would recommend a wholesale American approach for other societies. Rather it is to indicate that all I have said so far is not a fable, and if "contextualization" has become an acceptable theological method today, especially among the third-world theologians, it is no less a useful method in the area of moral and political theory. One thing, at least, is very clear: no single model can presume to be "the sole key to the ways that religion and the public should meet in a kinetic, pluralist society. The mix is too rich, the set of situations is too volatile, and the repository of plausible proposals from many sources is too well stocked to permit anyone's sense of having arrived at full resolutions."[87] What I am exploring here is only one model out of many plausible ones. Leo Pfeffer observes that the distinguishing feature of religious conflict and competition in the United States is that it "is carried on in the frame of reference of a written constitution which sets forth the basic rules for its resolution and a Supreme Court which interprets and applies these rules."[88]

Murray's Analysis of the American Consensus

Murray argues that it was the "American consensus" that furnished the animating principles undergirding the First Amendment. This consensus is constitutional, "its focal concept is the ideal of law," and its ultimate root is "the ideal of the sacredness of man, *res sacra homo.*"[89] He construed the American experiment with democracy as both the consequence and an expression of this consensus. There were four essential principles which, according to Murray, were necessary to the foundation of the American republic.

First was the belief that the nation, in all its activities, "looks to the sovereignty of God as the first principle of its organization."[90] Besides the radical distinction between this affirmation and the Jacobin tradition of Continental Liberalism, which ideologically exiled God from its political arena, Murray appraised the American consensus for its ability to address the basic question of political legitimacy. The consensus rooted the American political system in its people's self-understanding which, as it were, was a religious one. As Seymour M. Lipset has asserted, "legitimacy involves the capacity of the system to engender and maintain the belief that the existing political institutions are the most appropriate ones for the society." In effect, "groups will regard a political system as legitimate or illegitimate according to the way in which its values fit in with their primary values."[91] Thus for Murray, there was no neutral American civil tradition. Everyone brought certain commitments—religious or secular (or both)—into the understanding of the American proposition.

The second underlying principle was the declaration of the purposes of government as political, in the sense that the right to command depends on adherence to the law—that the king or government officials are subject to the order of law, not purely creators of it. And third was the Thomistic social authorization principle, "the claim that the people are the ultimate judges of the king's justice," and that the validation of the moral content of law is carried out by the people.[92] This third principle is particularly central to Murray's theory of religious liberty and of all political and civil liberties generally. Contrary to the argument of the American Catholic right that an abstract notion of religious truth legitimizes political authority, Murray contends that it is the people, otherwise referred to as political society or body politic—that is, "civil society organized through various institutions and beliefs for the attainment of the common good"—who are the source of ethical legitimization and limitation of state authority.[93] And, for Murray, a people never exists as an abstract essence; rather, they are the product of historical growth and decay: "A people grows out of the moral soil of the country's history. 'We the people' is a human thing, of flesh and blood, ensouled by a community of ideas and purposes; it has a common life, organized into myriad of interlocking institutions, slowly built up in time, which impart to this life a structure and a form."[94] The fourth foundational principle was the belief that "only a virtuous people can be free." That is, it is only when people are inwardly governed by the recognition of the universal moral law that government can fully operate in its pursuit of its limited common good.[95]

These principles, cumulatively considered, are what Tocqueville speaks of as "habits of the heart," a phrase later employed by Robert Bellah and his colleagues to decry the increasing decline of the "Republican virtues" in America.[96] James Madison, one of the American Founding Fathers, was particularly at pains to demonstrate the political relevance of the fourth foundational principle—the idea of a virtuous people. He regarded it as the chemistry of citizenship. In his judgment, a republic that was merely a procedural democracy, where certain rules protected those who exclusively pursued their own private interests, would never succeed. Government will survive only if its citizens are animated by some common concern for the public good—"the real welfare of the great body of the people"—which, Madison declared, "is the supreme object to be pursued." More poignantly, he asked, "Is there no virtue among us? If there be not, no form of government can render us secure. To suppose that any form of government will secure liberty or happiness without any virtue in the people is a chimerical idea."[97] In the next two chapters, I shall take up this issue, especially the difficulty of forging common bonds in new nation-states such as Nigeria.

The thrust of Murray's argument is that America's founding fathers did not seek to protect America's freedoms by mechanical checks and balances alone. They relied on the civic-mindedness and self-restraint of the country's citizens. Without republican virtue, disorder would arise, and people would use their elected institutions to promote injustice. Thus, "men who would be politically free must discipline themselves."[98] Niebuhr corroborates this view when he states that "no society can maintain its health if the individuals who compose it do not have some sense of responsibility for their fellow men."[99]

Other features of America's political culture have both complemented and strengthened the effectiveness of the four principal elements. There is the fact of a written constitution explicitly ratified by the people. "By the constitution," Murray explains, "the people define the areas where authority is legitimate and the areas where liberty is lawful. The constitution is therefore at once a charter of freedom and a plan for political order."[100] Another characteristic is the principle of consent, more strongly specified as consent to legislation through representative government. This consent involved "a great act of faith in the moral sense of the people," in their ability to "judge, direct, and correct" the processes of government.[101]

Finally, Murray shows that the means by which citizens' participation in government has been defended are such democratic institutions as free speech and free press. The animating principle here is that "the state is distinct from society and limited in its offices toward society"—the principle that distinguishes "the order of politics" from "the order of culture" and that ultimately emphasizes "the incompetence of government in the field of opinion." Government is not the judge of truth in society; to the contrary, it submits itself to the truth of society. Murray regards all these provisions as "social necessities" and they constitute the "conditions essential to the conduct of free, representative, and responsible government."[102]

These principles constitute what Murray calls the "American Proposition," otherwise understood as the people's unflinching commitment to constitutional government within a democratic framework. The religion clauses fall within this larger framework. What the clauses affirm is essentially echoed in the two-pronged doctrine of Religious Liberty promulgated at Vatican II, a declaration for which Murray was the chief architect. The Vatican statement declares that "all men are to be immune from coercion on the part of individuals or of social groups and of any human power, in such wise that in matters religious no one is to be forced to act in a manner contrary to his own beliefs. Nor is anyone to be restrained from acting in accordance with his own beliefs, whether privately or publicly, whether alone or in association with others, within due limits."[103]

The specification of the institutional consequences of these clauses, and by extension, of the religious liberty doctrine, has been a source of historical controversy even among the people who have so long treasured the political framework that gave birth to the clauses. There were two extreme sectarian views, one religious and the other secularist, which Murray and Niebuhr found to be inadequate renditions of religious liberty, and as such, inhospitable to the type of political life envisioned by the doctrine.

The Confessional State

A confessional state exists where one religion "assures uniformity and is most intimately and inseparably united with the whole of political life."[104] This was the mainline Roman Catholic position before Vatican II. On the American scene, it was strongly advocated by the Catholic right, whose chief exponent was Joseph C. Fenton.[105] This position can be stated in the following syllogism:

> The Roman Catholic faith is the true religion.
> It is good for people to believe what is true.
> The state is obligated to promote the common good.
> Therefore, the state is bound to promote Catholic belief, and
>   wherever possible to establish Catholicism as the religion of
>   the state.[106]

Within this tradition of thought, the possession of truth by the Catholic Church provides a ground for her moral and legal right to establishment, and confers the duty upon the state to institutionalize that right. There are two major consequences of this view. First, the relationship between the state as a sphere of political authority and the church as a sphere of spiritual authority is nonegalitarian. The Church is superior, by virtue of her monopolistic access to and possession of truth, to the state. The second implication is the legal repression of heresy, and in this case, of all non-Catholic notions of truth. Truth, abstractly construed, and not the human person, is the subject of right. This is a classicist conception of truth, rooted in a kind of theological epistemology according to which truth is understood "as objective truth 'existing out there' apart from history and formulated in verbally immutable propositions. Truth remains unchanged even in its formulations but can find different applications in different historical circumstances."[107]

The continuing pluralization of the world, which Roman Catholicism can neither suppress nor ignore, has led to modified versions of this position. What emerged was a clear case of what Ibrahim called the "politics of arithmetic."[108] Roman Catholicism conceded that those not sharing this faith were free to believe and practice what they wished as private individuals (and not citizens). The state could not violate an individual's personal freedom of conscience in matters of belief and practice by any form of coercion. But only Catholic believers could enjoy public religious freedom, and they had a right to it because they alone possessed the truth. As Murray explained,

> This conscience, which is the Catholic conscience, possesses the fullness of religious freedom, because religious freedom is rooted in objective truth. It is a positive concept. It is the social faculty of professing and practicing what is true and good, as the true and good are objectively proposed by the eternal law of God (both natural and positive) subjectively manifested by a rightly and truly formed conscience, and authentically declared by the Church.[109]

This religio-political situation is known in the Catholic circle as the "thesis" or ideal relationship of church and state, in which Catholic principles could be applied without qualification. Where this was not possible—i.e., where Catholics were a minority of the population—a "hypothesis" situation existed. In this latter situation, Murray also explained,

> the Church forgoes her right to legal establishment as the one religion of the state, with its juridical consequence, legal intolerance. The Church, however, gives no positive approval to the resultant constitutional situation. *Per se* the situation is an evil, but it may be regarded as the lesser evil than the evils which would result from application of the thesis. Therefore it may be tolerated, *per accidens* and in practice.[110]

In terms of religious liberty, what the "thesis-hypothesis" position meant was tolerance whenever necessary and intolerance whenever possible. Necessity and possibility were determined by whatever was thought to be more conducive to public peace. An important aspect of this doctrine was the judgment that tolerance itself is an evil, a lesser evil that must be accepted in communities sharply divided by religion.

The Secularist State

This position was chiefly represented by the Jacobin tradition of the French philosophers, who made an illicit application of the Enlightenment secular philosophy to the French political culture. The Enlightenment thinkers for the most part believed that human beings have been endowed by their creator with certain rights, among which is the right (and the duty) to seek truth and happiness. They largely took it for granted that there is a truth to be discovered about humanity and the universe, and that happiness depends on determining it and acting on it.[111]

By contrast, the French liberal thinkers denied that there is a truth about life in this sense and consequently that there is a happiness for which all humans look. Ultimate ends are irreducibly plural and reflect the plurality of individuals and societies. The term *plural society* was deployed to mean not just that we differ about the ends of life but that there is no rational way of achieving agreement about them.

This position not only presupposed the atomism of human existence, it also reified belief in the absolute autonomy of individual reason, regarding it as "the first and the sole principle of political organization." Logically deriving from the position was an advocacy for a domestication and privatization of religion. The secularist state construed religion as an enterprise "quite irrelevant to public affairs."[112] What this view thus offered was an exclusively political definition of life. It denied the validity of human spirituality as well as of any cultural or religious demands on human existence. Nothing is meaningful except by its reference to the state. The state impinges on human life as a matter of right, since according to the secularist prescriptions, the state was the source of its unlimited authority, of the order of justice and of all laws and rights. The cardinal assertion of the secularist state is, according to Murray:

a thorough-going monism, political, social, juridical, religious: there is only one Sovereign, one society, one law, one faith. And the cardinal denial is of the Christian dualism of powers, societies, and laws—spiritual and temporal, divine and human. Upon this denial follows the absorption of the Church in the community, the absorption of the community in the state, the absorption of the state in the party, and the assertion that the party-state is the supreme spiritual and moral, as well as political authority and reality. It has its own absolutely autonomous ideological substance and its own absolutely independent purpose: it is the ultimate bearer of human destiny. Outside of this One Sovereign there is nothing. Or rather, what presumes to stand outside is "the enemy."[113]

Within this framework, religious freedom was understood as freedom from religion. Religion must be somehow eliminated or made to be noneffective. If it were left to exist, it would be due not to an inherent right, but only to the concession of the state. In other words, the state itself determined what religion was to be and what role it was to play in society.

Contrary to these two inadequate deductions from the religion clauses, I will examine and discuss the arguments that the clauses be seen as an appropriate moral response to a given sociological problem, and an embodiment of a juridical principle proper to the life of a political community.

Religious Pluralism, Religion Clauses, and Social Ethics

Two distinctive interpretations of the religion clauses (and of the religious liberty doctrine they endorse) were offered by the main thinkers whose ideas I am exploring in this chapter. On the one hand, the clauses are seen as a prudent political response to a given sociological situation. On the other hand, they are regarded as norms of political morality that establish ethical boundaries within which different sectors of society can locate both their limits and possibilities. I have designated these interpretations as the articles of peace and the juridical principle theses.

Religion Clauses as Articles of Peace

Murray observes that there were four dominant interacting "conspiracies" (a term used by Murray to refer to religious traditions) at the founding of the United States, namely, the Protestant, Catholic, Jewish, and Secularist groups.[114] Today, the number of these "conspiracies" has considerably increased. Besides "the real issues of truth" that seem to divide these different groups, there were also the "secondary issues of power and prestige." The groups sought to "have influence on the course of events, on the content of the legal order, and on the quality of American society." But more frightening was the fact that "to each group . . . its influence seem[ed] salvific."[115]

Evidently, this trend is as yet persistent as it is global in scope. N. J. Demerath and Rhys H. Williams, whose illuminating studies place the political impact of religion in the context of patterns of differentiation and secularization in society, have observed that organized religion has become but one voice among many trying to influence a bureaucratized government that has its own institutionalized agendas.[116] And, in his own attempt to explain this dynamic of religion's involvement with power, Gustavo Benavides claims that the religious spheres have become "ideological battlefields—to which one gains access by using metonymic and metaphorical chains as ladders, and in which multiple mirrors and models are in constant competition."[117] These explanations clarify Murray's point that "a structure of war and passion" was the tragic pattern of interaction among America's conspiracies.[118] James Hunter recently characterized this pattern as "culture wars," which are about "the struggle for domination . . . a struggle to achieve or maintain the power to define reality."[119]

In addition to these confessional differences, there was the significant presence of the secularists, who represented a current of thought that was at odds with the customary assumptions of the religious majority. Although Murray attempted to differentiate the American version of secularism from the organized and militant atheism of the Jacobin mold, he was at pains to show that America too was not spared from people who believed that religion was a purely private matter and were offended by any attempt to establish a public presence or influence for religious concerns.

In order for all these conspiracies to limit their warfare and pave the way for an enlarged atmosphere for dialogue, it was necessary to contrive a political arrangement capable of offering a basis for that "highest political good, the unity which is called peace."[120] This was the requirement fulfilled by the disestablishment and the free exercise clauses. "These institutions," Murray writes, "came into being under the pressure of their necessity for the public peace."[121] The clauses are undistorted mirrors of a good law because they were cognizant of the necessity or utility to preserve the public peace under a given set of conditions. He strongly believes that "all law looks to the common good, which is normative for all law. And social peace, assured by equal justice in dealing with possibly conflicting groups, is the highest integrating element of the common good."[122] More significantly, the clauses did not seek to achieve national unity at the expense of individual or corporate religious freedom. They were premised upon the conviction that civil unity ought not "hinder the various religious communities in the maintenance of their own distinct identities." And, mutatis mutandis, "the public consensus, on which civil unity is ultimately based, must permit to the differing communities the full integrity of their own religious convictions."[123] The first amendment to the Constitution was thus for Murray "a great act of political intelligence," making it possible for the various religious communities and people of no religion to maintain their own separate identities and to pursue freely the practice of the faiths they professed while at the same time living together in harmony.

Criticizing those who would like to interpret these clauses as signaling an ideological triumph for any of the competing conspiracies, Murray insists that the religion clauses are, first and foremost, articles of peace and not of faith. They are not "dogmas, norms or orthodoxy" that require "a religiously motivated assent," nor do they pretend "to answer any of the eternal human questions with regard to the nature of truth and freedom or the manner in which the spiritual order of man's life is to be organized or not organized."[124] It suffices only to see the peace of a pluralistic society secured by the First Amendment as "altogether a moral norm. . . . One may not, without moral fault, act against these articles of peace."[125]

Given the historical and sociological complexity that prevailed at the time of their adoption—the great mass of the unchurched, the multiplicity of denominations, the problems of economic trade, and the background of widening religious freedom in England—any other course of action would have proved catastrophic for the nation. There was thus a "mark of inevitability," the American "special social context," which made the political institutions that developed "the only plausible option."[126]

Murray further defends the religion clauses as conducive to social peace on the basis of subsequent American experience, which has abundantly confirmed the wisdom of these clauses. Three aspects of this collective experience are germane to Murray's argument. First is the acknowledgment that "political unity and stability are possible without uniformity of religious belief and practice, without the necessity of any governmental restrictions on any religion." Second, there was the American experience that "stable unity, which means perduring agreement on the common good of man at the level of performance, can be strengthened by the exclusion of religious differences from the area of concern allotted to government." Third, and most important of all, was the benefit religious groups have derived from this atmosphere of free political institutions.[127] Since no single religion was established, it was considered to be in the interest of each religion to be tolerant of all in order to continue to experience toleration for itself.

This argument is typical of most liberal accounts of the relation of religion to political life. When fully elaborated, it would be discovered that it still leaves unresolved many of the nagging questions raised by this problematic. It may therefore be helpful to broaden the intellectual context within which the "articles of peace" argument had been proposed. John Locke is now regarded as the first major proponent of this argument. In his treatise on toleration, he affirmed that human freedom and equality are the central values in public life. But because the citizens of pluralistic societies hold different convictions about God and ultimate moral purposes in human life, if we are to treat them as equals we must protect the freedom of all to hold these convictions. In public life, therefore, theological and metaphysical beliefs cannot be invoked as normative for the way society is organized. To do so would be to violate the freedom and equality of at least some citizens.[128]

John Rawls has refined this theory by developing a notion of "overlapping consensus" based on "a reasonable conception of justice."[129] By *overlapping consensus*, he means a conception of justice that applies to a particular subject, namely the basic structure of a modern constitutional democracy—society's main political, social, and economic institutions. The conception of justice contained in the overlapping consensus does not claim to be the whole of morality. It is not a "comprehensive" conception of morality that "includes conceptions of what is of value in human life, ideals of personal virtue and character, and the like, that are to inform much of our conduct (in the limit of our life as a whole)."[130] According to Rawls, religious moralities as well as philosophies such as those of Kant, Mill, and Marx embody just such comprehensive, even metaphysical, views of the full meaning of the good life. Because there seems to be no reasonable hope of overcoming the plurality of theological and metaphysical conceptions of the good life, a political conception of justice must avoid any claim to be comprehensive. Rather, an account of political justice demands that we deal with the historic controversies connected with religion, philosophy, and metaphysics by "the method of avoidance." "We simply apply the principle of toleration to philosophy itself."[131]

Unlike the bias of Continental Liberalism, which Murray finds objectionable, Rawls states that this form of toleration should not be construed as skepticism about, or indifference to, the truth of comprehensive visions of the full human good. He acknowledges that there would be no possibility that religious believers could affirm such a skeptical theory without denying their own deepest convictions. He states that disputes about religious or metaphysical questions must be avoided in politics "because we think them too important and recognize that there is no way to resolve them politically."[132]

On the positive side, Rawls hopes that diverse religious and philosophical traditions can find reasons within their own belief systems for affirming the political conception of justice he proposes, namely one that regards all persons as free and equal. An "overlapping consensus" will be achieved only to the extent that the diverse comprehensive moral and religious traditions of a society can affirm this more limited political idea of justice on the basis of their own fuller account of the good.[133]

Nevertheless, Rawls insists that matters of public morality—those that fall within the domain of the overlapping consensus of a democratic society—must be adjudicated by what he calls public reason. He identifies this with "the shared methods of, and the public knowledge available to, common sense, and the procedures and conclusions of science when these are not controversial."[134] Thus in the actual practice of public life, comprehensive religious, philosophical, and moral conceptions of the good life are privatized.[135] Moreover, Rawls states, appeals to comprehensive doctrines of the good must be avoided both in arguments about the basic structure of society and in the formulation of more specific social policies.[136]

These conclusions clearly violate religious liberty as a normative theory. In the search for a desirable political structure of a religiously pluralistic society, it does not help to restrict religious convictions to playing second fiddle. Such a restriction is precisely what the communities of faith are protesting against. Privatization of religion in the name of democracy turns democracy into a kind of tyranny. Murray called this totalitarian democracy.[137] It is also a kind of religion that Niebuhr named idolatry. As Vatican II's Declaration on Religious Freedom put the matter, "It comes within the meaning of religious freedom that religious bodies should not be prohibited from freely undertaking to show the special value of their doctrine in what concerns the organization of society and the inspiration of the whole of human activity."[138] Murray's commentary on this passage clarifies its original intent. "Implicitly rejected here," he explains, "is the outmoded notion that 'religion is a purely private affair' or that 'the Church belongs in the sacristy.' Religion is relevant to the life and action of society. Therefore religious freedom includes the right to point out this social relevance of religious belief."[139]

While these objections are obviously instructive for established democracies, they are more strongly so for societies still groping in political uncertainty. A more inclusive interpretation of religious liberty has to be able to clarify not only the political limits of religion, but also the moral limits of the state, as well as specifying the sorts of attitude that can sustain these limits. These issues are addressed in the interpretation of religious liberty as a juridical principle.

Religious Liberty: A Juridical Principle

There are two aspects of this interpretation, namely the religious and the political. Under the conceptual umbrella of the religious correlate, Murray attempts to clarify the locus of religious freedom, which for him is located in the social and civil orders. Freedom of religion is a constitutional guarantee to "the people," taken individually, collectively, and in assembly, of immunity from all external coercion in religious matters. This liberty, as it is found in a constitutional democracy, is essentially comprised of "freedom of conscience" and "the free exercise of religion." Freedom of conscience refers to the individual's human and civil right to be unhindered by any external or constraining force in matters religious. "It is the freedom of personal religious decision."[140] And no individual or group within society has the right to exert coercion in any form whatsoever to influence such religious decisions.

The validity of this freedom is established by the convergence of theological, ethical, political, and legal arguments, in spite of the fact that religious liberty is primarily a juridical notion. Theologically, freedom of conscience is supported by an unbroken tradition of the necessity of freedom in the act of faith. Central to this understanding is the conviction that "the response of human beings to God transcends the order of politics and cannot legitimately be brought under the control of the coercive powers of government."[141] The political argument affirms the essentially limited nature of governmental power, limited as it were, to "an obligation to protect and support the transcendent dignity of the human person." It consists in the immunity of conscience from restraint or constraint by powers of state or society in matters of belief or unbelief, independent of whether consciences are true or erroneous. "The truth or error of conscience is not relevant to the constitutional question of religion."[142]

The free exercise of religion has both personal and corporate referents. At the personal level, where the chief concern is about an individual's personal relation with God, the validity of this freedom is coextensive with that of the freedom of conscience, in that "a man may not be coercively constrained to act against his conscience, nor may a man be coercively restrained or impeded from acting according to his conscience."[143] The corporate correlate of the personal freedom of religious expression has three facets: "the right of religious communities within society to corporate internal autonomy," "freedom of religious association," and "freedom of religious expression"— that is, "the right, both of individuals and of religious bodies, to immunity from coercion in what concerns the public worship of God, public religious observances and practice, the public proclamation of religious faith, and the public declaration of the implications of religion and morality for the temporal affairs of the community and for the action of the public powers."[144]

Here we are given a clue as to the sorts of roles religious people can play and the sorts of arguments they can make in the public square. Their arguments must not be theological, but ethical, which means they should be able to indicate the "implications of their beliefs" for political life. Citing John A. Coleman with approval, Perry says that "the most important place for theological symbols in public debate is more as an ethical horizon and set of value preferences than in specific and concrete policy discussion."[145]

Within this interpretive framework, Christians, Jews, Muslims, and others may be aware of their distinctive identities, each acknowledging, as Barth put it, that "on this side of the eschaton their faith is . . . only one note among many other invocations and exclamations that are hardly in harmony with it, but call for notice just as loudly, or even more so."[146]

Yet this does not preclude that elements of a faith can be

recognized as true or its moral claims taken as guides for action in the experience of other communities as well. What we need, according to Robin W. Lovin, is "a criterion of public truth that is different from the criterion for a correct interpretation of one's own tradition, a criterion that requires corroboration of one's claims in the critical scrutiny of another community of meaning and which holds back from claims to this sort of truth until that corroboration is forthcoming."[147]

This is a dispositional requirement that invites a certain kind of attitude in a religiously and morally pluralistic context. It bears upon our estimate of others, our method of retrieving religious insights, and our conduct of public or political debate. With respect to the first aspect, Niebuhr emphasizes the finiteness of human knowledge and the contingency of religious truth as embodied in particular doctrinal formulations. The epistemological limit of religious sensibility underlies the distinction generally made between *religious faith* and *religious beliefs*. Faith is "trust in the ultimate meaningfulness of life," a response to the mystery of the divine, which has to do with visions and values. On the contrary, beliefs are creedal propositions, that is, "faith mediated by—understood and expressed in the medium of—words, whether concretely, in stories, or abstractly, in concepts and ideas."[148] So conceived, faith may be distorted when reduced to conceptual formulations. Thus, criticizing the manner in which a religious community lives in relation to other religious communities does not necessarily mean rejecting the intensity of its vison and the depth of its commitment, which is rooted in faith.

Human beings easily succumb to two forms of religious pride: "the efforts to deny the finiteness of our perspectives [and] to hide and obscure the taint of interest and passion in our knowledge."[149] To overcome this pride, people must cultivate the dialogic virtue of "fallibilism," which is a religious spirit of humility that demands of each religion, or each version of a single faith . . . to proclaim its highest insights while yet preserving an humble and contrite recognition of the fact that all actual expressions of religious faith are subject to historical contingency and relativity. Such a recognition creates a spirit of tolerance and makes any religious or cultural movement hesitant to claim official validity for its form of religion or to demand an official monopoly for its cult.[150]

Niebuhr insists that tolerance in religion must not degenerate into "an irresponsible attitude towards the ultimate problem of truth." Skepticism and fanaticism are two forms of this attitude. Both forms fall short of Niebuhr's two criteria of tolerance, namely, "the ability to hold vital convictions which lead to action; and also the capacity to preserve the spirit of forgiveness towards those who offend us by holding to convictions which *seem* untrue to us."[151]

Two additional tests of tolerance that are also "dialogic virtues" are public intelligibility and public accessibility. They are the necessary antidotes for fanatical and dogmatic tendencies. Public intelligibility requires that a person aspires to make his or her position sufficiently "comprehensible to those who speak a different religious or moral language—to the point of translating one's position, to the extent possible, into a shared ('mediating') language." To cultivate the habits of offering religious arguments that are publicly accessible is to engage in a practice that seeks neither sectarian nor authoritarian support for one's position. Explaining this, Perry says that "a defence of a disputed position is sectarian if (and to the extent) it relies on experiences or premises that have little if any authority beyond the confines of one's own moral or religious community. A defence is authoritarian if it relies on persons or institutions that have little if any authority beyond the confines of one's own community."[152]

Concerning the mode of employing religious resources for

public purposes, Murray appeals to Bernard Lonergan's hermeneutic of "historical consciousness." Lonergan had developed a theological method that emphasized a "turn to the subject," a recognition that all knowledge is inseparable from the people who do the knowing. And since all "knowers" are immersed in the flow of history, coming to knowledge of the truth is always historically and socially situated.[153]

In his deployment of this hermeneutic, Murray argues that cultural factors, historical circumstances, and political immaturity, all shaped the varied political theories contained in past encyclicals, and he contends that contemporary interpretations of these teachings "must proceed from an historical point of view. Nothing is more unhelpful than an abstract starting point."[154] He accused the conservatives for transmuting conditions that were transient and contingent into metaphysical truths. There is a great deal of agreement between Murray and Ibn Khaldūn on this methodological question.

Murray argues that a change of emphasis has been effected in moral theory with the birth of democracy. Two themes emerge from this new political consciousness that the church can ill afford to ignore: the juridical concept of the state, and the concept of the dignity of the human person. These new developments make necessary a redefinition of the church-state relationship. The mistakes of the conservatives, he says, are two: archaism and anachronism. On the one hand, to miss the modern developments in the state of the question, primarily the development of personal and political consciousness, entails an archaic return to a situation that is no longer existent or definitive. Similarly, to read the new solution back into the past encyclicals would be anachronistic—that is, any attempt to criticize the past understandings of or solutions to church-state relations would be inappropriate. We cannot accuse the past of a mistake that we only understood as a result of new understandings or solutions in the present. What has taken place in the twentieth century, according to Murray, is the development of personal and political consciousness, in consequence of which the age-old question is being redefined, which therefore must be answered in light of all the significant contemporary factors that inform the question. According to Murray,

> the common consciousness of men today considers the demand for personal, social, and political freedoms to be an exigency that rises from the depths of the human person. It is an expression of a sense of right approved by reason. It is therefore a demand of natural law in the present moment of history. This demand for freedom is made especially in regard to the goods of the human spirit. . . . In a particular way, freedom is felt to be man's right in the order of his most profound concern, which is the order of religion.[155]

In view of this social and political reality, Murray asserts that the problematic with regard to religious freedom has changed. It is no longer the exclusive rights of truth and its correlate, legal tolerance and intolerance. Rather, "the question today is whether public care of religion is not only limited by a necessary care for the freedom of the Church, but also limited to a care for the religious freedom of the Church together with a care for religious freedom for all peoples and all men."[156] These dialogic virtues, conjoined with the appropriate hermeneutical method, offer a promise for constructive contributions of religion to political life—a right protected by the free-establishment clause.

The second aspect of Murray's interpretation of the religious clause as a juridical principle is the political correlate, which he understands as a constitutional government. According to him, a government of limited power is based on four principles. The first is the distinction between the sacred and the secular spheres of life. He derives this distinction from the teachings of Pope Gelasius I and from John of Paris, who had affirmed the existence of two autonomous societies, distinct in their origin and ends.[157] The temporal originates not in the spiritual but in nature, and ultimately in God. The state evolves as a necessary and useful institution for furthering the justice, peace, and well-being of a society. The spiritual order is directed to humanity's highest end, which is supernatural in character. Because of the primacy of that end, the spiritual enjoys a primacy in *dignity,* but extends to nothing that is not necessarily related to Christ's redemptive work.

Given this distinction, Murray states that there could no longer be direct involvement of one in the sphere of the other, working directly toward the realization of the other's ends. The spiritual power is limited to spiritual matters and terminates at the conscience of the individual believer. However, its activity does produce "aftereffects" in the temporal order, and this it achieves through the citizen. It is through the conscience of the individual who is both citizen and Christian that the spiritual power has a reach into human affairs.[158] Similarly, since the state is limited in its action by its origin and finality, it can only assist the church indirectly by supplying the temporal conditions and occasions for the church's realization of its ends. This it does by actualizing its own ends. The church cannot demand or expect anything more than this from the state. It can only require that the state act according to the necessities of its own nature.

More precisely, with regard to state assistance to the spiritual power in carrying out its proper mission, it is necessary only that the state guarantee the church the freedom to pursue its ends in its own way. "What the Church required of political power," Murray asserts, "was the freedom to touch the *res sacrae* of human life, those aspects of human person which are related to eternal life. Ultimately, the *res sacrae* reduce to one reality, the human person oriented to both temporal and eternal ends."[159] The state must organize what it did not create, what it finds already there in society. Through the citizen, who holds membership in religious groups, the state finds not only Catholics or Protestants but a plurality of sects. It follows that the state cannot repress heresy or attempt to maintain or establish religious unity in society because such action is beyond its finality.[160]

The second principle is the distinction between society and state. Within a constitutional tradition and a dialogic political life, the state ought to see herself only as an agency within society, playing "a limited role" and performing "certain limited functions—through the coercive discipline of law and political power—for the benefit of society." A constitutional government understands itself as "only one order within society—the order of public law and political administration," whereas civil society "designates the total complex of organized human relationships on the temporal plane, which arise either by necessity of nature or by free choice of will, in view of the cooperative achievement of partial human goods by particular associations or institutions."[161]

In short, within civil society, there are autonomous or semi-autonomous sources of moral as well as of technical direction, which are best left with as much freedom as possible, not only in relation to the state, but to society at large. Some of these are fairly individualistic, such as the family, but some are complexes of institutions that extend through the full spatial and cultural range of a particular society, such as religion and economy. The state, then, is limited by society, and society itself is limited by the moral, cultural, and technical efficiencies of its own parts. Murray describes this form of structural relations as resting on the "principle of subsidiarity." To deny this principle and the structural distinctions it prompts is "to espouse the notion of government as totalitarian."[162]

The third principle is the distinction between the common good and public order, and this distinction is entailed by the previous distinction. Society writ large, comprised of individual citizens, has the moral obligation to pursue the common good, which includes "all the social goods, spiritual and moral as well as material, which man pursues here on earth in accord with the demands of his personal and social nature." Public order is a more limited concept and is the responsibility of the state. This notion of public order is meant to highlight the two-pronged nature of the function of civil law: a moral and a limited function. Civil law is not morally required to "enforce every humanly beneficial activity or to coercively forbid every moral evil." Principally, its role, which is limited but nonetheless crucial, is to ensure the basic conditions of social existence: public peace, justice, and those aspects of morality on which social consensus exists."[163] Government intervention in religious matters is both justified and limited by the principle of public order. The bearing of this principle upon frequent government intervention and involvement in religious matters in Nigeria will be taken up in chapter 4.

The fourth and final principle is both a political truth and a primary method of political procedure. As political truth it is simply "freedom under law." Precisely, it means that "the freedom of the people is a political end, prescribed by the personal consciousness among the people. The freedom of the people is also the higher purpose of the juridical order, which is not an end in itself. Furthermore, freedom is the political method per excellentiam, prescribed by the political consciousness among the people."[164] Any political society that depends "on force and fear to achieve its ends" has deviated "both from political truth and from the true method of politics."[165] Murray argues that religious institutions cannot press for freedom if they are not prepared to regard freedom as a moral value that should permeate all realms of life. Religious freedom and all other civil and political freedoms make up a whole cloth; they are all interrelated, interdependent, and inseparable—"in fact, they are identical. They stand or fall together." Religious freedom "is required for human quality of society," while the political framework that makes it possible (that is, constitutional government or democracy) "is a requirement for a human and humane society."[166]

My aim in this chapter has not been to underestimate the enormity of strains that religious diversity can place on political society but to show that those strains can and ought to be managed if collective life is to make any sense. Toward this end, I have endeavored to demonstrate the importance of political institutions and political attitudes in any efforts to mitigate the potentially deleterious effects of religious factionalism. The success of any political solution to religious pluralism is not measured by an escape from or a disdain for pluralism but by joint deliberative efforts aimed at stimulating and structuring intergroup communication and promoting accommodative habits of thinking, decision making, and behavior in the population. I have also tried to show that a democratic framework and a pluralist outlook, inspired and nurtured by an ecumenical political ideal, offer a great deal of promise on how to achieve this goal. The theoretical and practical significance of the chapter is the emphasis it places on the moral gap between a form of collective life that encourages mutual coexistence and the the form of life that discourages, impedes, and otherwise frustrates it.

Notes

1. Kenneth Post and Michael Vickers, *Structure and Conflict in Nigeria, 1960-1966* (London: Heinemann, 1973), 5.

2. Peter Morton-Williams, "The Fulani Penetration into Nupe and Yoruba in the Nineteenth Century," in *History and Social Anthropology,* ed. I. M. Lewis (London: Tavistock Press, 1968), 4.

3. Sturm, *Community and Alienation,* 11.

4. See Ogbu U. Kalu, "Religions in Nigeria: An Overview," in *Nigeria since Independence: The First Twenty-Five Years,* vol. 9, *Religion,* ed. J. A. Atanda, Garba Ashiwaju, and Yaya Abubakar (Ibadan: Heinemann, 1989), 22.

5. Ernst Troeltsch, *Religion in History,* trans. James Luther Adams and Walter F. Bense (Minneapolis: Fortress Press, 1991), 109.

6. David Martin, *A General Theory of Secularization* (New York: Harper and Row, 1978), 18-24.

7. John Markoff and Daniel Regan, "Religion, the State, and Political Legitimacy in the World's Constitutions," in *Church-State Relations: Tensions and Transitions,* ed. Thomas Robbins and Roland Robertson (New Brunswick, N.J.: Transaction Books, 1987), 161.

8. Ibid., 165.

9. Alfred T. Hennelly and John Langan, eds., *Human Rights in the Americas: The Struggle for Consensus* (Washington, D.C.: Georgetown University Press, 1982); Henry Shue, *Basic Rights: Subsistence, Affluence, and U.S. Foreign Policy* (Princeton: Princeton University Press, 1980); Osita C. Eze, *Human Rights in Africa: Some Selected Problems* (Lagos: Nigerian Institute of International Affairs, 1984); Stanley Hoffman, "Reaching for the Most Difficult: Human Rights as a Foreign Policy Goal," Daedalus 112 (1983): 19-49.

10. R. A. Joseph, "National Objectives and Public Accountability: An Analysis of the Draft Constitution," in *Issues in The Nigerian Draft Constitution,* ed. Suleimanu Kumo and Abubakar Aliyu (Zaria, Nigeria: Ahmadu Bello University Press, 1977), 1.

11. *The Constitution of the Federal Republic of Nigeria* (Daily Times Publications, 1979), section 10.

12. Federal Government of Nigeria, *Report of the Constitution Drafting Committee Containing the Draft Constitution* (Lagos: Times Publications, 1976), 1:v-vi.

13. John Stuart Mill, "Utilitarianism," in *John Stuart Mill: A Selection of His Works,* ed. John M. Robson (New York: Odyssey Press, 1966), 209. Italics in original.

14. Joel Feinberg, *Social Philosophy,* Foundations of Philosophy Series (Englewood Cliffs, N.J.: Prentice-Hall, 1973), 61.

15. Markoff and Regan, "Religion, the State, and Political Legitimacy," 164.

16. Murray, *We Hold These Truths,* 18. Murray uses "public civility," "public philosophy," and "public consensus" interchangeably *salva veritate.*

17. Sidney Verba, conclusion ("Comparative Political Culture") to *Political Culture and Political Development,* ed. Lucian W. Pye and Sidney Verba (Princeton: Princeton University Press, 1965), 516.

18. Gabriel A. Almond and Sidney Verba, *The Civic Culture* (Boston: Little, Brown, 1963).

19. Lucian Pye, *Aspects of Political Development* (Boston: Little, Brown, 1966), 104.

20. Dudley, *Introduction to Nigerian Government and Politics,* 22, 70.

21. Reinhold Niebuhr, "Leaves from the Notebook of a War-Bound America," *Christian Century* 56 (15 November 1939), 1405. Throughout his prodigious academic career, which spanned several decades, Niebuhr insisted that to understand politics is to recognize the elements of power that underlie all social structures—the play of power that may be obscured or submerged but cannot be eliminated. For a clear expression of this argument, see his *Christianity and Power Politics* (New York: Scribner's, 1940).

22. S. E. Finer, *Comparative Government* (Harmondsworth, England: Penguin Books, 1970), 15.

23. Robert A. Dahl, *Modern Political Analysis* (Englewood Cliffs, N.J.: Prentice-Hall, Inc., 1963), 6.

24. Harold Lasswell, *Politics: Who Gets What, When, How* (New York: Meridian Books, 1958).

25. Dudley, *Introduction to Nigerian Government and Politics,* 15.

26. Perry, *Love and Power,* 4.

27. David Nicholls, *The Pluralist State* (London: Macmillan, 1975), 13.

28. Ibid., 3.

29. Robin W. Lovin, "Perry, Naturalism, and Religion in Public," *Tulane Law Review* 63 (1989): 1531-32.

30. Murray, *We Hold These Truths*, 90.

31. Perry, *Love and Power*, 84.

32. Walter Lippmann, *Essays in the Public Philosophy* (Boston: Little, Brown, 1955), 79.

33. Murray, *We Hold These Truths*, 9.

34. Perry, *Love and Power*, 85.

35. John Courtney Murray, "Leo XIII: Two Concepts of Government: Government and the Order of Culture," *Theological Studies* 15 (March 1954): 32.

36. John H. Hallowell, *The Moral Foundation of Democracy* (Chicago: University of Chicago Press, 1954), 35-36.

37. Murray, *We Hold These Truths*, 132; cf. Figgis and Laski in chapter 1.

38. John Courtney Murray, "Free Speech in Its Relation to Self-Government," *Georgetown Law Journal* 37 (May 1949): 658.

39. Murray, *We Hold These Truths*, 87.

40. John Courtney Murray, *The Pattern for Peace and the Papal Peace Program*, pamphlet of the Catholic Association for International Peace (Washington, D.C.: Paulist Press, 1944), 11. Until recently, the doctrine of natural law had been much discredited in both philosophical and religious ethics. Frederick S. Carney identified eight different objections that have been historically raised against this doctrine, and to which he responded by proposing a revisionist conception of natural law understood as "a continuing process of reflection upon how human life—relationally understood—can best be preserved and fulfilled." According to Carney, any adequate natural law ethics must be cognizant of "the historicity of man and the consequent relativity of all material moral norms." See Frederick S. Carney, "Outline of a Natural Law Procedure for Christian Ethics," *Journal of Religion* 47, 1 (January 1967): 26-27.

41. Lippmann, *Public Philosophy*, 76-77.

42. Reinhold Niebuhr, "Democracy, Secularism, and Christianity," in *Christian Realism and Political Problems* (New York: Scribner's, 1953; Fairfield, N.J.: Augustus M. Kelley, 1977), 101-3 (page references are to reprint edition).

43. Murray, *We Hold These Truths*, 80.

44. Ibid., 91-92.

45. Perry, *Love and Power*, 44–45.

46. Ibid., 45.

47. Mouw and Griffioen, *Pluralisms and Horizons*, 56.

48. Max L. Stackhouse, *Creeds, Society, and Human Rights: A Study in Three Cultures* (Grand Rapids, Mich.: Eerdmans, 1984), 2.

49. Ibid.

50. Perry, *Love and Power*, 45.

51. Joseph L. Allen, "Power and Political Community," *Annual of the Society of Christian Ethics* (1993), 14.

52. Murray, *We Hold These Truths*, 25.

53. Ibid., 21–22.

54. Perry, *Love and Power*, 30.

55. Ibid., 31.

56. S. Hampshire, *Two Theories of Morality* (Oxford: Oxford University Press, 1977), 49.

57. Allen, "Power and Political Community," 14.

58. Murray, *We Hold These Truths*, 18.

59. John Murray Cuddihy, *The Ordeal of Civility: Freud, Marx, Lévi-Strauss, and the Jewish Struggle with Modernity* (Boston: Beacon Press, 1987), 235; idem, *No Offense: Civil Religion and Protestant Taste* (New York: Seabury Press, 1978), 108.

60. Sturm, *Community and Alienation*, 15.

61. John Courtney Murray, "The Issue of Church and State at Vatican II," *Theological Studies* 27 (December 1966): 592.

62. John Stuart Mill, *Essays on Politics and Culture*, ed. Gertrude Himmelfarb (Garden City, N.Y.: Doubleday, 1962), 52.

63. Ibid., 53.

64. Neuhaus, *Naked Public Square*, 61.

65. Perry, *Love and Power*, 91.

66. Ibid.

67. Ibid.

68. Michael Walzer, *Spheres of Justice: A Defense of Pluralism and Equality* (New York: Basic Books, 1983), xii–xiii.

69. Hunwick, *Religion and National Integration in Africa*, 7.

70. Niebuhr, *Children of Light*, 119–52. It is common knowledge that democracy has had varied meanings, forms, and goals. For a good account of the various understandings of democracy, see Robert

A. Dahl, *A Preface to Democratic Theory* (Chicago: University of Chicago Press, 1956).

71. Reinhold Niebuhr, *The Contribution of Religion to Cultural Unity*, Hazen Pamphlet no. 13 (1945), 6.

72. Reinhold Niebuhr, *The Nature and Destiny of Man*, vol. 2, *Human Destiny* (New York: Scribner's, 1943), 247-57.

73. Niebuhr, *Children of Light*, 46-47.

74. Niebuhr, *Human Destiny*, 258.

75. *The Federalist Papers*, with an introduction by Clinton Rossiter (New York: New American Library, 1961), 77-84.

76. Niebuhr, *Christian Realism and Political Problems*, 14, 51.

77. Perry, *Love and Power*, 100.

78. Alvin Rabushka and Kenneth A. Shepsle, *Politics in Plural Societies: A Theory of Democratic Instability* (Columbus, Ohio: Charles E. Merrill, 1972).

79. Ibid., 462.

80. Cynthia Enloe, *Ethnic Conflict and Political Development* (Boston: Little, Brown, 1973).

81. Ali A. Mazrui, "Pluralism and National Integration," in *Pluralism in Africa*, ed. Leo Kuper and M. G. Smith (Berkeley: University of California Press, 1971), 334, 346.

82. Omo Omoruyi, "Representation in Federal (Plural) Systems: A Comparative View," in *Readings on Federalism*, ed. A. B. Akinyemi, P. D. Cole, and Walter Ofonagoro (Lagos: Nigerian Institute of International Affairs, 1979), 372.

83. Richard L. Sklar, "Democracy in Africa," in *Political Domination in Africa: Reflections on the Limits of Power*, ed. Patrick Chabal (Cambridge: Cambridge University Press, 1986), 19.

84. Young, *Politics of Cultural Pluralism*, 141.

85. Ibid., 526.

86. Perry, *Love and Power*, 45. Perry's citation here is from *The Williamsburg Charter: A National Celebration and Reformation of the First Amendment Religious Liberty Clauses* 8 (1988). The italics are, however, mine.

87. Martin E. Marty, foreword to *Religion and American Public Life: Interpretations and Explorations*, ed. Robin W. Lovin (New York: Paulist Press, 1986), 4.

RELIGIOUS PLURALISM AND THE NIGERIAN STATE

88. Leo Pfeffer, *God, Caesar, and the Constitution: The Court as Referee of Church-State Confrontation* (Boston: Beacon Press, 1975), 3.

89. Murray, *We Hold These Truths*, 87–88.

90. Ibid., 40.

91. Seymour M. Lipset, "Social Conflict, Legitimacy, and Democracy," in *Legitimacy and the State*, ed. William Connolly (New York: New York University Press, 1984), 89.

92. John Courtney Murray, "Leo XIII on Church and State: The General Structure of the Controversy," *Theological Studies* 14 (March 1953): 22.

93. John Courtney Murray, ' "The Problem of The Religion of the State,' " *American Ecclesiastical Review* 124 (May 1951), 350.

94. Ibid., 351.

95. Murray, *We Hold These Truths*, 47–48.

96. Robert Bellah et al., *Habits of the Heart: Individualism and Commitment in American Life* (Berkeley: University of California Press, 1985).

97. *Federalist Papers*, 288–94. The last two decades have witnessed an increased scholarly interest in "the public question" especially as it bears upon various aspects of human existence. It is not always clear, however, whose idea of the public we are talking about, or whose public that particular proposals will serve. For a discussion of strictures against unguarded uses of the term public, see John F. Wilson, "The Public as a Problem," in *Caring for the Commonweal: Education for Religious and Public Life*, ed. Parker J. Palmer, Barbara G. Wheeler, and James W. Fowler (Macon, Ga.: Mercer University Press, 1990), 9–22.

98. Murray, *We Hold These Truths*, 48.

99. Reinhold Niebuhr, "A Dark Light on Human Nature," *Messenger* 13 (27 April 1948): 7.

100. Murray, *We Hold These Truths*, 44.

101. Ibid., 45.

102. Ibid., 46.

103. National Catholic Welfare Conference, *Dignitatis Humanae* (Washington, D.C.: National Catholic Welfare Conference, 1956), ch. 1, para. 2.

104. Troeltsch, *Religion in History,* 109.

105. For a good account of the debate between Fenton and Murray, see Donald E. Pelotte, *John Courtney Murray: Theologian in Conflict* (New York: Paulist Press, 1976), 3–73; Charles E. Curran, *American Catholic Social Ethics: Twentieth-Century Approaches* (Notre Dame, Ind.: University of Notre Dame Press, 1982), 172–232.

106. David Hollenbach, *Justice, Peace, and Human Rights: American Catholic Social Ethics in a Pluralistic Context* (New York: Crossroad, 1988), 102.

107. Curran, *American Catholic Social Ethics,* 185.

108. Ibrahim, "Politics of Religion in Nigeria," 77–79.

109. John Courtney Murray, *The Problem of Religious Freedom* (Westminster, Md.: Newman Press, 1965), 7.

110. Ibid., 12.

111. Walzer, *Spheres of Justice,* 243–48; Basil Mitchell, introduction to *Law and Justice, Christian Law Review* 82/83 (1984): 87.

112. Murray, *We Hold These Truths,* 40.

113. John Courtney Murray, "The Church and Totalitarian Democracy," *Theological Studies* 13 (December 1952): 531.

114. Murray, *We Hold These Truths,* 33.

115. Ibid., 30.

116. N. J. Demerath and Rhys H. Williams, "A Mythical Past and Uncertain Future," in *Church-State Relations: Tensions and Transitions,* ed. Thomas Robbins and Roland Robertson (New Brunswick, N.J.: Transaction Books, 1987), 77–90.

117. Gustavo Benavides, "Religious Articulation of Power," in *Religion and Political Power,* ed. Gustavo Benavides and M. W. Daly (New York: State University of New York Press, 1989), 6.

118. Murray, *We Hold These Truths,* 30.

119. James Davidson Hunter, *Culture Wars: The Struggle To Define America* (New York: Basic Books, 1991), 52.

120. Murray, *We Hold These Truths,* 34.

121. Ibid., 67.

122. Ibid.

123. Ibid., 55.

124. Ibid., 58, 59.

125. Ibid., 62–63.

126. Ibid., 66–68.

127. Ibid., 80–81.

128. John Locke, "A Letter Concerning Toleration," in *A Letter Concerning Toleration in Focus,* ed. John Horton and Susan Mendus (London: Routledge, 1991), 12–56.

129. John Rawls, "The Idea of an Overlapping Consensus," *Oxford Journal of Legal Studies* 7 (1987): 2.

130. Ibid., 3, n. 4.

131. Ibid., 12–13.

132. John Rawls, "Justice as Fairness: Political Not Metaphysical," *Philosophy and Public Affairs* 14 (1985): 230.

133. Rawls, "Overlapping Consensus," 6–7.

134. Ibid., 8.

135. Ibid., 15.

136. Ibid., 20.

137. Murray, "Church and Totalitarian Democracy," 532.

138. *Dignitatis humanae,* 4.

139. John Courtney Murray, "Religious Freedom," in *The Documents of Vatican II,* ed. Walter M. Abbott and Joseph Gallagher (New York: American Press, 1966), 683, n. 11.

140. Murray, *Problem of Religious Freedom,* 24.

141. Hollenbach, *Justice, Peace, and Human Rights,* 12.

142. Murray, *Problem of Religious Freedom,* 38.

143. Ibid., 25.

144. Ibid., 25–26.

145. Perry, *Love and Power,* 90.

146. Karl Barth, *The Christian Life* (Grand Rapids, Mich.: Eerdmans, 1981), 7.

147. Robin W. Lovin, "Religion and American Public Life: Three Relationships," in *Religion and American Public Life: Interpretations and Explorations,* ed. Robin W. Lovin (New York: Paulist Press, 1986), 24.

148. Perry, *Love and Power,* 73.

149. Niebuhr, *Human Destiny,* 214.

150. Niebuhr, *Children of Light,* 134–35; cf., Perry, *Love and Power,* 59–61, 100.

151. Niebuhr, *Human Destiny,* 219; the italics are mine.

152. Perry, *Love and Power,* 106.

153. Bernard Lonergan, *Insight* (New York: Philosophical Library, 1958).

154. John Courtney Murray, "Government Repression of Heresy," *Proceedings of the Third Annual Convention of the Catholic Theological Society of America* (1948): 33.

155. Murray, *Problem of Religious Freedom,* 18-19.

156. Ibid., 48.

157. Gelasius I was pope from 492 to 496. Just less than a century after St. Augustine battled the Donatists, Pope Gelasius attempted to define more precisely the relationship between the church and the state. Where St. Augustine emphasized the need for church and state to work together, Gelasius stressed their separate spheres. In his letter to Emperor Anastasius I, he said, "There are indeed, your Majesty, [two powers] by which this world is mainly ruled: the sacred authority of pontiffs and the royal power." See Aloysius K. Ziegler, "Pope Gelasius I and His Teachings on the Relation of Church and State," *Catholic Historical Review* 27 (1942): 412-37.

158. John Courtney Murray, "Contemporary Orientations of Catholic Thought on Church and State in the Light of History," *Theological Studies* 10 (June 1949): 223.

159. John Courtney Murray, "Leo XIII: Separation of Church and State," Theological Studies 14 (June 1953), 208.

160. Murray, "Government Repression of Heresy," 83-84.

161. Murray, *Problem of Religious Freedom,* 29.

162. Ibid.

163. Ibid., 28-29.

164. Ibid., 30.

165. Ibid., 31.

166. Ibid., 81-82.

Chapter 3

Quests for Order, Freedom, and Social Justice: Religion, Politics, and the State in Nigeria, 1900–1966

THE CONTOURS OF contemporary political discourse in Nigeria bear the unmistakable stamp of religion. The increasing scholarly interest in the role of religion in the country's politics is a direct consequence of the political assertiveness of religion, which has become more noticeable in the last two decades. While this resurgence of intellectual interest in the religious dimensions of Nigerian politics is a welcomed corrective for the gulf that has long existed between religious behavior and political theory, it is important to emphasize that religious politics is not a recent occurrence in Nigeria.

This chapter traces the history of this phenomenon, a history that has been traversed by many and culturally different dramatis personae. The diversity of religions, the nature of the political landscape, and the divergence in the goals of the significant actors have shaped the ways in which religion, politics, and the state have interacted in Nigeria. My aim is to decipher some patterns in these relationships; and for this purpose, I shall draw upon Robin Lovin's three categories of understanding that people bring to bear upon the question of how religious faith is to be related to public life.

First, there are some people who see the social and political significance of religion essentially in terms of its maintenance of order. This characteristically Durkheimian view of religion supposes that "religious commitments . . . provide a system of shared meanings which make public moral choices possible, and without which even basic forms of civility and social restraint are jeopardized."[1] Modern proponents of civil religion, Robert Bellah in America[2] and Jacob Olupona in Nigeria, could be appropriately placed in this category. Olupona has in fact argued in several of his works that "any coherent society must rest on a set of moral beliefs which ground the political order on a transcendent basis."[3]

Other thinkers see religion as a guarantor of freedom. This view rests on an awareness of a center of ultimate value beyond the claims of the state: "The idea that persons have rights given by God protects both individuals and their communities of identity against excessive claims by the government."[4]

Religion provides for still another group of people the possibility for new forms of social justice. This form of religious thinking evinces a trust in the possibility of righting past wrongs and reforming social relationships "along new and more equitable patterns." An essential dimension of this view is that the possibility of change and reform "depends in large part on the way that religious patterns of self-transcendence render a way of life subject to challenge by the moral claim of others, and give those who make such claims some confidence that they can be understood and received."[5]

I will examine the patterns of historical interaction among religion, politics, and the state in Nigeria within the context of these underlying ethical concepts of order, freedom, and justice. An additional methodological interest of this chapter is to demonstrate the intersection of ethics and historical analysis. If part of what it entails in the study of history is an assertive and self-conscious attempt to understand how the past was formed or distorted, then one cannot ignore entirely or forever the enterprise of moral judgment, and in dealing with that "one has to move, however deftly or reluctantly, from demonstrable propositions to matters that correspond to actual experience."[6]

This chapter covers the era of the colonial rule through the First Republic, which ended in 1966. Periodization has of course been a very controversial subject among Africanist scholars. As I mentioned in chapter 1, students of precolonial Nigerian states, most ably represented by the Ibadan history school, argued for a de-emphasis of colonialism in the country's history in order to spotlight the links between the precolonial past and the realities and aspirations of contemporary Nigeria. But there have also been varying degrees of critical vigilance against the inscription of cultural norms and traditions as comforting but enervating myths of pure origins, and as uncontaminated matrices of the self. Among the notable critics is John Peel, who argues that European links with Africa antedated the period of the official political annexation of most African states, and that both the present and the precolonial Nigerian past "were shaped by external contact."[7] The late-nineteenth-century colonial experience not only served to intensify these links, it also helped to give them a political form. Hence, the justification for starting from that colonial political reality. With respect to geographical scope, I shall limit myself to the north and the west, the two regions where the dynamism of religious politics has been most manifest. A. E. Afigbo, E. C. Amucheazi, and D. I. Ilega provide an excellent guide for understanding this phenomenon in eastern Nigeria.[8]

It is common knowledge that Nigeria's political and religious scene reflects an untidy reality, a reality that advisedly warns us against the tendency to force the country's situation into "a preformulated paradigmatic framework."[9] An important point to demonstrate, therefore, is that religion has been central to how the Nigerian people understand themselves. This task is particularly important, given the standard argument that "until independence in 1960, religion was not a significant factor in national politics," rather, "ethnic rivalry, regionalism and competition for resources . . . dominated the direction of political activities."[10]

Religion and Ethnicity

Studies have shown that the historic formation of most of Nigeria's ethnic groups not only had specific religious roots, but also that their continuing self-fashioning and self-definition are heavily influenced by their religious assumptions. Of course, there is nothing peculiar to Nigeria about this religious underpinning of identity.[11] Leading anthropologists have long emphasized the role of religion in codifying people's identity. Religion offers not only a comprehensive world view, but also an all-embracing social identity. It creates these identities and sacralizes them through what Hans Mol calls "myths, rituals, and the processes of objectification and commitment."[12] It is also empirically demonstrable that Nigeria is peopled by over four hundred ethnic groups, each possessing a distinct language, set of social customs, and belief. I can deal with only a representative sample here.

In his study of the cultural roots of the Yoruba, an ethnolinguistic group of western Nigeria, John Peel identifies "*olaju* or 'enlightenment,' a complex of development values rooted in Christianity and Western education" as the efficient cause for the emergence or formation of Yoruba identity.[13] In precolonial times, up till the advent of the Christian missions, Yorubahood was a singularly elusive concept.[14] Save in the legendary penumbra of the eponymous ancestor legend, the collectivity now bearing the name Yoruba have never been organized in a single political unity. The Yoruba label only applied to the old Oyo kingdom, now one of the major constituents of the present Yoruba people. The operative identity terms, at the precolonial baseline, related to the names of the major kingdoms, such as Ijebu, Ife, Ijesha, Ekiti, and so on.[15]

The term came into use in the late nineteenth and early twentieth centuries to describe returned slaves of western Nigerian origin; and two of these, Samuel Crowther and Samuel Johnson, were major artisans of Christian evangelization and the establishment of British authority in Yorubaland. Through the efforts of Crowther and Johnson, the major ingredients of Yorubahood—language and culture—were developed. In a pioneering ethnographic work on the Yoruba, upon which Peel himself largely draws, Reverend Samuel Johnson underscored the primacy of Christianity in the emergence and formation of Yoruba identity. Johnson's conclusion to his monumental work was a retrospective and fitting tribute to the pacificatory role of the Christian ministers during the early nineteenth-century intertribal wars in Yorubaland. With hope for a much stronger and more unified Yoruba under the banner of Christianity, he prayed for peace to

> reign universally, with prosperity and advancement, and that the disjointed should all be once more wielded into one under one head from the Niger to the Coast as in the happy days of ABIODUN, so dear to our fathers, that clannish spirit disappear, and above all that *Christianity* should be the principle religion in the land—paganism and Mohammedanism having had their full trial-should be the wish and prayer of every true son of Yoruba.[16]

Successive generations of Yoruba political elite have continued to cast their manifestos in Christian idioms.[17]

Similarly, the Igbo in eastern Nigeria have historically affirmed the centrality of Christianity to their ethnic identification. Although the precolonial and stateless Igbo society, governed according to clannish and gerontocratic principles, was loosely knit together by the traditional cultic systems such as the *Aro-Chuckwu* cult, and notwithstanding the nostalgic desire for the revival of traditionalism portrayed in the works of such novelists as Achebe and Echewa, neither the indigenous cultic systems nor Islam has had "the ghost of a chance in disputing the Igbo heart with Christianity."[18] It is this pervasive and hegemonic presence of Christianity in eastern Nigeria that made it easy for the defunct Biafra Republic to claim an exclusively Christian identity as political propaganda during the Nigerian civil war (1967–1970), although the degree of religious motivations behind that war will probably remain undecipherable for years.[19]

In the northern region, the role played by Islam in the construction of Hausa-Fulani social and political reality has also been copiously documented.[20] The contemporary political orientation of this tribal grouping was largely informed by "Shaikh Uthman dan Fodio, the caliphate which he inspired, and the jihad which he led."[21] Certainly, Islam had existed for several centuries in northern Nigeria before Fodio executed his jihad in 1804. The first Islamic expedition to that part of the country took place in the eleventh century, in the area of Kanem-Borno, part of the present northeastern Nigeria. By the fourteenth century, Islam was already firmly established in the whole of Hausaland.[22] This pre-jihad existence of Islam in the North raises some questions about the raison d'être of the 1804 holy war. Was Fodio's jihad an exclusively religious expedition or were there other motives behind it?

Crowder argued that judging from the composition of the reformers and the patterns of their activities, economic and political factors overshadowed the ostensibly religious underpinning of the jihad. He pointed out that none of the three greatest achievements of the jihad—namely, the establishment of a uniform system of government through a vast area of Nigeria that for centuries beforehand had been torn by internecine wars, the stimulation of commerce under what might be called the Pax Fulani, and the literary revolution it stimulated—had an unambiguous religious goal.[23]

A different reading of the jihad has, however, concluded that it must first be seen within the context of the succession of reforming movements that profoundly affected the Muslim world during the latter part of the eighteenth and the nineteenth centuries. The common objective of these movements was to seek a return to the pure and pristine faith of Islam, purged of heresies and accretions.[24] Thus Fodio's overriding aim was to establish a purer form of Islam in what he considered a predominantly corrupt and decadent society. In other words, the 1804 jihad was not aimed at converting non-Muslims, but at reforming lax Muslims. Theologically conceived, its vision of a new life was probably less concerned with the *kufr* (unbelief) of pagans than with the *kufr* of those Muslims who opposed the jihad.[25]

The preceding account of the religious roots of ethnic formation is by no means intended to suggest that region and religion coincide homogeneously in Nigeria. A closer, and more nuanced scrutiny, of Nigeria's geopolitical landscape reveals a complex situation of overlapping and interstitial relationships. As proselytizing religions, both Christianity and Islam have always sought to transcend regional boundaries. Encapsulated within the northern region, for example, were the vast non-Muslim populations in the middle belt and southern Zaria. Even in the far north, a region formerly considered to be an uncontested Islamic stronghold, Christianity continues to make substantial gains. This modern incursion into *Dār al-Islam* is partly responsible for many of the riots and disturbances that have occurred in northern Nigeria in recent years. Islam had likewise been firmly established, as far back as the eighteenth century, in the northern and western parts of Yorubaland, especially, "in the lands of the old Oyo Empire and in towns flooded with Oyo refugees on its southern fringe—Ibadan, Iwo, Oshogbo, etc."[26] Many Yoruba people had converted to Islam in the eighteenth and nineteenth centuries partly to resist colonial incursion from the coast, and partly through the long-distance Muslim trading networks, especially via Kano.[27] Even in the east, where Christianity had enjoyed a monopoly of cultural hegemony, the historic divisions between Protestantism and Catholicism as well as within each of them have been one dimension of cleavage in intra-Igbo politics.[28]

An example of this disjunctive connection between region and religion in Nigeria is Abner Cohen's study of Hausa ethnicity in the Yoruba town of Ibadan, a classic of West African ethnography. The study shows how intrareligious differences can be consequential for ethnic identifications. Cohen gave a fascinating account of the process in Ibadan by which the Muslim Hausa trading community became differentiated from the native Yoruba, among whom Islam has spread very rapidly in this century. The separateness of Hausa linguistic-cultural identity found reaffirmation in rallying to the Tijaniyya *tariqa* (brotherhood), which provided a religious vessel for ethnic segmentation. In the course of only two years, 1951 and 1952, the overwhelming majority of Ibadan Hausa joined Tijaniyya, and the reason for this mass conversion was that

the Tijaniyya provided solutions to some of the political problems they faced as a result of the coming of party politics. The process was of course neither rational nor intended by individuals. It was "vehicled" in a series of countless small dramas in the lives of men. . . . Thus on the one hand intensive social interaction which the Tijaniyya brought, creates strong moral obligations between members of the same community and between them and members from other communities in the Hausa diaspora, while on the other hand it inhibits the development of similar moral obligations between Hausa and Yoruba. The political consequences of such a situation are far-reaching, . . . with the rise of the Tijaniyya, Hausa identity and exclusiveness, which were imperilled by the coming of party politics, are now cast in a new form and validated in terms of new myths.[29]

In spite of (and indeed because of) these puzzling manifestations of religious identities, it can be argued that at both the local and national levels, religious vocabularies had been central to the processes of political negotiations and power brokerage in Nigeria. But no single religion has provided the overarching language of political discourse. Multiple religious maps are drawn on Nigeria's wider political atlas. Besides the splinters of new religious and quasi-religious movements, most of which are (though not exclusively) foreign in both origin and rituals, Christianity, Islam, and the traditional religions are recognized as Nigerians' main religions.[30] But only Christians and Muslims have been involved in the vortex of powerful and organized political structures.

Whether the political marginalization of the indigenous faiths was historically inevitable or whether it was an act of cultural infidelity is a topic of intense debate among the Africanist scholars.[31] Olusola Akinrinade and M. A. Ojo contend that the beliefs, rituals and symbols of the traditional religion have long regulated the diverse spheres of the African people's life, and "proved an integrative apparatus for social cohesion."[32] Jibrin Ibrahim blames the lack of civility in contemporary Nigerian political terrain on the intolerance of the two universal religions that "have always seen things in a binary and reductionist fashion—good and evil, God and the devil, etc." He argues that the distinctive virtue of the traditional religions is "tolerance," which Nigerians would be wise to reclaim by resolving to free themselves from the tyranny of Christian and Islamic cosmologies that he regards as "imposed paradigms."[33]

Granted that there are certain accommodationist and integrative ingredients in the traditional faiths that are worth retrieving as part of a cumulative effort to inject toleration into Nigerian politics, it remains improbable that the indigenous religions could compete effectively with the other world religions in the context of modern politics. First, those religions "are inseparably linked to the hearth," and as such, cannot be "readily translated into more generalized identity systems conceived on a scale which can be meaningful in contemporary social and political arenas." Besides this localized and rural feature of the traditional faiths, they are also "incapable of generating the cultural entrepreneurs to provide ideological content to folk cults."[34]

Another relevant point is the myth of a unified and organicist precolonial African cosmos, which many scholars are now debunking. The normative and proleptic call for what Biodun Jeyifo caustically refers to as "return to the source" is unfortunately premised upon a partial representation of that past. Realistically speaking, African traditional religion can hardly be referred to in the singular sense because religious practices differ from group to group. John Onaiyekan rightly points out that "even within the same broad linguistic group of Yoruba or Ibo there could be appreciable differences."[35] In his effort to justify a myriad of divinities characteristic of the indigenous African religion, E. Bolaji Idowu portrays that religion as a "diffused monotheistic" one, another way of admitting that pluralism is at the core of African culture.[36]

Religion and Public Order in Nigeria

The British Colonial Policy of Religious Paternalism

Nigeria as a nation is a child of British colonialism. Its modern history appropriately begins on 1 January 1914, when two disparate territories—the northern and southern protectorates —were amalgamated under the administrative leadership of Lord Lugard. Since the amalgamation merely and arbitrarily lumped together peoples of divergent cultures and conflictual traditions, it became necessary to evolve modalities that would help to guarantee order and maximize peace. Lugard instituted the Indirect Rule System to ensure a hospitable environment for the accomplishment of the political and economic objectives of his home government. He defined this system as

> the rule through the Native chiefs who are regarded as an integral part of the machinery of Government with well-defined powers and functions recognized by Government and by law and not dependent on the caprice of an Executive Officer. The recognized indigenous rulers were to be supported and their authority upheld by the Residents (i.e., the colonial officers responsible for the emirates and the provinces at large). These rulers were thus not independent but must act as delegates of the governor, whose representative was the resident.[37]

Given the reality of some contiguity between geopolitical boundaries and religious groups during this period, the Indirect Rule System amounted to a policy of convenience, a sort of political expediency contrived to provide cultural therapy for the wounds of political subjugation. In the opinion of many contemporary students of Nigerian politics, the system did not signal any bureaucratic generosity on the part of the British; rather there was a mark of inevitability in its adoption. In fact, others have charged it with cultural insubordination and political manipulation. The Indirect Rule System was merely "a pragmatic way of resolving the problems that arose from a shortfall of personnel, money, communications, etc."[38] Even in the north, where Williams adjudged the system to be "quite successful,"[39] it was later to be discovered as a carefully crafted administrative system with considerable humiliating consequences for different strata of the society. The emirs were stripped of real political power, and what power they wielded "derived from the centralized colonial chain of bureaucratic command." Within the society, the system "reinforced and exacerbated communal tensions even where none had existed previously." Suffering most from these tensions were the non-Muslims of the middle belt, who were relegated to a second-class status. As a historical occurrence, Matthew Hassan Kukah declares the system to be a paradoxical mix: "Not only did it enhance the status and the unchecked powers of the emirs, it disillusioned the common people on both sides who had gallantly fought on the side of the British as part of the colonial military machine, informers and guides, believing (wrongly) that the victory of the British over their age-old oppressors, would terminate their sufferings and degradation."[40]

The northern part of the country was already an established theocracy by the time it was occupied by the British in 1900.[41] The irony of the British occupation of the north is that the same political system that was disrupted was legitimized to protect Islam from the incursion of Christian missions. The colonial administration underwrote Islam in this region and used it as the basis of political authority in local administration. The Native Authority System (NAS) was woven around the emirates, with the emir as a spiritual head. Each emir became "the *defensor fidei* within his area of authority."[42]

This move was intended to ensure that unity and order prevailed amid the process of political transition that was then underway, as well as to allay any identity-related anxieties. The incumbent political hierarchy was defeated but not humiliated; peace with not only honor but advantage within the British framework was provided to the Fulani elite. "Mesmerized by the mobilizing force of Islam and conscious of the thinness of the red line of British forces," Crawford Young remarks, "the colonizer gave careful deference to hierarchy, language, and religion."[43]

At the installation of the newly appointed Sultan of Sokoto in March 1903, Lugard promised that his rule would be just and fair and that all persons would be free to worship God as they pleased. He also promised that his government would not interfere with Islam, a promise fulfilled in the embargo he placed on the activities of the Christian missions in the north. Islamic religious integrity was affirmed as a prerequisite for the legitimacy of British political authority within the northern territory. The emirates' acceptance of the British rule actually derived from the Islamic principle of *taqiya*, which enjoined Muslims "to do business with the British by . . . showing regard to them with the tongue and have intercourse with them in the affairs of the world, but never love them in our hearts or adopt their religion."[44]

When Lugard was accused by the Christian missionaries of privileging Islam at the expense of Christianity, he retorted that it would be "unwise and unjust to force missions upon the Mohammedan population for it must be remembered that without the moral support of the Government these missions would not be tolerated. And if they were established by order of the Government the people have some cause to disbelieve the emphatic pledge I have given that their religion shall in no way be interfered with."[45]

In both the east and the west, the colonial administration adopted a different strategy to achieve the same purpose—a stable order. There existed in these regions a replay of the Constantinian drama of the fourth century, when the Bible and the sword were entwined in an unholy romance. The missionaries, no less than the government, claimed to be agents of civilization, with each side attempting to outwit the other in achieving its self-serving goals: "the missionaries colluded with the colonial government when it suited their interests," and, in return, the government sought their assistance to Christianize subjugated peoples on the supposition that "Christians were more loyal to the British than non-Christians."[46]

The missionaries were disappointed to see this modus operandi discredited in the north. They had expected the government "to remove the Fulani obstacle by force" so as to "pave the way for the massive conversion of the Hausa." But before this Caesaro-ecclesial alliance turned sour, the government belief in the political utility of Christianity demonstrated in the south had already shaped the way the missionaries projected their political role and religious objectives. Those of the Church Missionary Society (CMS) who went to the north projected themselves as "knights-errant of British imperialism, believing that by winning the North for the British the christianization of the territory would be hastened." The disdain which they had for the indigenous religions in the South was similarly unleashed upon the Islamic faith in the north. A case in point was one Dr. Walter Miller, who believed that Islam was not a blessing but a curse for northern Nigerians, "for this religion, wherever one has seen it, seems to blight a people and throw over them a mantle of darkness and moral crookedness which they can never throw off." He was intransigent in his conviction that any attempt to improve the northern people "other than those of first giving them the light of the Gospel of Jesus Christ will be an utter failure."[47]

Interpretations of the posture of the British officials toward religion in Nigeria have been considerably and, of course, understandably varied. V. Y. Mudimbe makes a very penetrating observation in this regard: "although in African history the colonial experience represents but a brief moment from the perspective of today, this moment is still charged and controversial, since, to say the least, it signified a new historical form and the possibility of radically new types of discourses on African traditions and cultures."[48] There are analysts who argue that the acorns from which the country's great oaks of social and political problems eventually grew were sown by the British colonial authorities; and that when they left, their successors in the corridors of power enthusiastically watered the little acorns and, indeed, sowed more.[49] Adigun Agbaje discredits the worth of the colonial policy because it throve on a double-standard morality. He accuses the administrators of protecting Islam in the north, while in the south they maintained "the 'pure autonomy' perspective which posited a rigid demarcation of state from religion and insisted that religious considerations be discouraged in the political arena."[50]

Agbaje himself was quick to note the contestation of his assertion by Muslim scholars who argue that what the colonizers transported to Nigeria was "a state system flavored with Western, hence Christian, precepts."[51] Not only through education, but also through "its initiation and acceleration of social change . . . ; its provision of a basis for societal reintegration on a new and larger scale; and its stimulation of racial and political consciousness," Christianity entrenched itself as a major religious presence through the unofficial support of the colonial government.[52] The Muslims blame this situation for the wide educational gap that existed between the north and the south.[53]

In the southern provinces, most of the educational institutions were in the hands of Christian missions because of the inability or unwillingness of colonial authorities to meet the great demands made on them by various communities. And, as it should be expected, Christian missions were happy to provide these eductional facilities because they served as major avenues of conversion. In the north, schools were largely in the hands of the government, particularly in the emirates, where there was a deliberate policy to control missionary penetration. The northern Muslims were not only suspicious but also contemptuous of Western education. They associated it with Christianity and so feared that embracing it was a danger to their religious beliefs. They also considered that education in government institutions was devoid of moral content and lacked those values which only an Islamic educational system could inculcate.[54]

Peter B. Clarke has shown that this disdain for Western education was not limited to the northern Muslims. The Bamidele movement in Ibadan, western Nigeria, attracted those Muslims who were caught in the crisis of traditionalism and the requirements of the secular state. A member of this movement reportedly expressed his indignation at the growing secularization of the state being caused by Western civilization: "Western education . . . has come to naught . . . it has been an increasing source of prolific affliction and poverty. Many formerly employed are now unemployed. A man who formerly ate from a table now eats from a leaf. . . . Our fathers were not Europeanised and could carry out their responsibilities."[55]

Amid the welter of these conflicting interpretations, several points do seem to emerge. As I have shown through my discussion of Ayandele's work, the British colonial attitude toward religion defies simplistic assessment. It is fair to say that a situation of political paternalism existed in both regions. The dual imperative faced by the administration was to balance public order with religious freedom. Given the relative strength of the two dominant religions in the regions in which each was strong, and the novelty of the incipient political system, there was hardly any other alternative for the government than a delicate balance between modest partiality and distributive fairness. Religious freedom was ceded to the Muslims in the north, and to a fair degree, to the Christians in the south, while the government superintended the political space to ensure that anarchy and chaos did not engulf the country. The aftermath in the postcolonial period has been a country that is neither dominantly Islamic nor dominantly Christian but one that contains elements of both in rough parity.

Ayandele interprets this posture as political neutrality, a sort of equal deal for all, and places the stance within the general context of social and political liberalism developing in Britain and other parts of the world during this period.[56] Clarke provides a very crisp, and perhaps more accurate, rendition of the British colonial policy toward religion in Nigeria: "Colonial policy towards [religion] generally, to the extent that one can talk about such a policy, was based on various positivist, evolutionary notions of human, cultural, social and religious development. It was infused with pragmatism. Rather than being formally and rationally thought out beforehand, it was often no more than an ideological justification for a policy dictated by circumstances."[57]

It is also fair to say that the colonial government encouraged the attitude of mutual suspicion and parochialism that has characterized religious interaction ever since this period. Because of its fear of cultural contamination, the government precluded the possibility of religious, cultural, and cognitive negotiation. Each regional compartment developed with the idea that its traditional ways of looking at the world were the only plausible ones; every group was encouraged to take its worldview for granted. The commensality and connubiality that are quintessential for civic peace and religious coexistence were inchoatively blocked through a system of coercive balkanization and irreverent ideology. It cannot be totally arbitrary to see a strong connection, as some scholars are inclined to do, between the prevalence of political corruption in Africa and the moral vacuum created by the absurdity of colonialism.[58]

All this has provided a potentially explosive background for disputes on the nature of the Nigerian state and the extent to which politics and religion could be separated therein. Contrary to Western experience, in which debates about secularity take place principally within the context of the dominant Christian values, common grounds are yet to evolve in Nigeria; rather the debate has tended to occur among groups with major perspectival differences—Christians, Muslims, traditionalists, and the secularists.[59]

In particular, the colonial approach places the relationship between Christians and Muslims at a potentially crucial position in the definition and maintenance of Nigeria's federalism along with ethnic, cultural, and regional considerations. This colonial legacy is undoubtedly one source of Nigerians' present moral and political disillusionment—a situation that has led some people, especially at the moments of political adversity and homicidal religiosity, to call into question the legitimacy of the territorial frame of politics, to decry the artificiality of a united Nigeria, and to doubt the possibility of civil collaboration among its solidary groups.[60] Ibrahim A. Gambari contends that "in general, the British were content to reflect, and indeed to increase, the indigenous sources of division and disunity which they found in Nigeria rather than to reduce them."[61] H. O. Davies also shares this general feeling of disaffection with colonialism by suggesting that "if the British created Nigeria, British colonial policy largely contributed to its remaining a mere geographical expression."[62]

The Incoherence of Nationalist Politics

For many of the formerly colonized societies, the struggle for political independence was seen as a sacred and moral duty. In Nigeria, the all-encompassing existential objectives of this struggle were first articulated by the southern political elite, many of whom were products of Western education purveyed by Christian missions. The events of the two world wars in which some of the colonized peoples participated had exposed the false pretensions of the colonizers' world to moral and cultural superiority. A chain of constitutional changes was triggered in Nigeria, beginning in the early 1940s, followed by the emergence of political parties, and culminating in the belated decision of the British overlords to grant independence in 1960.[63] Up till today in northern Nigeria, the period from about 1946 to 1966 is referred to as *Zaamanin siyasa* (time of politics).[64]

The 1946 Richards Constitution accomplished, inter alia, three things: it established a confederate Nigerian state, partitioned it into three regions among the major ethnic groups, and lifted the ban on the formation and activities of indigenous political parties.[65] The three political parties that emerged afterward neatly coincided with the partitioning format. In the west was the Action Group (AG), the Northern People's Congress (NPC) was dominant in the north, and the National Council of Nigerian Citizens (NCNC) was the cadre party in the east.

The implication of this arrangement was that for a considerable length of time before national independence in 1960, the Nigerian peoples "were denied common legislative experience fundamental for the creation of a common outlook on the nation."[66] This in turn had far-reaching consequences for the nature of the relationship between religion and state within the context of a united nation, as each region was shaped by the wishes of the dominant political party. Even after the 1954 Constitution changed Nigeria to a federation, the tripartite regional structure continued as the modus vivendi of participation in political life and governance.[67]

A Theocratic Experiment under Ahmadu Bello

While the political elite in the south looked forward to independence with what in fact turned out to be an exaggerated hope, the north became apprehensive of the possible dissolution of its cultural and political unity. On realizing the inevitability of national self-rule, fear, rather than hope, became its constant companion. Several studies have shown that the voyage to Nigerian independence was embarked upon by mismatched sets of pilgrims with radically different objectives.[68] The northern intellectuals were preoccupied with Islam, and how it "ought to be interpreted in the new and challenging circumstances of post-colonial independence."[69] Thus, when Ahmadu Bello (otherwise known as the Sardauna of Sokoto) became the political leader of the North, first as the president of the Northern Peoples' Congress (NPC), and later the regional premier, he and his political colleagues launched a spiritual adventure as a climax of the political bid to transform the region into the religious empire thought to have been lost as a result of the British conquest.[70]

The Sardauna resorted to the evocation of two interlocking sets of metaphors, idioms, and symbols to establish and to consolidate the organic unity needed to prevent any forms of political and economic outpacing of the north by the south.[71] First, he started the *northernization* campaign, itself a reaction to the federally promulgated decree of *Nigerianization,* which was intended to facilitate the integration of Nigerians into all arms of the administration to enhance their acquisition of the skills needed for the running of the affairs of state.[72] The NPC saw the Nigerianization decree as a southerners' ploy to translate their educational advancement into political and material gains. According to one northerner, "too many southerners are in mission colleges. Government must not relax, but go through and enforce Northernization."[73] The complaints of Alhaji Yashe and the like encouraged the Sardauna's government to adopt the Northernization policy which was intended to "ensure for Northerners a responsible proportion of posts in the Federal Public service, to ensure for Northerners a reasonable proportion of posts in all statutory corporations, to ensure the number of Northerners in commercial, industrial, banking, and trading concerns in the region."[74] The Tafawa Balewa-led Federal Government, perceived by many in the south as a political veneer of the NPC, capitulated to the Northernization campaign by redeploying southerners working in the north then as federal civil servants. Needless to say, the southerners were combatively and unrepentantly despised by the north. As one student of northern politics and culture explains, the expatriates had a much better chance of being employed by the northern government than did southern Nigerians. According to C. S. Whitaker, "recruitment was based on an order of preference that stipulated northerners first, expatriates second [on the grounds that they could be employed on 'contract terms' that would permit the government to replace them at the first opportunity], southern Nigerians last."[75]

Having effectively fenced off the southern incursion into the north, the Sardauna also had to deal with the question of the political hopes of the non-Muslim population in his region. The manner of his response to this situation exposed the contradictions contained in the Northernization policy. On the one hand, the Sardauna assured the people of his region of an ecumenical political stance. In his State of the Region address given in 1957, he stated that "subject only to the requirements of law and public order, the Regional Government has no intention of favoring or advancing any religion at the expense of another. All persons in the Region are, as they have always been, absolutely at liberty to practise their beliefs according to their conscience without fear or favor, let or hindrance within the limitations outlined above."[76] A handful of minority elites (mostly Christians) were ritualistically initiated into the NPC, and political appointments were handed down to a token few of them. The NPC's slogan "One North, One People, Irrespective of Religion" became propaganda for concealing the internal fissures within the region.[77]

On the other hand, the Sardauna and his team had an unal-

loyed commitment to important Islamic principles of governance. These include a distaste for the Western European notion
of universal franchise. Traditional Islamic political process
"proceeds by 'selection' not 'election'"; and this "selection takes
place within a ruling oligarchy, with the aid of the ʿulamā, the
Muslim literates." They were similarly uncompromising in their
belief in the unalterability of the sharīʿa, insisting that "it is not
up to man to manipulate this; but only to interpret and apply
it." Furthermore, they held to the exclusivity of the traditional
jamāʿa, the Islamic political body, and because of this, "some
Muslims, particularly those of the traditional class of the ʿulamā,
have difficulty in accommodating non-Muslims on a basis of
equality, within the political framework of a predominantly
Muslim society."[78]

In his own studies, Kukah concluded that the Sarauta system
in the north, which holds that political legitimacy is rooted in
royal birth—holy descent from the Caliphate Founder—or
through appointment by the royal scions, naturally tilted the
power equation in favor of the Muslim political elite.[79] Not
only was it considered imperative that the leadership of the
NPC, and by implication, of the northern region, remained "in
the hands of a person of royal birth,"[80] the assumption of any
important political position must also be based on religious
qualifications. The Muslims' apprehension of the religious loss
to be sustained if a Christian was entrusted with a leadership
position in the region was epitomized in the poem of St'adu
Zungur, a Hausa-Fulani and a staunch member of the NPC:

As for the Christian, what he desires is gain,
To cast you, our mallams aside,
And to cause you to stop applying our Sharīʿa,
Which Allah sent down through our Prophet.[81]

Another Islamic metaphor carefully deployed by Ahmadu Bello
to project himself as a faithful trustee of his ancestors' cali-

phate was the idea of the *umma* (Muslim community or Islamic state). Evoking this religious vocabulary had a tremendous affective impact on his people, for it not only symbolizes "their cultural and religious unity," but also "differentiates them from their non-Muslim southern Nigerian political rivals, who seek independence not within a secure Islamic frame but within that of feared republicanism."[82] Political opposition within the region, economic challenge from the south, and the cultural disillusionment of the few liberal Muslims, were all cast in religious terms. Zungur argues that "the plight of northern Nigeria—its educational and technological backwardness and its vulnerability to non-Muslim, southern Nigerian domination—was due to the Muslims' own failure to live up to their Islamic heritage."[83]

In other words, Zungur and his likes strongly believed that the north could only have a meaningful socioeconomic and political development within the framework of Islamic principles. Following the secularist-cum-Christian path of the south would only ensure continued cultural disarray of the north and its continued domination by the south. To stem the tide of this unhappy state of affairs, the government of northern Nigeria busied itself developing pan-Islamic links throughout the period of nationalist and pan-Africanist struggles.

The contemporary row over the religious factor in Nigerian foreign policy owes much to these earlier links. Through the efforts of the Sardauna, pilgrimage affairs became a national responsibility.[84] Pilgrims' offices were built in Khartoum, Jidda, and El Obeid; and on the attainment of independence, the federal government accorded the Jidda office and its officials diplomatic status.[85] Several studies have documented the economic and political costs of the *hajj* on the Nigerian government. In purely economic terms, pilgrimage, whether Muslim or Christian, remains an enigma in Nigeria; for in the judgment of one theorist, it is difficult to believe that the religious significance of this ritual still has any credibility.[86] Responding to the accusation that the NPC-led regional and federal governments were trying "to set up a theocratic state," the Sardauna responded that "while pilgrimage is a personal matter, the joint cooperation of the Northern Regional and Federal Governments is necessary to provide safeguards for Nigerian pilgrims."[87]

Besides these efforts to procure international support for the political agenda of Islamizing the Nigerian state, the Sardauna also involved his government in other religious activities aimed at consolidating the Muslim north as a political fortress. He launched extensive and vigorous conversion campaigns in his region, fearing that "if the North was allowed to split religiously, either in terms of Christian-Muslim, or among the various Muslim groups," it might fracture into small "ineffective political communities."[88] Individuals and villages were promised a life more abundant and status befitting if they embraced the cultural core of the region, namely, Islam and its de facto political party, the NPC. Power, prestige, and mobility institutions were sturdily monopolized by the Hausa-Fulani-NPC amalgam. In effect, aspirant subordinate individuals and groups within the region became cultural catspaws of religio-political subterfuge. The conversion effort "was advanced by giving out Christian girls to Muslims to marry, basing promotion in the civil service on religious affiliations and using traditional chiefs as conversion agents."[89]

In his further use of the apparatus of state for religious ends, Ahmadu Bello founded in 1961 the Jamī'a Na*sr al-Islām (Society for the Victory of Islam), an educational and missionary organization for training and sponsorship of missionaries to all parts of Nigeria. This society engineered the resuscitation of Qur'anic education and its integration into the Western educational system. Expatriates were brought from Pakistan and many Middle East countries to teach Arabic and Islamic subjects.[90] These institutions replicated the erstwhile Christian missionaries' strategy of coalescing academic with missiological goals.

The Sardauna's deft use of his royal, religious, ethnic, and political resources as incorporative mechanisms earned him an international prestige unsurpassed by any other member of the northern oligarchy. A plethora of honorary titles was conferred on him by several world Muslim leaders. He reached the zenith of his spiritual ambition by becoming the vice president of the World Islamic Council, at whose 1964 congress he announced the growing success of his conversion campaigns in Nigeria:

It will please you to hear, dear brothers, that in my endeavour to expand the religion of Islam I have, by the grace of Allah, been able to convert some 60,000 non-Muslims in my region to Islam within a period of five months, that is, from November 1963 to March 1964. Prior to this remarkable achievement, I have successfully been able to build several mosques in as many suitable centres as possible having regard to the resources at my disposal. . . .[91]

The Sardauna was, however, prevented from enthroning himself as an absolute suzerain in both political and religious terms. There were strong protests mounted against his political and religious ambition, both within his region as well as in the rest of the federation. Of greater significance was the fissure within the northern Muslim community itself, a phenomenon that challenged the thesis of some contemporary conservative Muslims that there could be only one way of relating Islam to the state. It is thus apposite at this juncture to discuss the patterns of religio-political protests in both regions of the federation.

Religion and Protest:
The Quest for Freedom and Social Justice

The nature and structure of political protest in Nigeria will be explained here through an interpretation of religion as a symbol system. Crawford Young has suggested that "group categorizations are [usually] perceived through characterization in symbolic form."[92] Anthropologists generally define symbols as "the universal unit for human communication."[93] As political paradigms, symbols provide the vehicles through which political demands are articulated, and they serve as the objects around which mobilization and countermobilization occur.[94] Conflicting interpretations of the symbolic order thus have a tangential relationship to the structure of social conflict and tensions. As Victor Turner explains, symbols are polysemic or multivocal, that is, they have many referents or multiple meanings at the same time. In other words, "certain dominant or focal symbols conspicuously possess the property of multivocality which allows for the economic representation of key aspects of culture and belief."[95]

Religion best illustrates the multivocality of symbol systems. On the one hand, it can provide a cultural platform for the formation of social cement.[96] Historically, this has sometimes taken the form of sacralization of the status quo, a religious involvement in the general "enterprise of world construction," in short, an attempt to project secular events as "mimetic reiterations of cosmic realities."[97] On the other hand, religion can also serve "as a rallying symbol with which the disenfranchised minimally manifest their opposition to the political order and the prevailing socio-economic decadence in the society."[98]

Within the context of Nigerian regional politics, in which religious and ethnic differentiation was crucial to the definition and distribution of political and material benefits, the political process became a competition between the groups of the "center and those of the periphery."[99] One major structural flaw in Nigerian triangular politics noted above was that while the three major communal groupings accounted for only two-thirds of the Nigerian population, the administrative structure of the country until 1967 served to nearly eclipse the remainder. Each of the three regions existing at the time of independence and serving as units of the Nigerian Federation was dominated by one of the major configurations. Edo, Urhobo, Itsekiri, and Midwestern Igbo in the western region; Tiv, Igala, Idoma, Nupe, and others in the north; Ibibio, Efiks, Ijaws, and others in the east were placed in a very exposed and dependent position by the three-cornered communal federation of the first phase of independence.

In each of these regions, as well as in the entire federation, religion provided the language, the values and the institutions "through which groups struggle and over which groups contend, both within and between religious communities."[100] The wailings of the minorities were about their domination by the regional power blocs, and an insistence upon political freedom and social justice. In fact, it was the political articulations of the minorities' religious discontents that "led to the Constitutional provision of the Bill of Rights in Nigerian law."[101]

Despite the disparity in the regional diffuseness of these protests, there was a common unifying element in the manner of their expression. Alternative political parties were formed coinciding with religious and ideological convictions. Such was to be expected, given the political climate of the time, which encouraged party activities, as well as the more theoretical fact that political parties are "organized attempts to get power"[102] (power here understood as control of the government).

Religion and Protest in the North

There is a near consensus among scholars that the coherence of religious protests in the north was given organizational direction by political parties. Different antiestablishment parties emerged in this region. The most significant of the Islam-inspired ones were the Northern (later Nigerian) Elements Progressive Union (NEPU), Kano People's Party (KPP), and Bornu Youth Movement (BYM).

NEPU was led by Mallam Aminu Kano, who, together with a number of young northern men who studied under him, have come to be identified as progressive Muslims. Their party was ideologically committed to the participation of the commoners (*talakawa*) in government, the rights of women to participate fully in economic and political development, the provision of better welfare services in the north, and the need for honesty in personal and public affairs. These progressives also criticized the emiral aristocratic institution as it had evolved in northern Nigeria. They regarded it as having no place in Islamic thought, and insisted that the kingship traditions were merely "custom," part of a feudal legacy that should be extirpated.[103] In terms of religious patronage, it was closely associated with the populalist Tijaniyya order of Sufis, in opposition to the Qadiriyya order, upon whose infrastructure the establishment party, the NPC, was built.

The discontent of the BYM dates back to the antagonism between the Sokoto caliphate established by Fodio and the Bornu imamate.[104] Bornu—recently divided into Bornu and Yobe states—has been characterized through much of the nineteenth and twentieth centuries by its insistence on autonomy from Sokoto, and by its identification with non-Sufi forms of Islam. At its inaugural meeting on 26 June 1954, the BYM clearly articulated the political grievances of the northeastern people, especially their desire to secede from the region and become a separate state that would comprise the Bornu, Adamawa, and Plateau provinces.[105]

However, none of these antiestablishment parties doubted that political reform must be conducted within the framework of Islamic *Weltanschauung*.[106] All of them, as well as the NPC, "manipulated Islamic ideas and symbols in support of their positions."[107] At nearly all election times, the southern-based political parties have misconstrued the depth of the political divisiveness among the northern Muslims. They have thought that, by reason of a semblance of political ideologies, they can erode the northern Muslims' belief in "the Islamic Sharīʿa [as] the basis of legitimate government."[108] For example, presidential aspirants from the south have usually picked their running mates from the north in the hope of breaking the northern political solidarity, but as Chief Obafemi Awolowo's 1983 experience clearly demonstrates—when his own political party (the UPN) failed to capture a single northern state—the Islamic vision of the state, well articulated by the northern Muslims, remains a defiant obstacle against any enduring north-south political alliance.

Reacting to the frustrations of the southern politicians at the persistent elusiveness of any enduring political alliance between them and the opposition political parties in the north, Ahmadu Bello boasted of the impenetrability of northern Muslims' solidarity. "Islamic brotherhood," he said, "is stronger than blood."[109] This has been the normative understanding of the northern Muslims. For both the ruling elite and the marginalized masses, Islam provides the glue necessary to maintain the dominance of the north in national politics.[110] To illustrate this point, Kukah explains that "the objections of NEPU to emirate rule was mainly against its oppression, not its very existence."[111] And, by way of self-definition, all the ethnolinguistic groups in the Bornu area have long regarded

Islam as the central organizing principle of their identity and value system.

Muslim-led parties were, however, not the only political parties that sprang up in the north. In the "lower" north, otherwise known as the Middle Belt, there has been a homogenous opposition against the Hausa-Fulani hegemony and its Islamic underpinnings. For instance, during the *Zaamanin siyasa* that terminated at the eve of the civil war (1967–1970), the United Middle Belt Congress (UMBC), led by a Christian, Joseph S. Tarka, provided the organizational direction for the demands of this region. The UMBC was the political vanguard of the Northern Nigeria Non-Muslim League (NNML), whose formation in 1950 "was aided by the Christian missions, namely, the Sudan Interior Mission (SIM) and the Sudan United Mission (SUM)."[112]

Notwithstanding the political misjudgment of the Willink Commission—set up in 1958 to look into the fears of the Minorities and make recommendations to the government for incorporation, if need be, into the Independence Constitution then in the making—the non-Muslims in the north complained against all sorts of discrimination, ranging from "various restrictions imposed on Christians, such as denial of land to build Churches, restriction in the circulation of Christian literature, freedom of worship, association etc., degrading treatment to traditional rulers for not being Muslims, and other forms of cultural domination."[113] Without a doubt, the current thirty-state arrangement of the Nigerian Federation underscores, more than any other factor, the moral import of geopolitical freedom and the saliency of the so-called Minority groups in Nigerian political calculations. Reflecting the mood and perspectives widely shared across the country, President Babangida explained in his broadcast to the nation on the occasion of the repartitioning of Nigeria into a thirty-state arrangement that government decisions to create more states have usually been based on three mutually reinforcing principles, namely, "the principle of social justice, the principle of development, and the principle of a balanced federation."[114]

Religion and Protest in the West

Regarding politics in Yorubaland, there is a certain predilection among analysts to conclude that confessional identification has not been politically relevant.[115] "Factional splits among the Yoruba," another scholar suggests, "cannot be correlated with Christian-Muslim divisions."[116] At the conclusion of his inquiry on the place of religion in Yoruba politics, David Laitin, now reputed to be the chief proponent of this thesis, argues that ancestral-city identity, not religion, is the keystone of Yoruba politics. According to him, "ancestral city remains the primary focus for political identification within Yoruba politics: nearly all political actions and positions are examined in Yorubaland through the lens of an ancestral city's color."[117]

I wish to challenge that interpretation. In what follows, I will argue that a careful study of Yoruba politics would reveal certain religious characteristics in the composition of aggrieved constituencies in this region. While it may be true that "at no level is [any Yoruba] community fixed or monolithic," it is equally incontrovertible that the spread of Christianity and Islam among the Yoruba "has been such that they are *both* significantly present in most communities *and* also, to a fair degree, regionally concentrated."[118]

The Action Group (AG) and its successor, the Unity Party of Nigeria (UPN), both led by Jeremiah Obafemi Awolowo, were perceived in certain quarters as Christian parties. Citing the symbolism of the University of Ife established by the AG government, the structure of political conflict between the AG and the Muslim Adelabu-led local party called Mabolaje (Don't spoil the honor), and the concentration of the political allies of the northern-based parties "in the predominantly Muslim, Oyo-Yoruba area, from Ibadan through Ogbomosho up to Ilorin," Peel concludes that "there was a distinctly Christian undertow" to the political messages of the AG and the UPN. It was not just that key leadership positions in these parties were held by Christians, but that the parties' programs were "so clearly a continuation of the Christian enterprise of Yoruba ethnicity."[119] The policy priority given to education by the AG and the UPN, and the iconography of the UPN in the 1979 election (a lighted torch, signifying light over Nigeria), was an extension and a perpetuation of the *olaju* (enlightenment) philosophy begun by the Christian missions.[120]

Besides these cleavage patterns in Yorubaland, there have also been specific political protests expressed against the alleged Christian agenda of the ruling parties. The Muslims saw the Christian elite as a major stumbling block to their progress. An early start in the acquisition of Western education secured for the Christians extensive control of politics, education, the judiciary, and the civil service.

In the 1950s the National Muslim League (NML) and the United Muslim Party (UMP), protested against the government's neglect of Muslim schools, its deliberate exclusion of the Arabic language from the curricula of most elementary schools, its silence over the coerced conversion of Muslim children who attended Christian mission schools, the systematic persecution of Muslims by Christians, and the inadequate representation of Muslims in the Western Region Executive Council and in the Western House of Chiefs.[121] Even those Muslim parliamentarians in the Western Region House of Assembly felt that the administration had denied them a fair share, and regarded them "as inferior and as a tool to be used for voting."[122]

In September 1954 the UMP forwarded a petition to the federal government in protest against attacks on Muslims in the programs and management of the Nigerian Broadcasting Service. It complained of deliberate provocations by Christian preachers, discrimination in the allocation of time to Muslim preachers, preference for Christian staff in the broadcast of religious programs, and inadequate salary of the Muslim Religious Broadcasting Assistant compared with his Christian counterpart.[123]

A clear example of how religious sentiments had been warped to further fuel political divisiveness among the Yoruba was an editorial response of the *West African Pilot,* a newspaper founded by Dr. Nnamdi Azikiwe to promote the interest of the NCNC, to religious conflicts within the AG-controlled region. In 1954 the paper and its patron party condemned the preference for Christian ceremonies by the government. It stated very emphatically that

> too long has Officialdom displayed a preference for the Christian form of worship in a population predominantly Muslim with the result that loyal citizens and public men who are followers of Islam are, by force of circumstances, made to attend a place of worship and participate in a devotional service in which a human being—a Prophet—is addressed as God, and the Only One God of the Universe is addressed as Trinity.[124]

While the paper and its party did not ask the government to declare the country a Muslim state, "even though the overwhelmingly Muslim population of the country makes such declaration a foregone conclusion," its members wanted Muslim dignitaries to be invited to state reception and banquets at the Government House, and they wanted the government to give equal recognition to both religions, to put an end to the prominence of bishops and archbishops in state functions at the expense of imams and chief imams, and to organize state services in the mosques.[125]

In his reaction to the Muslims' allegation, Awolowo focused more on his party than on the government and the state, a posture that further aggravated the Muslims' chagrin. According to H. O. Danmole, "Awolowo directed his attention to the religious nature of the party (NML) rather than the grievances expressed by the party."[126] His main concern was to maintain unity and order, which in the climate of the period, meant the political hegemony of his party. Muslims' agitation for policy reform that would secure them a right to public expression of their religion and a fairer treatment in the distribution of the "regional cake" seemed to have fallen on Awolowo's deaf ear. Disregarding the intensity of the Muslims' feelings, he accused them of attempting to create religious fanaticism, which could lead to religious violence, communal strife, and bloodshed. He thus threatened that his government would enact a law that would make it an offense to use religion against an opponent during an electioneering campaign and for the formation of political parties.[127]

Awolowo came to realize later the significance of religion in the region's politics, as well as in the country as a whole. This dawned on him after his party lost to the NPC in the 1959 general elections. Assessing the performance of the AG in that year, Richard L. Sklar suggests that "Muslim hostility to the AG may have been a factor in the defeat of the Action Group candidates in the sixteen Federal constituencies in the Yoruba area—one-third of the total number of Yoruba constituencies in the Western Region."[128] Even the quick fix that Awolowo tried to make in 1958 by establishing the Pilgrims' Welfare Board in the western region was too late to dissuade Yoruba Muslims from "look[ing] over their shoulders to the Hausa and beyond them to the Middle East," and from espousing "the idea of a separate Central Yoruba State, where Muslims would predominate."[129]

Conclusion

This chapter has focused mainly on delineating the dominant paradigms for understanding religion-state relations in Nigeria from the colonial period to the early years of independence. I have tried to show that no uniform paradigm existed throughout the period covered. Two important issues for socioethical reflection emerge from these interactive patterns. First was the level and quality of the country's political culture—that is, the prevailing patterns of political interaction and political institutions. While territorial unity was achieved through the amalgamation of regional units, no equivalent effort was made at the level of civic and political orientations. The institutionalization of regional political structures, each with its own value systems and philosophy of law and government, appeared to have ill prepared Nigerians for the challenges of nation building that devolved on them at independence. By the independence period, a common political ground or framework within which the diverse religious allegiances could find both their freedom and their limits had not been sufficiently stimulated. This lack of a commonly accepted philosophy of government has continued to strain Nigeria's political development.

The second issue was the pattern of state-society relationship. Throughout this period, the state enveloped the civil society in such a manner that the definition of the proper role of the various constituents within the latter was considered to be the exclusive preserve of the state. Each regional government not only bolstered its hold on power by the canopy of the dominant religion within its frontier, but also defined the parameters of acceptable religious behavior. The victims of these arrangements were the regional minority religious groups whose freedom was curtailed and public influence stultified.

Thus, both between the state and the various religious bodies, as well as among the religious communities themselves, there was a resistance to pluralism and its liberal democratic ethos. The colonial and postcolonial Nigerian state favored a monistic model of political community, one in which multiple sources of moral and religious insights were viewed as impediments to the commonweal. The regional variations in the political patronage of religious institutions further complicated the task of defining the proper relationship between religion and the emergent Nigerian state.

The last two decades have witnessed some attempts at political innovation. The most significant one, as we shall see in the next chapter, is the recognition that meaningful social engineering and political cohesiveness would require a new philosophy of government and law, one that has a mix of consensual and pluralist ingredients. The goal of this new orientation is to ensure that Nigeria become "neither a naked public square where all religion is excluded, nor a sacred public square with any religion established or semi-established but a civil public square in which citizens of all religious faith, or none, engage one another in continuing democratic discourse."[130]

Ironically, the emergence of fundamentalist religious precepts has stunted the initial fruits of this innovative effort, forcing the state to renege on its pledge to make a pluralist climate a respectable feature of public life. This paradoxical mixture of a more inclusive public ethos and of a narrow religious sentimentality is the subject of the next chapter.

Notes

1. Lovin, "Religion and American Public Life," 9.
2. Robert N. Bellah, "Civil Religion in America," in *Beyond Belief: Essays on Religion in a Post-Traditional World* (New York: Harper and Row, 1970), 168–89.

3. Jacob K. Olupona, "Religious Pluralism and Civil Religion in Africa," *Dialogue and Alliance* 2, 4 (1988–89): 41. The idea expressed here had been long articulated by Emile Durkheim. See Durkheim, *The Elementary Forms of the Religious Life* (New York: Free Press, 1915), 427.

4. Lovin, "Religion and American Public Life," 9.

5. Ibid.

6. Lamin Sanneh, *Encountering The West: Christianity and the Global Cultural Process: The African Dimension* (Maryknoll, N.Y.: Orbis Books, 1993), 27.

7. Peel, *Ijeshas and Nigerians,* 3.

8. A. E. Afigbo, "The Missions, the State and Education in South-Eastern Nigeria, 1956–1971," in *Christianity in Independent Africa,* ed. Edward Fashole-Luke et al. (Bloomington: Indiana University Press, 1978), 176–92; E. C. Amucheazi, *Church and Politics in Eastern Nigeria, 1945–1966: A Study in Pressure Group Politics* (Lagos: Macmillan, 1986); D. I. Ilega, "Religion and Godless' Nationalism in Colonial Nigeria: The Case of the God's Kingdom Society and the N.C.N.C.," *Journal of Religion in Africa* 18, 2 (1988): 163–182.

9. William D. Graf, *The Nigerian State: Political Economy, State Class, and Political System in the Post-Colonial Era* (London: James Currey, 1988), xi.

10. Olusola Akinrinade and M.A. Ojo, "Religion and Politics in Contemporary Nigeria: A Study of the 1986 OIC Crisis," *Journal of Asian and African Studies* 4, 1 (Fall 1992) 46. Cf. Ibrahim Gambari, "The Role of Religion in National Life: Reflections on Recent Experiences in Nigeria," in *Religion and National Integration in Africa,* ed. John O. Hunwick (Evanston, Ill.: Northwestern University Press, 1992), 88.

11. Cohen, *Custom and Politics in Urban Africa;* idem, *Two-Dimensional Man: An Essay on the Anthropology of Power and Symbolism in Complex Society* (London: Routledge and Kegan Paul, 1974); Jacob K. Olupona, *Kingship, Religion, and Rituals in a Nigerian Community: A Phenomenological Study of Ondo Yoruba Festivals* (Stockholm: Almqvist and Wiksell International, 1991); idem, "Religion and Politics in the Second Republic," in Nigeria's Second

Republic: Presidentialism, Politics, and Administration in a Developing State, ed. Victor Ayeni and Kayode Soremekun (Lagos: Daily Times Publication, 1988), 121-34; J. N. Paden, *Religion and Political Culture in Kano* (Berkeley: University of California Press, 1973); J.D.Y. Peel, "The Cultural Work of Yoruba Ethnogenesis," in *History and Ethnicity,* ed. Elizabeth Tonkin, Maryon McDonald, and Malcolm Chapman (London: Routledge, 1989), 198-215; C. S. Whitaker, *The Politics of Tradition: Continuity and Change in Northern Nigeria, 1946-1966* (Princeton: Princeton University Press, 1970).

12. Hans Mol, *Identity and the Sacred: A Sketch for a New Social-Scientific Theory of Religion* (Oxford: Basil Blackwell, 1976), x; Olupona, "Religion and Politics in the Second Republic," 124; Young, *Politics of Cultural Pluralism,* 51.

13. Peel, "Cultural Work of Yoruba Ethnogenesis," 201.

14. Obafemi Awolowo, Awo: *The Autobiography of Chief Obafemi Awolowo* (Cambridge: Cambridge University Press, 1960), 165-66.

15. N. A. Fadipe, *The Sociology of the Yoruba* (Ibadan: Ibadan University Press, 1970), 29-42.

16. S. Johnson, *The History of the Yorubas, from the Earliest Times to the Beginning of the British Protectorate* (Lagos: CMS Bookshops, 1921), 642. The italics are mine.

17. Peel, "Cultural Work of Yoruba Ethnogenesis," 210-13.

18. E. A. Ayandele, "The Collapse of 'Pagandom' in Igboland," in *Nigerian Historical Studies* (London: Frank Cass, 1979), 169; Chinua Achebe, *Things Fall Apart* (London: Heinemann, 1958); T. Obinkaram Echewa, *I Saw the Sky Catch Fire* (New York: Plume, 1993); F. K. Ekechi, *Missionary Enterprise and Rivalry in Igboland, 1857-1914* (London: Frank Cass, 1972).

19. A. Bolaji Akinyemi, "Religion and Foreign Affairs: Press Attitudes towards the Nigerian Civil War," *Jerusalem Journal of International Relations,* 4, 3 (1980): 56-81; Cynthia Sampson, "'To Make Real the Bond Between Us All': Quaker Conciliation During the Nigerian Civil War," in *Religion, The Missing Dimension of Statecraft,* ed. Douglas Johnston and Cynthia Sampson (New York: Oxford University Press, 1994), 88-118; A. F. Walls, "Religion and the Press in 'the Enclave' in the Nigerian Civil War," in *Christianity in Inde-*

pendent Africa, ed. Edward Fashole-Luke et al. (Bloomington: Indiana University Press, 1978), 207-9; Laurie S. Wiseberg, "Christian Churches and the Nigerian Civil War," *Journal of African Studies* 2, 13 (1975): 297-331.

20. R. A. Adeleye, *Power and Diplomacy in Northern Nigeria 1804-1906: The Sokoto Caliphate and Its Enemies* (New York: Humanities Press, 1971); Louis Brenner, "Muhammad al-Amin al-Kanimi and Religion and Politics in Bornu," in *Studies in West African Islamic History,* vol. 1, *The Cultivators of Islam,* ed. John Ralph Willis (London: Frank Cass, 1979), 160-76; M. Hiskett, *The Sword of Truth* (Oxford: Oxford University Press, 1973); D. M. Last, *The Sokoto Caliphate* (London: Longman, 1967); F. A. Salamone, "Becoming Hausa: Ethnic Identity Change and its Implications for the Study of Ethnic Pluralism and Stratification," *Africa* 45, 4 (1975): 410-24.

21. Louis Brenner, "The Jihad Debate between Sokoto and Borno: An Historical Analysis of Islamic Political Discourse in Nigeria," in *Peoples and Empires in African History: Essays in Memory of Michael Crowder,* ed. J. F. Ade Ajayi and J.D.Y. Peel (London: Longman, 1992), 21.

22. S. A. Balogun, "Islam in Nigeria: Its Historical Development," in *Nigeria Since Independence: The First Twenty-Five Years,* vol. 9, *Religion,* ed. J. A. Atanda, Garba Ashiwaju, and Yaya Abubakar (Ibadan: Heinemann, 1989), 54, 55.

23. Michael Crowder, *The Story of Nigeria,* 2d ed. (London: Faber and Faber, 1966), 97, 106.

24. Thomas Hodgkin, *Nigerian Perspectives: An Historical Anthology, West African History Series* (London: Oxford University Press, 1960), 131-32.

25. M. Last, "Some Economic Aspects of Conversion in Hausaland (Nigeria)," in *Conversion to Islam,* ed. Nehemia Levitzion (New York: Holmes and Meier, 1979), 247-65.

26. Peel, "Cultural Work of Yoruba Ethnogenesis," 209-10.

27. T. G. O. Gbadamosi, *The Growth of Islam among the Yoruba 1841-1908* (Atlantic Highlands, N.J.: Humanities Press, 1978).

28. Amucheazi, *Church and Politics in Eastern Nigeria,* 3.

29. Cohen, *Custom and Politics in Urban Africa,* 152, 159.

30. Nigeria, *Report of the Political Bureau*, 186.

31. E. A. Ayandele, *The Missionary Impact on Modern Nigeria, 1842-1914: A Political and Social Analysis* (London: Longman, 1966); Segun Gbadegesin, "Traditional African Religiosity: Myth or Reality?," in *African Philosophy: Traditional Yoruba Philosophy and Contemporary African Realities* (New York: Peter Lang, 1991), 83-104; E. B. Idowu, *Towards an Indigenous Church* (Oxford: Oxford University Press, 1965); V. Y. Mudimbe, *The Invention of Africa: Gnosis, Philosophy, and the Order of Knowledge* (Bloomington: Indiana University Press, 1988); Terence Ranger, "The Invention of Tradition in Colonial Africa," in *The Invention of Tradition*, ed. Eric Hobsbawm and Terence Ranger (Cambridge: Cambridge University Press, 1983), 211-62.

32. Akinrinade and Ojo, "1986 OIC Crisis," 45.

33. Ibrahim, "Religion and Political Turbulence in Nigeria," 29.

34. Young, *Politics of Cultural Pluralism*, 52-53; cf. Robin Horton, "African Conversion," *Africa* 41 (1971): 85-108.

35. John Onaiyekan, "Recent History of Religions in Nigeria: Some Myths and Realities," in *The Economic and Social Development of Nigeria: Proceedings of the National Conference on Nigeria since Independence*, vol. 2, ed. M. O. Kayode and Y. B. Usman (Zaria: ABU Press, 1983), 363; Jeyifo, "For Chinua Achebe," p. 53.

36. Idowu, *African Traditional Religion*, 168. A historical argument in support of a pluralistic Yoruba cultural universe is J. F. Ade Ajayi and R. S. Smith, *Yoruba Warfare in the Nineteenth Century* (Cambridge: Cambridge University Press, 1964).

37. F. J. D. Lugard, *Political Memoranda* (London: Frank Cass, 1970), 296, 297.

38. Kukah, "Religion and Politics in Northern Nigeria," 15.

39. Williams, "State, Religion, and Politics in Nigeria," 196.

40. Kukah, "Religion and Politics in Northern Nigeria," 15.

41. B. J. Dudley, *Parties and Politics in Northern Nigeria* (London: Frank Cass, 1968); Paden, *Religion and Political Culture in Kano;* Whitaker, *Politics of Tradition*.

42. C. N. Ubah, "Islamic Culture and Nigerian Society," in *Traditional and Modern Culture: Readings in African Humanities*, ed. Edith Ihekweazu (Enugu, Nigeria: Fourth Dimension, 1985), 353.

43. Young, *Politics of Cultural Pluralism*, 227.

44. Kukah, "Religion and Politics in Northern Nigeria," 14-15.

45. Lugard, *Political Memoranda*, 124.

46. Kalu, "Christianity and Colonial Society," 183.

47. E. A. Ayandele, "The Missionary Factor in Northern Nigeria 1870-1918," in *The History of Christianity in West Africa*, ed. O. U. Kalu (London: Longman, 1980), 139.

48. Mudimbe, *Invention of Africa*, 1.

49. Bayo Williams, "The Paradox of a Nation," *Newswatch* (Nigeria), 3 October 1985, 7; Leo Dare, "Political Change in Nigeria," in *Social Change in Nigeria*, ed. Simi Afonja and Tola Olu Pearce (White Plains: Longman, 1986), 71-91.

50. Agbaje, "Travails of the Secular State," 290.

51. Ibid.

52. James S. Coleman, *Nigeria: Background to Nationalism* (Berkeley: University of California Press, 1958), 96-97.

53. Nigeria, *Report of the Political Bureau*, 29-30.

54. J. F. A. Ajayi, *Christian Missions in Nigeria 1841-1891: The Making of a Modern Elite* (London: Longman, 1965); E. A. Ayandele, *Missionary Impact on Modern Nigeria*; Babs A. Fafunwa, *History of Education in Nigeria* (London: Allen and Unwin, 1974).

55. Peter B. Clarke, *West Africa and Islam: A Study of Religious Development from the Eighth to the Twentieth Century* (London: Edward Arnold, 1982), 228.

56. Cited in A. E. Afigbo, "Christian Missions and Secular Authorities in South-Eastern Nigeria from Colonial Times," in *The History of Christianity in West Africa*, ed. O. U. Kalu (London: Longman, 1980), 189.

57. Clarke, *West Africa and Islam*, 193.

58. See Gbadegesin, *African Philosophy*, 137-60; Mudimbe, *Invention of Africa*, 44-64.

59. In the next chapter, I will analyze and discuss the confusion that the use of the term *secularity* has introduced into Nigerian political discourse.

60. Awolowo, *Awo*, 165-66.

61. Ibrahim A. Gambari, "British Colonial Administration," in *Nigerian History and Culture*, ed. Richard Olaniyan (Essex: Longman, 1985), 168.

62. H. O. Davies, *Nigeria: Prospects for Democracy* (Weidenfeld and Nicolson, 1961), 91.

63. Coleman, *Nigeria;* Billy Dudley, *Instability and Political Order: Politics and Crisis in Nigeria* (Ibadan: Ibadan University Press, 1973); Richard L. Sklar, *Nigerian Political Parties: Power in an Emergent African Nation* (Princeton: Princeton University Press, 1963).

64. Mervyn Hiskett, "Islam in Hausa Political Verse Propaganda from 1946 to Northern Nigerian Independence," in *Christian and Islamic Contributions towards Establishing Independent States in Africa South of the Sahara: Papers and Proceedings of the Africa Colloquium,* Bonn-Bad Godesberg, 2–4 May 1979, ed. J.D.Y. Peel (Stuttgart: Institut für Auslandsbeziehungen, 1979), 100.

65. Gambari, "British Colonial Administration," 159–75.

66. Nigeria, *Report of the Political Bureau,* 27.

67. Williams, "State, Religion, and Politics in Nigeria," 327.

68. Coleman, *Background to Nationalism;* A. H. M. Kirk-Greene, *Crisis and Conflict in Nigeria: A Documentary Sourcebook,* 2 vols. (London: Oxford University Press, 1971); John P. Mackintosh, ed., *Nigerian Government and Politics* (London: Allen and Unwin, 1966).

69. Hiskett, "Islam in Hausa Political Verse," 100.

70. Kukah, "Religion and Politics in Northern Nigeria," 48–83.

71. John N. Paden, *Ahmadu Bello, Sardauna of Sokoto: Values and Leadership in Nigeria* (London: Hodder and Stoughton, 1986), 279–312, 529–78.

72. D. J. M. Muffet, "The Coups D'état in Nigeria, 1966: A Study in Elite Dynamics" (Ph.D. diss., University of Pittsburgh, 1971); idem, *Let Truth Be Told* (Zaria: Hudahuda, 1982).

73. Interview with B. A. Yashe, *Nigerian Citizen,* 24 April 1962.

74. *Nigerian Citizen,* 4 April 1960.

75. Whitaker, *Politics of Tradition,* 401.

76. E. P. T. Crampton, "Christianity in Northern Nigeria," in *Christianity in West Africa: The Nigerian Story,* ed. Ogbu Kalu (Ibadan: Daystar Press, 1978), 88.

77. B. J. Dudley, *Parties and Politics in Northern Nigeria* (London: Frank Cass, 1968), 116–63.

78. Hiskett, "Islam in Hausa Political Verse," 101.

79. Kukah, "Religion and Politics in Northern Nigeria," 17.

80. Paden, *Ahmadu Bello,* 153.

81. Cited in Mervyn Hiskett, *A History of Hausa Islamic Verse* (London: School of Oriental and African Studies, 1975), 109.

82. Hiskett, "Islam in Hausa Political Verse," 106.

83. Ibid., 105.

84. Paden, *Ahmadu Bello,* 286.

85. Ibid., 293.

86. D. A. Oyeshola, "Religious Obstacles to Development in Africa," *Orita* 23, 1 (1991): 45. See also Olajide Aluko, "Nigeria's Foreign Policy," in *Nigerian History and Culture,* ed. Richard Olaniyan (White Plains: Longman, 1985), 217; Bukar Bukarambe, "Nigeria and the Arab World," in *Nigeria's External Relations: The First Twenty-Five Years,* ed. G. O. Olusanya and R. A. Akindele (Ibadan: University Press, 1986), 420–35.

87. Paden, *Ahmadu Bello,* 284.

88. Ibid., 303.

89. A. E. Ekoko and L. A. Amadi, "Religion and Stability in Nigeria," in *Nigeria since Independence: The First Twenty-Five Years,* vol. 9, *Religion,* ed. J. A. Atanda, Garba Ashiwaju, and Yaya Abubakar (Ibadan: Heinemann, 1989), 115.

90. Paden, *Ahmadu Bello,* 299–303.

91. Ibid., 533, 540.

92. Young, *Politics of Cultural Pluralism,* 141.

93. Olupona, *Kingship, Religion, and Rituals,* 149.

94. Charles D. Elder and Roger W. Cobb, *The Political Uses of Symbols* (New York: Longman, 1988), 9, 129.

95. Victor Turner, *Drama, Fields, and Metaphors* (Ithaca: Cornell University Press, 1971), 50.

96. Kenneth Thompson, *Beliefs and Ideology* (London: Tavistock, 1986), 61; Bryan Wilson, *Religion in Sociological Perspective* (Oxford: Oxford University Press, 1982), 32–36.

97. Peter L. Berger, *The Sacred Canopy: Elements of a Sociological Theory of Religion* (Garden City, N.Y.: Doubleday, 1969), 13–37, 47; another significant work in this area is David Martin, *The Breaking of the Image: A Sociology of Christian Theory and Practice* (Oxford: Blackwell, 1980).

98. Olupona, "Religion and Politics in the Second Republic," 121.

99. The concept of "center and periphery" was first used by Edward Shils. I got the idea, however, through its application by David Martin to a sociological study of the geopolitical relationship among Rome, Ireland, and England. The "center" considers itself as the symbolic fount of cultural civilization and political power, and the peripheries are expected to defer to it for various kinds of ideological direction. See David Martin, "Preliminary Excursus on Centre and Periphery" (Southern Methodist University, mimeographed); later revised and published in *Festschrift for Edward Shils* (Chicago: University of Chicago Press, 1988).

100. Henry Bienen, "Religion, Legitimacy, and Conflict in Nigeria," *Annals of the American Academy of Political and Social Science* 483 (1986): 50.

101. Ikem B. C. Ngwoke, *Religion and Religious Liberty in Nigerian Law: From the Colonial Days to 1983* (Rome: Pontificia Universita Lateranense, 1984), 54.

102. E. E. Schattschneider, *Party Government* (New York: Rinehart, 1942), 35.

103. Dudley, *Parties and Politics in Northern Nigeria,* 80; Sklar, *Nigerian Political Parties,* 95.

104. See Brenner, "Jihad Debate between Sokoto and Borno."

105. Dudley, *Parties and Politics in Northern Nigeria,* 89.

106. Ibid.; Paden, *Religion and Political Culture in Kano;* Whitaker, *Politics of Tradition.*

107. Paden, *Religion and Political Culture in Kano,* 312–13.

108. Hiskett, "Islam in Hausa Political Verse," 103.

109. Paden, *Ahmadu Bello,* 285.

110. Bienen, "Religion, Legitimacy, and Conflict in Nigeria," 59.

111. Kukah, "Religion and Politics in Northern Nigeria," 19.

112. Williams, "State, Religion, and Politics in Nigeria," 270.

113. Federal Government of Nigeria, *Report of the Commission Appointed to Enquire into the Fears of the Minorities and the Means of Allaying Them* (London: Her Majesty's Stationery Office, 1958), 36–46.

114. See Ibrahim Babangida, "Agitation for New States Is Healthy," in *Guardian,* 28 August 1991, 5.

115. Laitin, *Hegemony and Culture,* xi; Sklar, *Nigerian Political Parties,* 247.

116. Bienen, "Religion, Legitimacy, and Conflict in Nigeria," 54.

117. Laitin, *Hegemony and Culture,* 121.

118. Peel, "Cultural Work of Yoruba Ethnogenesis," 212. Italics in original.

119. Ibid., 210–12.

120. Ibid., 201.

121. *Minority Commission Report,* 26–26.

122. Western Region Government, *Western House of Assembly Debates: Official Report,* Ibadan, 1958, 477.

123. *West African Pilot,* 8 and 11 October 1954.

124. National Archives Ibadan, C.S.O. 26/2955, U.M.P. to the Chief Secretary to the Government, 18 August 1954.

125. *West African Pilot,* 11 October 1954.

126. H. O. Danmole, "The Religious Factor in Nigerian Politics: Awolowo and the Muslims, 1957–1983," in *Obafemi Awolowo: The End of an Era?* ed. Olasope O. Oyelaran (Ile-Ife, Nigeria: Obafemi Awolowo University Press, 1988), 881.

127. *Minority Commission Report,* 11.

128. Sklar, *Nigerian Political Parties,* 250.

129. Peel, "Cultural Work of Yoruba Ethnogenesis," 212; see also Danmole, "Religious Factor in Nigerian Politics," 886.

130. Perry, *Love and Power,* 45; see also chap. 2 of the present work.

Chapter 4

Seeking A Common Political Ground: Secularity and the Sharīʿa Debate

> . . . harmony, cooperation and "unity" have manifestly not characterized social and political life in post-independent Nigeria. No effective formulas have been found to bring ethnic competition, class conflict, social diversity and the like into a "higher," productive synthesis. Most adult Nigerians have directly and poignantly experienced protests, riots, even massacres, civil war and coercive military rule, and thus know at first hand the results of faulty integration.
>
> —William Graf, *The Nigerian State*

THE CENTRAL ARGUMENT in this chapter is that the debate about the relationship between religion and the Nigerian state, which took off in 1976, should be seen within the context of a larger concern, especially as voiced among the Nigerian elite, to develop a public ethic capable of serving as a common standard of political judgment for Nigeria's citizens and its varied groups. After discussing what might count as the origin and content of this public ethic, I analyze the "religion debate" as it has revolved around the two controversial concepts of secularity and the *sharīʿa*, both of which "were as much about laying the foundation stones for the future direction and character of Nigerian society as anything else."[1] The collective concern to actualize democratic polity both made possible the debate, and provided the ethical norms for articulating and negotiating interests for those significantly involved in it.

Nigeria in Search of a Public Philosophy

Nigeria's experience of the civil war, which ended in 1970, had a redemptive and soteriological impact on the nation's psyche. A Nigerian sociologist of religion has observed this irony in the nation's history. Jacob K. Olupona traces the origin of the civil religion of the emerging Nigeria to this experience: "Out of the disintegration disclosed in that war came paradoxically the ideas, symbols, and rituals of Nigerian civil religion, the purpose of which was to achieve integration where none existed."[2]

More germane to my purpose here is the nature of the orientations of the country's successive post-1970 governments. None of them has doubted the feasibility of establishing a nation-state with public purposes beyond individual gratification and cultural parochialism. In fact, since the military first seized power in 1966, its leaders have always justified their intervention in politics in terms of attempting to "nurture a national political culture which allows for democratic involvement at all levels of government, while at the same time strengthening a larger, national system, which is more than the sum of its parts."[3]

In his opening address to the fifty members of the Constitution Drafting Committee (CDC) on 18 October 1975, the head of Nigeria's military government, General Murtala Ramat Muhammad, declared, "It is important that we avoid a reopening of the deep splits which caused trauma in the country." Part of the "trauma" of the country—which was to be averted—included the tendency to regard the winning of elections as "a life and death struggle which justified all means—fair and foul"; the fact that "the interest of the party leaders came to supplant the interest of the public and indeed the interest of their parties, because once in power there was hardly any question of public or party accountability"; and the fact that "orderly succession to power was virtually impossible."[4] In a similar vein, President Babangida, shortly after assuming office as head of state in August 1985, inaugurated a seventeen-member Political Bureau, headed by Professor Sylvanus Cookey, whose terms of reference included "the review of Nigeria's political history, identifying the basic problems which led to failure in the past and suggesting ways of resolving and coping with these problems" and the identification of "a basic philosophy of government which will determine goals and serve as a guide to the activities of government."[5]

Besides the structural and institutional responses to Nigeria's problem of pluralism and integration, mainly through the country's federalist arrangements now considered to be a "sacred cow,"[6] there has also evolved in the country, albeit unformalized and arguably intangible, a sort of public philosophy couched in ethical terms and transcendent principles.[7] This new approach to Nigeria's politics is guided by the premise that "any viable society presupposes a certain degree of unity of purpose and that such unity should find expression in the philosophy undergirding its public life."[8] Hence the almost fanatical attempts by the state, through its managers, to express, encourage, and institutionalize a shared set of ethical values in order to provide a common frame of reference for the diverse segments of the country.

Faced with the onerous task of creating community and encouraging civility among people who disagree about the more fundamental issues of human existence, the Nigerian state has intensified efforts to render "political life intelligible by seeing it, even at its most erratic, as informed by a set of conceptions —ideals, hypotheses, obsessions, judgments—derived from concerns which far transcend it."[9] The deontic and teleological urgency of a public philosophy was underscored by Cookey's study group when it noted that "a major problem with our experiments at nation-building has been the absence of an effective, well defined, properly articulated and popular philosophy of government for the country."[10] It went on to define a philosophy of government as "a statement of the principles of what is good or right for the society taken as a whole."[11]

The idea of public philosophy in the context of political discourse in Nigeria is undoubtedly fraught with conceptual imprecision and historical ambiguity. Murtala Muhammad's administration, whose successor midwifed the return of democratic politics in 1979, expressed its suspicion about the desirability of pontificating a national philosophy of government. It was reasoned then that from the viewpoint of the military, "the evolution of a doctrinal concept is usually predicated upon the general acceptance by the people of a national philosophy and consequently, until our people, or a large majority of them, have acknowledged a common ideological motivation, it would be fruitless to proclaim any particular philosophy or ideology in our constitution."[12]

From the perspective of that administration, a philosophy of government was construed narrowly in terms of political and economic indoctrination. The competing options on the Nigerian scene have been capitalism, socialism, democracy, communism, diarchy, and other traditional philosophies, although some of these systems are not mutually exclusive.[13] Driven by the singular aim to produce a constitution that would "be workable and acceptable to the majority of people," Muhammad opted for a pragmatic approach.[14]

Interestingly enough, it was this same administration that determinedly pushed the discussions of public affairs during the transition program to the level of basic ethical principles. Thus, to be able to understand the historical evolution of the idea of public philosophy in Nigeria, we would have to broaden our conceptual definition. As already used in this work, public philosophy will refer to "a body of positive principles which a good citizen cannot deny or ignore."[15] A broader definition of the concept is guided by the premise that the political processes of a society's public life ought to be wider and deeper than the formal institutions that are designed to regulate it, realizing that in most free, stable, and democratic polities, "some of the most critical decisions concerning the direction of public life are not made in parliaments and presidiums [but] in the unformalized realms of what Durkheim called 'the collective conscience.' "[16] This collective conscience is what the state has been trying to create in an attempt to forge, through constitutional mechanisms, a common ground for political judgment among Nigerian citizens. Babangida defined this consciousness as "the total conviction of a greater percentage of the general populace by not just believing, but also supporting objectively, certain principles laid down by their country."[17]

What are the content and structure of the emerging Nigeria's public philosophy? The first element of this public philosophy is the belief articulated in the preamble to the 1989 Nigerian constitution that the nation is under the sovereignty of God: "We the people of the Federal Republic of Nigeria, having firmly and solemnly resolved to provide for a constitution. . . . and to live in unity and harmony as one indivisible and indissoluble Nation under God."[18] Hackett and Olupona suggest that the presence of God-language in Nigeria's constitutions, the national anthem, and national pledge, and the invocations of nonsectarian religious and moral values in the speeches of Nigeria's post-civil war rulers, reveal an underlying belief that "the nation is not an ultimate end in itself but stands under transcendent judgement and has value only in so far as it realized, particularly and fragmentarily, at best a higher law."[19]

While this feature of public philosophy may signal an incipient evolution of civil religion in an attempt to provide a homogenizing faith for Nigeria's varied religious and nonreligious groups,[20] it suffices to see this phenomenon as only an attempt to "find an extrasocietal bedrock on which to ground present political arrangements."[21] The postindependence features of Nigerian political climate are such that "whatever the character of the regime, politics has continually had to work with or around religious realities rather than against them."[22] It would certainly be baffling if things had been different. For not only are people's desires to shape their political arrangements not self-justifying, it is also the case that "any coherent society must rest on a set of moral beliefs which ground the political order on a transcendent basis."[23] References to religious themes are an acknowledgment of the fact that there are no religiously neutral Nigerians, and as such, there cannot be a religiously neutral political life. They clearly exemplify what Clifford Geertz characterizes as "the politics of meaning" or what Charles Taylor describes as "the politics of recognition."[24]

If there is any justification for the introduction of the themes of *meaning* and *recognition* to political theory, it is that they serve to debunk the myth of an ahistorical state, a state that prescribes political norms that are alien to its citizens' cultural and historical experiences. Not only would such a state be antithetical to the real experience of the Nigerian people, it would ultimately be found to be based on its own narrowly defined value of life, thus revealing the hypocrisy of any attempt to establish a value-neutral state. Writing about a different society, Subrata Mitra argues that "no concept of the state is value free; the values inherent in the prevailing concept of the state determine the parameters of political, social and cultural engagement within a society. Religions often have a great deal to say about what values are incorporated into such a concept of the state."[25]

It is thus consistent with the intent of the emerging public philosophy in Nigeria to see the references to religious idioms in the country's constitution as an indicator of the desire to create for Nigeria's varied groups "an institutional structure

for the country that enough of its citizens would find sufficiently congenial to allow it to function."[26] And this aim to organize a cultural hodgepodge into a workable polity "is more
than a matter of inventing a promiscuous civil religion to blunt
its variety."[27] The civil religion thesis is no doubt attractive in
the contemporary Nigerian political climate because it represents an attempt to identify common ground among positions
that differ in significant particulars. But its main weaknesses
tend to be overlooked by its proponents. First, in seeking
common ground, civil religion often reduces distinctive traditions to a least common denominator. Second, in struggling to
articulate fundamental values and institutional patterns for the
society as a whole, civil religion may become an uncritical
apologist for existing arrangements.[28]

The second set of elements of the evolving public philosophy in Nigeria has focused on the important issues of statecraft. Central among these are attempts to generate respect for
the rule of law, that is, constitutionalism. While the country
has been ruled by the military for most of its life after independence, the popular verdict has always declared military
government to be a clear evidence of political immaturity.[29] To
many Nigerians, the military is a force that is arrayed against
the answering of the national question, for "by its incursion
into politics, the military has created its own Frankenstein
monster."[30] Charles Archibong contends that the ends of pluralism cannot be served in the country as long as the military
stays in power.[31]

The embarrassing realities of Nigeria's politics—notably,
the absence of popular mobilization, effective accountability,
basic rights, and individual freedoms—have been attributed to
a pervasive lack of democracy. The country's "existing patterns
of social differentiation and political organization have tended
to encourage a rather narrow base for decision-making and the
lack of popular debate over basic national development poli-

cies and their implementation."[32] The natural consequences of this situation have been a consistent pattern of ruptured social relations and repetitive, ill-fated development policies.

It is not without significance that both the Second Republic (1979–1983) and the aborted Third Republic were brainchildren of military regimes. The military juntas themselves have appeared to be the best articulators of their illegitimacy to govern.[33] General Obasanjo, a former Nigerian head of state, saw military rule as an "aberration" because of "its fast and at times unconventional means of achieving results in the quickest way."[34] Also included among the many recommendations received by the Babangida administration from the Political Bureau, which Babangida himself commissioned, was one that would undoubtedly have embarrassed his regime. The bureau adjudged that "military rule is itself a departure from the normal political process, and it is not surprising that it has created [some] precedent of arbitrariness in public policy formulation and implementation."[35] The bureau advisedly reasoned that "military intervention in politics legitimized the use of violence as an instrument for changing a government."[36]

Since he left office, Obasanjo has consistently decried the continued invasion of Nigeria's political arena by the military. He has regularly called for the full democratization of the country's polity, not only because "democracy takes institutional pluralism for granted," but also because "it embodies more than any other form of power an immanent tendency of man towards freedom and thereby remains the best and the most humane form of power."[37]

At the institutional level, a democratic polity is deemed desirable because of its potential "to check, balance, and decentralize political power as extensively and innovatively as possible," as well as "to reduce both the stakes in any electoral contest and the scope for behavioral abuses."[38] Despite all the empirical evidences to the contrary, especially "the powerful statist and authoritarian tendencies," Nigerians are generally possessed of "strong pluralist values and structures," constantly propelling them to profess democracy as a political credo.[39] A significant number of them have come to trust democratic polity as the most rational way to solve many problems of public life. For instance, the failure of Babangida's Structural Adjustment Program (SAP), originally conceived to bring about sustainable development for the country, was considered inevitable by many political pundits because it sidestepped the democratic process, which required "that citizens be involved in any program of change and transformation."[40]

This disenchantment with military superimposition has necessitated a paradigm shift in the theories of governance in Nigeria. Contrary to the theories of the early 1960s concerning the alleged modernizing propensities of African military regimes,[41] there is now an increasing awareness among scholars that military rule does not necessarily lead to policies of socioeconomic change that would radically alter the nature of the political environment.[42] In fact, one scholar has characterized military intervention in politics as "a method of change that changes little."[43] Generally speaking, the military has been unable to bring about fundamental social change and a reordering of the power structure within Nigerian society because "the very factors which produce the army *coup d'etat* make it impossible for the army to produce a regime free from crisis."[44] Cultural parochialism and statism "have remained as strong during army rule as they have been during that of civilians."[45] Thus military rule has not always cured the political decay and the praetorian condition that constitute the predisposing conditions for military intervention. According to Whitaker, "Nigeria's version of a praetorian mission to purge, reform, unify, and modernize hardly bestowed immunity from the realities and currents of Nigerian problems and conflicts."[46]

The third element of Nigeria's evolving public philosophy

is the definition of the nature and purpose of government. Before the inauguration of the Second Republic, attempts were made by the CDC to formulate "fundamental objectives and directive principles of state policy" which were meant to inform the process of government. The committee blamed the failure of the previous regimes on the absence of such behavioral norms in the constitutions which guided them, notably, the 1954, 1960 and 1963 constitutions, all of which took for granted "the duties of the government towards its subjects."[47] The committee also blamed these past constitutions for the myopic assumption that "those who wield the power of the State will be conscious of, and responsive to, its obligations and responsibilities."[48]

Thus a statement of "fundamental objectives and directive principles of state policy" is an attempt at stating "how society can be organized . . . to the best advantage of all." Fundamental objectives refer to "those goals and long-term ends which a government," it is thought, "ought to commit itself to," while the directive principles of state policy refer to "those means by which the stated objectives are best to be achieved."[49] An example of "fundamental objectives" as stated in the 1979 constitution is the provision that "every citizen shall have equality of rights, obligations and opportunities before the law" (sec.17:2:a). Toward the realization of this and similar goal(s), the same constitution stipulates that "the composition of the Government of the Federation or any of its agencies and the conduct of its affairs shall be carried out in such a manner as to reflect the federal character of Nigeria. . . . there shall be no predominance of persons from a few states or from a few ethnic or other sectional groups in that government or any of its agencies" (sec.14:3); and "[the government shall] encourage inter-marriage among persons from different places of origin or different religious, ethnic or linguistic association or ties" (sec.15:3:c).

While recognizing that a society's objectives and values are neither static nor timeless, the committee was firmly of the opinion that the values it had in mind were fundamental enough to command a wide consensus in the community and not to be dismissed as ephemeral objectives or factional slogans. The committee justified the inclusion of these values on the merits of national integration. It concluded that "only an explicit statement of objectives and directive priorities which clearly sets the parameters of government and informs its policies and action can generate a spirit of cooperation, peace, unity and progress."[50]

This public ethic was deemed necessary in Nigerian society and in the federal constitution for two additional reasons. First, it was observed by the committee that in developing countries there had been an overwhelming preoccupation of public officers "with power and its material perquisites."[51] Second, certain sociological and economic facts about Nigerian life would make any alternative approach seem tragic. Some of these facts include "the heterogeneity of the society, the increasing gap between the rich and the poor, the growing cleavage between the social groupings, all of which combine to confuse the nation and bedevil the concerted march to orderly progress."[52]

In the attempt to avoid the charges of bland generality and vagueness in the stated fundamental objectives, the chapter on "Philosophy for Government" in the report of the 1986 Political Bureau specified more clearly the functions of the state, namely, the maintenance of order and public peace, and of a just and equitable political system.[53] The ultimate canon against which a just political system should be measured is the ability of the state to free its citizens "from the debilitating conditions which have shackled their lives and left them at the beck and call of the elites," as well as to "make laws designed to induce in everybody conformity of behavior whose aggregate effect will be to promote the well-being of all the people."[54]

In addition to guarding against the tendency to impose "on society a rigid system of egalitarianism,"[55] the state must also aspire to prevent the ills of "prebendalism," which Richard Joseph claims have infested Nigerian polity. Prebendal politics refers to

> patterns of political behavior which rest on the justifying principle that [public offices] should be competed for and then utilized for the personal benefit of office holders as well as of their reference or support group. The official public purpose of the office often becomes a secondary concern, however much that purpose might have been originally cited in its creation or during the periodic competition to fill it.[56]

As submitted by the bureau, the norms of equity and accountability are breached when a political system allows actors who play roles in public affairs "to pass the privileges attached to these roles from themselves to their families and thereby perpetuate the domination of the affairs of the nation by a small group of people."[57]

The drafters of both the 1979 and 1989 constitutions of Nigeria believed that a constitution had to be more than merely a code of justiciable rules and regulations. Above everything else, it must be able to provide normative standards against which the activities of government and the behavior of public officers can be measured and evaluated.[58] In short, a constitution is supposed to be "a charter of government," for only then would Nigeria's constitution be able to fulfill its proper role of seeking to "unite society into one nation, bound together by common attitudes and values, common institutions and procedures, and, above all, an acceptance of common objectives and destiny."[59]

Finally, the fourth element of the emerging public philosophy emphasizes the cultivation of a dialogic and tolerant political attitude as a method for organizing the collective life. The Ethical Revolution program of Shehu Shagari, the president of

Nigeria's Second Republic, and the War against Indiscipline program of Muhammadu Buhari and Tunde Idiagbon, the military duo who ousted Shagari from office, were both rooted in the premise that "the construction of a democratic and decent society in Nigeria will require a transformation of values and behavioral orientations."[60] In his Independence Anniversary broadcast to the nation on 1 October 1976, the head of state, General Olusegun Obasanjo reminded Nigerians that while it is incontrovertible that "the constitution is clearly the starting point for what we believe will be a fresh, progressive and unifying political process, the constitution by itself will not solve all our problems."[61] He invoked such virtuous traits of character I earlier referred to as "chemistry of citizenship" as the only dependable panacea for national ills. "Solutions to our national problems," Obasanjo opined, "will be found only through sacrifice, understanding, and mature considerations at all times."[62]

Professor Jerry Gana also appraises the decision of the Babangida administration to commission a Political Bureau as marking "a significant milestone in the history of Nigeria," for "the activities of the Bureau legitimized public debate, encouraged open discussion of issues of historical relevance and reawakened the democratic spirit."[63] This revisionist approach to politics in Nigeria arises from the realization that "a deeply consultative process of political reconstruction" is the only way of creating and "restoring legitimacy to national institutions."[64] The process is indeed "a machine of representation" that not only bears "an imprimatur of broad, tentative, Nigerian approval," but has also been "deliberately designed to break the destructive association between competitive party politics and disintegrative tendencies."[65]

In short, then, the fourth element of the emerging Nigerian public philosophy is meant to raise the tone, morality and purpose of politics. It is a call for a fundamental change in the way

Nigerians define and practice politics, in the way they nego-
tiate between their narrow personal or cultural interests and
the imperatives of the common good, and in the methods they
employ to assert and enact their interests in the stream of the
collective whole. Normatively speaking, this means that

> politics must cease to mean warfare, with reliance on force rather
> than arguments. Politics must cease to mean political parties be-
> having more or less like armies in combat, with differences abso-
> lutized and polarized. Politics must become the politics of consent
> and consensus. Politics must become the politics of conviction and
> commitment. Politics must become the politics of compassion and
> accountability.[66]

These emerging criteria for evaluating political life in Nigeria set the parameters for the debate on religion and the state
that effectively began in 1976. Like any other issue of national
significance, the religion debate, in turn, provides the acid test
for the popularity of and commitment to the evolving public
philosophy. It must be admitted from the outset that there are
two major impediments to the flourishing of this public ethic,
and consequently, to the actualization of that "predictable political life," one that is bereft of "cynicism and apathy."[67]

The first impediment is the informational hiatus between
lofty ideals and empirical reality. Common wisdom dictates
that the physical conditions of a country have a causal relationship to the "ease of communications between areas, and thus
the ease of formation of a 'common public opinion.'"[68] Specifically, Seymour Martin Lipset explains that there is a correlation between the level of literacy or education in a country and
its level of political development: "Education presumably
broadens man's outlook, enables him to understand the need
for norms of tolerance, restrains him from adhering to extremist doctrines, and increases his capacity to make rational electoral choices."[69]

Although we cannot but grant the cultural and contextual relativity of Lipset's hypothesis, especially his problematic suggestion about the presumed moral superiority of the intelligentsia, yet the explanatory force of his proposition for the Nigerian situation cannot be ignored. In his own recent study of this issue, Matthew Kukah notes that up till today in Nigeria, notwithstanding Babangida's establishment of the questionable Directorate for Public Enlightenment and Social Mobilization (MAMSER), "discourse and articulation" of public issues still rely on the English language. This in effect means that "the larger segments of society" are mentally, politically, and ideologically quarantined from the political process. *The public associated with, and aware of, this philosophy is a restricted one.* Kukah rightly asserts that what passes for political discourse in contemporary Nigeria is, in the main, "elite dialogue which, conducted on the pages of the newspapers, the radio and television, has been a dialogue of the deaf."[70]

The second impediment is the recklessness of the ruling elites, especially their lack of commitment to the rules of the democratic game. This recklessness is abundantly revealed in the prebendal character of politics in Nigeria, and its immensely destructive consequences—corruption, violence, the zero-sum struggle for power. Larry Diamond stresses that this phenomenon is worsened by the fact that the masses themselves have come to accept prebendalism as an acceptable form of political game. Based on his extensive study of the Nigerian society, he observes that

> the expectation that state office can and will be used for corrupt gain has become the driving force behind the chief features of the political culture, at both the elite and mass levels: not only the violent, fraudulent nature of politics, but the strange schizophrenic attitude of the Nigerian people, their profound cynicism and alienation from electoral politics, and yet their ready, anxious mobiliza-

tion and involvement in the heat of scramble for whatever morsels the masses can scavenge from a system that has otherwise largely excluded them.[71]

Against this background, the tone and the pitch of the religion debate, and most important, its substance, seriously call into question Nigerians' preparedness to become a people *juris consensu et utilitatis communione sociatus*—a people united by a common agreement about laws and rights and a common desire for mutual, not just selfish, advantage. There has been, in particular, a widespread frustration arising from the failure of the state to provide legitimate means for diverse religious bodies to articulate and aggregate their demands or an adequate political vocabulary with which to engage in dialogue. It is to this reality that I now turn.

An Ambiguous Discourse on Religion in Nigeria

The fact that in little over a decade Nigeria has had two federal constitutions, clearly reveals the fragility of its civil unity and its status as a nation-state. It also explains, however fragmentarily, why the efforts to determine and clarify the official status of religion have moved frustratingly abortive. The main contention has centered on how to interpret the various guidelines on religion and state contained in the two post-civil war federal constitutions (1979 and 1989).

These guidelines, when examined, give a picture of a state simultaneously upholding two contrasting visions of democracy in an attempt to remain politically sensitive to the religious diversity of the country. On the one hand, we see an ethic of political neutrality, which is believed by many to be the most desirable posture for the Nigerian state if integration is to be facilitated and strengthened. On the other hand, we observe the irrepressible urge to recognize the cultural integrity of the country's diverse population. The standard argument in this regard is that if Nigerians' attempts at democracy are to be successful, they "must tailor democratic institutions to fit Nigeria's unique heritage and to overcome the structural problems that have defeated democratic government in the past."[72] While these two goals, namely, civil unity and cultural integrity, need not conflict, the manner in which they have been pursued in Nigeria has aroused suspicion that both cannot be simultaneously pursued by the state without threatening the public peace.

In the remainder of this chapter, I will examine how both the state and the public have grappled with the tensions between the demands for political neutrality and cultural recognition. These tensions are especially discernible at the conceptual and policy levels. I will also argue that the prevailing stalemate on articulating an acceptable political framework is due to lack of a comprehensive moral standard by which to reconcile the moral limits of the state with the particularistic "goods" of the citizens and their various cultural universes of meaning. Following the analysis of the concept of dialogic politics I offered in chapter 2, I will endeavor to show that these guidelines are not intrinsically incompatible with one another, and that the failure to see their coherence stems from the lack of sufficient political insight and imagination. Such insight and imagination are needed for groups to be able to reconcile their narrow interests with the common good, the value that the constitution sets out to promote.

The guidelines on religion and state in Nigeria are contained in sections 11, 37, 242, 259-61, and 272 of the 1989 constitution. Section 11, along the lines of the establishment clause in the First Amendment to the United States Constitution, prescribes that "the Government of the Federation or a state shall not adopt any religion as state religion." And section 37, subsections 1–4, outlines the boundaries of freedom of thought, conscience and religion, thus stating the free-exercise principle:

> Every person shall be entitled to freedom of thought, conscience and religion, including freedom to change his religion or belief, and freedom (either alone or in community with others, and in public or in private) to manifest or propagate his religion or belief, in worship, teaching, practice and observance.
>
> No person attending any place of education shall be required to receive religious instruction or to take part in or attend any religious ceremony or observance if such instruction, ceremony or observance relates to a religion other than his own or a religion not approved by his parent or guardian.
>
> No religious community or denomination shall be prevented from providing religious instruction for pupils of that community or denomination in any place of education maintained wholly by that community or denomination.
>
> Nothing in this section shall entitle any person to form, take part in the activity or be a member of a secret society.

Interpreting these seemingly simple and unambiguous precepts has proven to be as problematic as they were to formulate. What complicated the interpretive process was the reemergence of a once explosive subject centering on "the extent to which concessions, if any, should be given to Muslims in the country's judicial system, and the extent to which Muslims could demand 'balance' and 'fairness' for perceived state concessions to Christians"[73] without tearing the nation apart. An influential Muslim scholar has said that the question of the official status of the *sharīʿa* in the nation's judicial system is "the most important and complex political issue dividing Muslims and Christians in Nigeria."[74] A closer examination of the sections on the *sharīʿa* is thus in order.

Section 259, subsection 1, of the constitution provides for setting up *sharīʿa* courts at the level of the constituent states in the federation, while section 260, in outlining the qualifications of judges, or qadis (*qu*dāʾa*), within the *sharīʿa* system, insists that they be versed in Islamic law. Section 242, subsection 1 and section 272, subsection 1, outline the relationship between the *sharīʿa* court system and the common-law judicial system. Section 242(1) provides for appeals to the (Federal) Court of Appeal from the *sharīʿa* Court of Appeal with respect to questions of Islamic law, while section 272 provides that "in exercising his powers . . . in respect of appointments to the offices of Justices of the Supreme Court and Justices of the Court of Appeal, the President shall have regard to the need to ensure that there are among the holders of such offices persons learned in Islamic law and persons learned in customary law." With regard to jurisdiction, section 261 states that "the *Sharīʿa* Court of Appeal of a state shall, in addition to such other jurisdiction as may be conferred upon it by the law of the State, exercise such appellate and supervisory jurisdiction in civil proceedings involving questions of Islamic law where all the parties are Muslims."

The controversial question has been whether or not the establishment and the free-exercise clauses are violated by the provision for the *sharīʿa* court system in the constitution. Muslims, Christians, nonreligionists, and the government itself have answered this question differently. However, as should be clear by now, the locus of the controversy has resided mainly with the Christian and Muslim communities, with the government intermittently finding itself playing the role of umpire. Divergence between the Christian and Muslim positions has resulted from conflicting interpretations of the two principal clauses, and their positions have produced implications for the handling of some other seemingly less controversial issues (to be highlighted in a moment).

The report of the bureau, headed by Cookey, contains a lucid summary of the main "issues of conflict" as expressed during the debate on religion and state, which took place amid allegations that Nigeria had secretly joined the Organization of Islamic Conference (OIC). According to the report, Christians argued that

> the state should not be involved in religious matters; Nigeria should not be a member of the OIC and should withdraw from it; missionary schools that have been taken over by the government should be returned to their proprietors so that ethical and moral values could be properly taught to Nigerian children; [and] government should disengage itself from pilgrimage exercises.[75]

The bureau characterized the Muslims' position as being "diametrically opposed to what the Christian groups advocated." The Muslims insist that there can be no real separation of state and religion, and that any attempt to deny the country admission into the OIC would amount to denying the Nigerian Muslims their constitutional rights. They also would like to see *sharīʿa* courts established where there is a demand for them by the Muslims. Most especially, they demand that a *sharīʿa* Court of Appeal be established at the federal level to take care of appeals from state *sharīʿa* Courts of Appeal. Furthermore, they want continuing government involvement in matters relating to pilgrimage and the immediate termination of Nigeria's diplomatic representation at the Vatican.[76]

Amid these conflicting demands and the seemingly incompatible constitutional guidelines, we need a theoretical framework that will enable us to extract the moral and political issues involved in questions about religion and civil life in Nigeria. Such an interpretation is especially urgent when we bear in mind that it was the desire to construct and establish a democratic polity in the country that provided the moral context for the debate and the constitutional guidelines on religion and state. Given the content of the emerging and thriving public consensus in the country, that such a polity is morally preferable to its alternatives—for example, military dictatorship—an interpretation of political life is required that will underscore both the moral obligatoriness of these constitutional precepts and the attitudinal requisites for sustaining the envisioned polity. Such a framework will be attempted in the following sections. By examining the differing arguments in the country on this problematic, I hope to expose the relative strengths and weaknesses of the extant positions. But more germane to my analysis is the argument that the contending factions have more common ground than they realize, and that they could enlarge their political vision by revising their narrow theological perspectives. As J. L. Hooper has shown, "perspectives can be adopted which make the moral shaping of [one's] society impossible; likewise, other perspectives can be adopted which facilitate the moral forces necessary for an ethical and just society."[77] In short, the perspectives that culturally differentiated peoples bring to bear on issues of common concern will largely determine whether or not they are prepared to cultivate a consensual will necessary for the formation and nurturing of a common political community.

Guided by the tenets of dialogic politics, I wish to submit that the guidelines on religion and state in Nigeria's 1989 constitution be construed as complementary coguarantors of a single end, which is "to promote and assure the fullest possible scope of religious liberty and tolerance for all and to nurture the conditions which secure the best hope of attainment of that end."[78] Two animating principles, representing strands of prevailing concerns, can be discerned as undergirding this core value enshrined in that constitution. These are the principles of institutional separation and accommodation. I shall examine each of these in turn.

The Principle of Institutional Separation

In Nigerian political discourse, this principle has usually been invoked not so much to clarify the question about "who should have power," but more important, about "what kind of state Nigeria should be."[79] Geertz says that only such clarification can address the central issue of political legitimacy, since "for a state to do more than administer privilege and defend itself against its own population, its acts must seem continuous with the selves of those whose state it pretends it is, its citizens."[80] There is a near consensus that this is the principle explicitly expressed in section 11 of the constitution, which prohibits all tiers of the government from adopting any religion as the state religion. However, in the attempt to unpack the full scope of this principle, two vocabularies or terms have been employed that, with hindsight, now appear to have confounded rather than clarified the issue. These are *separation* and *secularity*.

Two different groups of Nigerians seem most comfortable with the use of these terms, namely, the Christians and the so-called progressive (Marxist) thinkers, although on quite different grounds. Both groups also appear doctrinaire in their defense of the terms, for in their judgment, separation and secularity are theological and ideological dogmas etched with a constitutional precept. Msgr. Adigwe argues that "the state [as] described in section 10 of the 1979 constitution and clause 11 of the 1988 draft constitution is by implication a secular state."[81] In their memorandum sent to the Constitution Review Committee in 1986, the Catholic Bishops of Nigeria defended Nigeria's secularity as "the only viable 'modus vivendi' for it to survive as a nation." They went further to define a secular state as one in which "there is no official religion but in which religion as such may nevertheless be treated with respect; and religious bodies and their activities are seen as purely social agents within the communities."[82]

In his keynote address delivered to the second assembly of the Christian Association of Nigeria (CAN) held in Kaduna in 1988, the Rt. Revd. E. B. Gbonigi, the Anglican bishop of Akure Diocese, rejected the dictionary definition of secularism, according to which it is seen as a "doctrine of public morality based on the citizens' well-being and exclusive of religious considerations." He characterizes Nigeria's secularity as "a form of separation between religion and state which allows for voluntary relationship and cooperation wherever and whenever necessary and possible."[83] Invoking the classical Protestant doctrine of the two kingdoms, Bishop Gbonigi defends church-state separation on the basis of their different functions. The state's duty is "to maintain justice, security, peace, relative wellbeing of its citizens," while the church is "primarily concerned with the inward and spiritual life of the people . . . , ordained and commissioned to preach the gospel of salvation."[84]

Bala Usman attributed the confusion over the interpretation of the nonadoption of religion clause to the imprecise way in which the clause is worded, in that the provision does not preclude the state from associating or identifying with any religion "as long as this stops short of adoption."[85] He proposes what he thought would have been a better definition of the principle of institutional separation: "The Federal Republic of Nigeria is a secular State and the State shall not be associated with any religion but shall actively protect the fundamental right of all citizens to hold and practice the religious beliefs of their choice."[86]

Segun Gbadegesin, formerly of the Philosophy Department at the University of Ife, Nigeria, supports Usman's addition of the concept of "secular state" to the actual wording of the constitutional concept, in that secularity is a principle that is morally defensible on three grounds. First, it presupposes the value of freedom of conscience, something nonexistent in a sacral society. Second, it encourages respect for individual autonomy. Finally, it presupposes "the belief that human beings are equal in the sight of God and therefore are equally capable of approaching Him for their various needs."[87] In short, for Usman and Gbadegesin, religion is a personal and private affair, and any attempt to conflate it with politics is seen as a threat to national stability and integrity, and secularity requires that this devilish force be uprooted.

It is precisely this conclusion that some Muslims find objectionable, even though "standard Islamic prescriptions are not necessarily any more convincing."[88] Mr. Justice Sambo, a Muslim judge, argued that there is an obnoxious danger in deriving secularity from the nonadoption of religion clause, because it implies that "both the Federal and State governments will have nothing to do with the divine religions of their people."[89] The clause did erect, in Sambo's interpretation, a wall of hostility between religion and the state, which he found repugnant on two grounds. First, it seems to suppose that "human reasoning and not revelation [religion] is the transcendent source of law," and second, it overlooks the fact that the "secular principle has no place in the Islamic lexicon."[90] To prescribe secularity for a country where "divine religion [referring to both Islam and Christianity] is a complete way of life for 99 percent of its population . . . is a rude shock."[91]

Besides the apparent cultural insensitivity of a secular interpretation, Nigerian Muslims also argue that to divorce religion from politics is to elevate the state to "a false absolute, an expression of *shirk* [the sin of associating partners with God]."[92] Justice Sambo reminded his fellow Nigerians that "the only solution to the chronic vices which have overcome Nigeria is for the nation to take a distinctive governmental stand on religious, moral and spiritual training of her peoples. . . . It is only divine religious injunctions backed by those who govern that can stabilize discipline, good morals and obedience to God, and constituted authority."[93]

Sambo insisted that it is not enough simply to provide for freedom of thought, conscience, and religion without explicitly writing the moral norms and theological principles of the country's two revealed religions into the constitution. He therefore made a definite call for a constitutional provision that "once a Nigerian declares for a divine religion, it is the duty of the state to see that such a declarant respects and lives in accordance with the teachings of the religion."[94]

There are other Muslims, however, who reject Justice Sambo's position for being too skewed and theologically imperialistic. Malam Mukhtar, son of Nigeria's first prime minister and a one-time imam at a Bauchi mosque, argued that establishing a religious state [Islamic or Christian] "is neither realistic nor possible" in Nigeria.[95] Much earlier, a similar view had been expressed by Alhaji Aliyu, the Magaji Gari, a senior councilor and kingmaker in the Sokoto Sultanate, who argued that "the call for an Islamic state is the misguided view of the radical academics," whose views, unfortunately, "the government tends to respect . . . because they come from university dons who are supposed to be knowledgeable."[96] Aliyu urged the creation and nurturing of a civil environment which would permit religion to serve as a moral catalyst, by enlarging public vision and accentuating the broader base of human community.[97]

Thus, the fear of a significant number of Nigerian Muslims is not necessarily, as many Christians tend to believe, that Islam is being prevented from becoming the official religion, but that the prevailing interpretations fail "to foster much more hospitable grounds for the setting of the religious agenda in public affairs."[98] What is more, the Muslim community in Nigeria is not politically and ideologically monolithic. As observed by Paden, nine different political values, representing categories of intrareligious identities, could be found among the Nigerian Muslims.[99]

In order to harmonize the divergent interpretations of the nonadoption of religion clause, I must correct two misconceptions that have obscured the meaning of the animating principle behind this clause, namely, that the principle of institutional separation requires a secular society (as the title of Bishop Gbonigi's paper confusingly suggests), and that it demands the exclusion of religion from political discourse.

First, the principle of separation should be understood in institutional rather than cultural terms. What it seeks to avoid is "an alliance of civil and ecclesiastical power"[100] that might threaten religious liberty, and not an evacuation of religious symbols and values from "the totality of cultural life and of ideation."[101] Muslims do have a cultural, historical, and theological reason to be suspicious of the continued use of "secularity" as a metaphor to conduct political discourse, if, as Soskice has powerfully argued, the language we use has a metaphorical force to depict the particular reality we want to construct or enact.[102]

Secularity, formerly regarded by many sociologists as a synonym of modernity, is generally understood as a state of affairs inevitably brought about by the forces of progress in history, principally science and technology.[103] But the term cannot be said to be religiously neutral, at least, from a historical perspective. Peter Berger argues that there is "an inherent connection between Christianity and the character of the modern Western world," such that "the modern world could be interpreted as a higher realization of the Christian spirit."[104] The German Catholic theologian, Johannes B. Metz, has in fact offered a positive defense of secularity of the world from a theological standpoint. It is a manifestation in history of the fact that God has "accepted" the world, by both de-divinizing and humanizing it, and in consequence, removed all the magical impediments to human creativity. For Metz,

> The secularity of the world, as it has emerged in the modern process of secularization and as we see it today in a globally heightened form, has fundamentally, though not in its individual historical forms, arisen not against Christianity but through it. It is originally a Christian event and hence testifies in our world situation to the power of the "hour of Christ" at work within history.[105]

In light of Nigeria's colonial past, during which "the Anglican Church provided religious legitimation for the polity and acted, unofficially, as the State Church,"[106] it seems not unreasonable for Muslims to contend that Nigeria, as is presently constituted, is neither Islamic nor secular.[107] The Muslims identified many spheres of the nation's public life to illustrate what they see as a preponderance of Christian symbols and values, all of which have been unquestionably accepted as the status quo. For instance, Muslims portrayed the common-law tradition underpinning the Nigerian judicial process as "more or less a Christian law," and they listed other such areas of contention where, but "for our own tolerance the law courts would have been full of suits by Muslims asking the courts to stop the government from the:

> observance of Saturdays and Sundays as free working days, which is a favor for Christians to worship without hindrance or in the alternative tell the court to compel the Government to declare Fridays as a free working day as well, to compensate the Muslims who constitute the majority of the people in this country;
>
> Use of cross symbol for our health institutions, which is a Christian symbol or in the alternative use the crescent as well to compensate the Muslims;

Use of the Reverend regalia as academic gown in our higher institutions or compel the government to adopt the use of *Alkimba,* the Islamic regalia, as alternative;

Use of Christian-oriented melody as our national anthem;

Use of Christian Gregorian Calendar which has no relevance to the need of the Muslims or in the alternative use the Islamic Calendar *pari pasu* with it;

Use of Christian calendar to name our School Holidays, e.g., Christmas Break, Easter Break, etc.[108]

The demand for a secular Nigerian state is, from the perspective of many Muslims, a disguise to "perpetuate Euro-Christian culture and neocolonialism," and an attempt to strip Nigeria's public square of transcendent moral values.[109] In fact, many Christians share this apprehension with the Muslims, and it is against this background that we can grasp the essence of the contemporary resurgence of religious vitality, erroneously characterized by many scholars as "fundamentalism."[110] Contrary to this pejorative designation, I would argue that this renaissance of religious interests is a manifestation of a genuine intention for the *"tajdid* (renewal)"[111] of Nigeria's public square that is increasingly becoming naked, of an irrepressible urge towards "a re-enchantment of the world, precisely because the disenchanted world is so cold and comfortless."[112]

For instance, the charismatic or "born-again" Christians in Nigeria, formerly thought of to be self-avowedly apolitical,[113] are now actively engaging in political discourse. Many of them have been trying to revise their attitudes to politics as a result of what they perceive in the country as a "chaotic moral field," notably, the prevalence of such practices "as bribery, corruption and the degeneration of the moral and material."[114] Ruth Marshall argues further that the doctrinal cornerstone of these reformist Christians, namely, the metanoiac "theme of personal and social rebirth," as well as the egalitarian and communal theme of "covenant," do provide them with a religious resource to engage in a "project of social reconstruction and transformation of power relations" and to directly challenge Nigerians' "way of doing politics."[115] The moral and sociopolitical significance of these movements in Nigeria, Marshall insists, lie in their serving as

> a powerful metaphor for new types of practice, as well as a symbolic and material resource for the elaboration of a conceptual challenge to the power monopolies . . . , for the creation of 'autonomous spaces' of practice which defy the oppressive logic of current 'power monopolies' (in which state violence and economic exploitation figure prominently), and for the articulation of strategies to create, exercise and legitimate new power relations and new opportunities for survival.[116]

Elizabeth Hodgkin shares this perspective in her own study of this phenomenon in Islam. Hodgkin defines the "increase in religious observance and fervor" among many African Muslims as "Islamism," the aim of which is to employ modern and intellectual resources "to bring Islam into every aspect of human life, political, economic and cultural."[117] And "many Islamists, or movements of Islamic revival," Hodgkin points out, "do not see the seizure of state power as among their aims."[118]

The point being established here is that what a significant number of Muslims are opposed to is the attempt to deduce from the constitution a secular principle that posits a rigid demarcation of religion and political life. They are not necessarily opposed to a functional separation of powers between civil and religious authorities. Of course, saying this is not intended to obscure the crucial stumbling block posed by the arguments of Justice Sambo and some other Muslim reformists, who are presenting Islam as "a holistic ideology, competent to address every activity of life and every sphere of human society."[119] A case in point is the position of the late Shaykh

Gumi, the leader of the antitraditionalist *Izala* movement, who once issued a controversial *fatwā* (authoritative ruling) stating that in contemporary Nigeria, "politics is more important than prayer" or going on pilgrimage, because politics ultimately controls the right to pray. According to him, "A Muslim who neglected [prayer] would have caused himself injury, but a Muslim who allowed the ship of state to sail anyhow, would have caused the whole society a major injury."[120] Gumi was strongly of the opinion that, were it not for the arbitrary incursion of the military into Nigeria's politics, the topmost political post in the country would always be occupied by a Muslim. And "if Christians do not accept Muslims as their leaders [and] Muslims cannot accept Christians as their leaders," then Nigeria will have to be divided.[121]

Gumi was not the only one associated with this immoderate position. He enjoyed the considerable support of numerous Muslim youth organizations and leaders, many of whom (e.g., Malam Ibrahim El-Zak Zaky) call for the demolition of the country's present political order, "including the constitution on which it is based" and they insist that "a *jihad* is necessary until *Sharī'a* is established as the governing law in Nigeria" and "Islam only" becomes the *religio licita*.[122] Perspectives like these not only make the path toward the construction of civil unity very difficult, but also blur the jurisdictional question that the principle of institutional separation purports to address.

At the same time, the concept of secularity is too weak, narrow, and confusing to capture the legal intent of the constitutional provision on the nonadoption of any religion as a state religion. Christian and strict separationists' arguments, which suggest the possibility of privatizing religion, have failed to clarify the ambiguity that has dogged the nonadoption clause. The 1986 Constitution Review Committee acknowledged this ambiguity, and called public attention to the fact that the concept of "a secular state" does not appear in the nation's constitution, as it might inadvertently project Nigeria as "a Godless nation." The committee explained the exigency of the non-adoption clause against the backdrop of the "multiplicity of religious groups in the country," as well as Babangida's prescription "to make provisions which will make government at every level . . . remain neutral, just, fair and even-handed in its treatment of all religious groups."[123] In short, the clause emphasizes the incompetence of the state in the realm of religious doctrines.

Needless to say, religion can become a disruptive and sometimes oppressive force in society, but confining it to private or small spaces increases the potential of its explosiveness, for "whether one professes the shema of Israel . . . , the Christian credo . . . , or the Muslim shahadah . . . , private religion is theologically self-contradictory. Because religion is about the ultimate good of the whole of human life, it will be untrue to itself if it accepts the private niche [to which some theorists would assign it]."[124] What the principle of institutional separation affirms is "the constitutional provision which forbids the making of any law, and therefore the taking of any executive action, that involves the interlocking of the official functions of the state with the official or institutional functions of any [religion]."[125] The issues it clarifies are about the public care of religion and the moral limits of the state; and that care, "in so far as it implies the care of souls, is not in any sense the function either of civil society or of the state. Second, the care of religion, in so far as religion is an integral element of the common good of society, devolves upon those institutions whose purposes are religious—the Church and the churches, and various voluntary associations for religious purposes. . . . Third, the care of religion in so far as it is the duty incumbent on the State is limited to the care for the religious freedom of the body politic."[126]

There is disagreement, however, on the scope of religious

liberty in Nigeria. I will now proceed to review the debate on this theme under the principle of accommodation.

The Principle of Accommodation

Arlin M. Adams and Charles J. Emmerich designate the concept of accommodation as a "free exercise doctrine" that may be defined as "an area of allowable and, in some cases, compelled governmental deference to the religious needs of people holding a variety of beliefs."[127] They explain further that, in any given instance of tension between civil duties and religious conviction (a phenomenon inevitable "in a society characterized by expansive government and religious pluralism"), "accommodation calls for a delicate balance between government's duty to promote the cohesiveness necessary for an ordered society and its responsibility to honor the religious practices of citizens by refraining from unnecessary or burdensome regulation."[128]

The *sharī'a* debate in Nigeria, which began in 1976 and has remained a key issue ever since, falls within the parameters of this principle. This debate has been well documented by W. I. Ofonagoro, David Laitin, and Ikem Ngwoke, and so needs no repeating here.[129] My concern is to distill the thrust of the main positions taken in the debate, and assess them from the ethical standpoint of dialogic politics.

What came out clearly in the debate is that Nigerians differ not only in terms of conceptual articulation of religious themes but also in the understanding of the moral responsibility of the state within a democratic framework. Essentially, the debate is about whether, and to what extent, the government should recognize and enforce the *sharī'a* (Muslim religious law). To the Muslims, the issue needs no debating if indeed the state is serious about guaranteeing religious freedom to all citizens of Nigeria. It is for them a theological and moral issue. The

Christians see the call for enforcement of the *sharī'a* as "part of a grand design to Islamize Nigeria."[130]

It is important to clarify the way in which the *sharī'a* has been used in this debate. First, the formal or orthodox Islamic understanding of the *sharī'a* wherein it means a sacred law, embracing the whole range of religious duties, "the totality of Allah's commands that regulate the life of every Muslim in all its aspects,"[131] and according to which the state is understood to be subordinate to the *sharī'a* was far removed from the historical experience of Nigerian Muslims. Historically, in Nigeria, the *sharī'a* has only been applied to issues of personal status, especially "various aspects of marriage and inheritance."[133]

Second, *sharī'a* courts, following the *Maliki* school, had existed in precolonial northern Nigeria, which upon the advent of the British and the subsequent Anglo-Fulani pact, were defined as customary or native courts, having authority to "administer native law and custom prevailing in the area of jurisdiction and might award any type of punishment recognized thereby except mutilation, torture, or any other which is repugnant to natural justice and humanity."[134]

This situation remained, though not without some judicial quagmires, until a few years before independence, when, first, a Muslim Court of Appeal was established in 1956, and later a *sharī'a* Court of Appeal was established in Kaduna, the northern regional headquarters, on 1 October 1960. Under this arrangement, crafted to fit the democratic scheme, appeals from the native courts in ordinary cases were lodged with the High Court of the Region (which operated under the common law), but in cases involving Muslim personal law (*sharī'a*) appeals went to the *sharī'a* Court of Appeal, which applied the law of the Maliki school as it was customarily interpreted in the area around the native court. Jurisdictional disputes between the High Court and the *sharī'a* Court of Appeal were resolved by a Court of Resolution. Decisions of the *sharī'a* Court of Appeal involving constitutional issues could be appealed further to the Federal Supreme Court.[135]

Prior to the 1976–77 transition program, the legitimacy of the arrangement described above was hardly challenged by the south, where the absence of the *sharī'a* was considered normal, thanks to the appreciable regional autonomy in the First Republic. Thus, before the preparations for the Second Republic effectively began, "the *Sharī'a* issue . . . was not a Federal issue affecting the public's perception of and interaction with the Federal administration and the Nigerian state."[136] The Pandora's box was opened when, during the debate, the Muslims sought what Birai had characterized as a "legal and geographical extension" for the *sharī'a*.[137]

First, they demanded constitutional provisions "for *Sharī'a* courts in the states, and state and federal *Sharī'a* courts of appeal."[138] In particular, they wanted the extension of the *sharī'a* court system to the southern part of the country. Through the Council of *'ulamā*, the Muslims vowed "to reject any new political order that does not recognize the uninhibited application of *Sharī'a* law in Nigeria."[139] Second, they contended that the present arrangement, which limits the application of the *sharī'a* to issues of personal status, was an unjust restriction on the religious freedom of the Muslims, for "while not a bit of the Constitution deprived the Christian from being Christian, every bit of the same Constitution can easily deprive the Muslim from being Muslim."[140] Areas in which a wider legislative scope was being sought for the *sharī'a* included sumptuary laws, the economy (especially banking and taxation), and education.[141]

Objections to the *sharī'a* were based on two grounds, one moral-political and the other jurisprudential. The Christians invoked the principles of institutional separation and state neutrality to counter the proposal that would commit the state to what they understood to be an official establishment of religion. The Catholic bishops of Nigeria argued that what "full religious freedom in fact and practice" means is that "government or any of its arms" must not be "employed to prosper or hinder any particular religion."[142] What was at stake, in the *sharīʿa* proposal, is the "equality" of all citizens "before the law," which they contend, would be breached by the inclusion of "religious laws or principles of any particular religion" in the constitution. Insisting that the *sharīʿa* legal system be seen as "purely and unmitigatedly a religious system espoused by only the adherents of one particular religion in this country," the bishops warned against foisting it on the nation "as this will run violently counter to the country's declared objective of remaining a secular state."[143] Msgr. Adigwe suggested that the entire sections dealing with the *sharīʿa* "be expunged in order to free non-Muslims from the burden of being involved in the building, financing and administering [of] a Muslim religious court."[144] There were several others who saw the elevation of the *sharīʿa* to the national level as a smokescreen for legitimizing multiple and perhaps conflicting judicial systems in Nigeria. A situation in which two legal systems, one Islamic and the other Christian, compete for legitimacy, offers a cultural recipe for national disintegration.[145]

The second reason for objecting to the *sharīʿa* proposal was the argument that there was a "fundamental ambiguity" in the nature of the demand. Laitin pointed out that judicial appeal procedures, "which normally thrive on more general rules, were often considered inappropriate in the Muslim context," because "the *Sharīʿa* law is based on a set of particularized rules of the Islamic tradition."[146] Muslims were perceived by the anti-*sharīʿa* groups to be "pushing for an institution which was hardly central to the Islamic experience."[147] In fact, for many minorities in the north, the Area Courts, which have historically claimed to be the judicial embodiment of the *sharīʿa* ideals, are still "seen as the vestiges of emirate rule and its oppression of the masses of their peoples."[148]

With these diametrically opposed views on the perception and definition of democracy, how might the retention of the *sharīʿa* court system in the constitution be justified? One way of seeing the merit of the present constitution is to argue that democracy itself permits the consideration of intensity (i.e., "the degree to which one wants or prefers some alternative") as an important measuring factor in a pluralistic setting where each side perceives "the victory of the other as a fundamental threat to some very highly ranked values."[149] As several students of Nigerian politics have noted, the degree to which non-Muslims preferred a *sharīʿa*-blind constitution was far less than that to which Muslims expressed their demand for an alternative, one that would give adequate recognition to their cultural value.[150]

Although a few Christians asked the government to provide for the operation of canon-law courts for the Christians,[151] a suggestion that Muslims were willing to accept "if Christians actually wanted them,"[152] a majority of the Christians did not take this demand seriously because the canon law, prominent mostly in the Catholic circles, "deals only with rules of liturgical worship and very private issues concerning priests."[153] While a culture-blind, nonaccommodating federal constitution might not pose any threat to the identity and cultural integrity of non-Muslim Nigerians, it would be too homogenizing for the Muslims, sacrificing cultural difference at the altar of civil unity.

The ultimate challenge for Nigerians, therefore, is how to broaden their notion of democracy, in such a way as to be able to deal with their conflicting demands without compromising the basic political principles on which their continued common existence can be assured. Charles Taylor has argued that the logic behind the vision of freedom and equality rests on the premise that "we owe equal respect to all cultures."[154] And quite apart from the generic identity of common humanity, each person or group of persons is also "unique, self-creating, and culture-bearing."[155] Taylor calls for a more vibrant and robust understanding of democracy, one that acknowledges that "human identity is partly shaped by recognition or its absence, often by the *mis*recognition of others, and so a person or group of people can suffer real damage, real distortion, if the people or society around them mirror back to them a confining or demeaning or contemptible picture of themselves. Nonrecognition or misrecognition can inflict harm, can be a form of oppression, imprisoning someone in a false, distorted, and reduced mode of being."[156]

A more vibrant and robust democratic culture is certainly congruent with the concept of dialogic politics; for in this kind of political context, people of different religions are conceivably able to uphold "the invariant defence of certain rights" (e.g., a uniform application of habeas corpus) and still "*recognize* the equal value of different cultures."[157] This model of democracy differs from the Lockean, contractual model, which is rooted in the conception of atomistic individuals creating their identities de novo and pursuing their ends independently of each other. To many religiously inclined individuals, Muslims and Christians alike, a political community is deliberative and democratic only if it recognizes and accommodates the worth of particularistic identities.[158]

Another perspective on the *sharīʿa* is to say that the constitution itself did not consider the principles of institutional separation and benevolent neutrality to be absolute, in that they were meant to be understood as logically entailing non-discrimination. For instance, section 16, subsections 1 and 2 of the 1989 constitution states that "the motto of the Federal Republic of Nigeria shall be Unity, Peace and Progress. Accordingly, national integration shall be actively promoted whilst discrimination on the grounds of place of origin, circumstance of birth, sex, religion, status, ethnic or linguistic association or ties shall be prohibited." This particular section of the constitution thus creates a permissible zone within which some particularized demands could be justified, and in this light, the *sharīʿa* is neither compelled by the free-exercise clause nor forbidden by the establishment clause.

Third, the Armed Forces Ruling Council (AFRC), formerly the highest legislative and executive body in the Babangida administration, invoked the balancing-of-interests principle, perched on the federalist structure of the country, to justify the inclusion of the limited application of the *sharīʿa* in the country. The council, speaking through Babangida, settled on federalism because of the firm belief that only such an arrangement could accommodate diversity and "guarantee justice for all Nigerians of whatever religious persuasion." In a multireligious society "founded on the principle of indivisible union," Babangida argued, "each section of our community must accommodate the others in the wider interest of our nation."[159]

He further explained that the principal rationale which undergirded the decision of the Constitution Review Committee was the need to avoid the two extreme positions: disallowing the *sharīʿa* courts altogether (the Christian position) or sanctioning the courts at the national level. Hence, the decision to give the court jurisdiction "only in matters relating to the Muslims' personal life; only states which wish to have such courts need establish them, and any state that does not require it will not have such a court." Thus, under the present arrangement and in contradistinction to the 1979 constitution, the *sharīʿa* courts "will hear cases involving only Muslims . . . , any person who is not a Muslim will not have anything to do with the *Sharīʿa* Courts."[160]

Quite apart from the efforts of the state to strengthen national integration, there is also at work here the principle of fairness and justice. On the one hand, the moral imperative to preserve civil unity was heeded by providing "an overarching set of values and mores for the entire nation" through the elevation of "common law to the status of a higher law,"[161] and the rejection of the authoritarian position to place the *shari'a* above the federal constitution. On the other hand, care was taken to ensure that common political goals did not lead to cultural indifferentism. As Babangida put the matter, "We must listen to the yearnings of Nigerians who want justice in their personal and family lives; we must listen to those who want government to provide instrumentality and institutions for guaranteeing justice to them within the ambit of the constitution."[162] Responding to those who might want to argue that this position violates the principle of state neutrality on religion, Babangida explained that "it is pointedly mischievous and manifestly wrong to equate *Shari'a* Courts with religious courts. If the truth be told, they are no more nor less than simply courts of justice to which many Nigerians look for Justice."[163]

Christians have hardly been convinced by this argument, as Babangida's own religious identity (Muslim) tends to place him in the role of a vanguard of the perceived aggressive Islamic onslaught on the entire nation. The title of the communique issued by the northern zone of the Christian Association of Nigeria (CAN), "*Shari'a* versus National Unity," aptly summarizes the collective grievances of the Christian community against the Babangida regime. CAN contends:

> Since the Babangida Administration came to power it has unashamedly and in utter contempt for national unity manifested its naked discriminatory religious posture through overt and covert acts of patronage and preference for Islamic religion. One is therefore left with no alternative but to conclude that the Babangida Administration is the principal agent for the islamization of Nigeria. This administration more than any before it has built up religious tension in this country of a dimension that is capable of obliterating the foundations of our corporate entity as a country.[164]

This same administration, and that of his immediate prede-
cessor, Buhari, have also been attacked by Christians for failing
to apply the federal character principle, which requires that
the "composition of the Government of the federation and the
conduct of its affairs reflect the federation, across the board."[165]
The Buhari regime's highest policy-making and legislative organ, the Supreme Military Council (SMC), was heavily criticized
for being dominated not only by northerners but also by Muslim
military officers. Christians also pointed to the same lopsided-
ness in the AFRC, the SMC's equivalent under the Babangida
administration. There were several other specific events which
appeared to have confirmed the fears of Christians that they
were under an Islamic siege. These included:

(a) the aborted attempt in 1986, apparently with the blessing of
the Muslim Federal Education Minister, to force the University of
Ibadan to relocate a cross from the site on which it was erected in
the early 1950s for a mosque that was completed only in the 1980s;
(b) the surreptitious manner in which Nigeria in 1986 joined the
Organization of Islamic Conference; (c) the promulgation in 1988
of a decree which turned the various Pilgrims' Welfare Boards at
state and Federal levels, which used to cater for both Christian and
Muslim pilgrims to the Holy Lands, into wholly Muslim affairs;
and (d) the spate of anti-Christian riots in the North up to 1987.[166]

The use of religious qualification for appointment into public offices, which the principle of institutional separation forbids, is said to be more rampant under the military regime.
Underscoring the mediating role of democratic institutions
and processes and the mellowing influence these have on those
entrusted with public responsibility, the 1986 Political Bureau
remarked that "it is easy for the doctrine of the separation of
organized religion and the state to be quietly set aside once
constitutional guarantees have been militarily annulled."[167]
Here lies the vicious circle in Nigeria's public debate!

The difficulty besetting the "religion debate" in Nigeria is more than what appears to be the doctrinal intransigence of the religious people. There is also the amorphous state, which is neither completely authoritarian nor constitutional. Yes, it is true that the failure to find a political form appropriate to the temper of the varied religious groups is partially related to the conceptual differences between these groups as to the very meaning of the state and the intermittently orchestrated democratic dream. It is, nevertheless, the case that the military image has long dominated public consciousness, eroding people's confidence in the viability and authenticity of the democratic framework within which issues and opinions can be openly debated. As Olupona aptly observed, the near eclipse of Nigeria's judicature by the brutal power of military decrees vividly illustrates the superficiality of constitutional tradition and the ethos of public dialogue in Nigeria, and points up vital areas in which more work still needs to be done.[168]

It is also important to note that the debate has so far focused on the attitude of the state toward religion in a pluralistic context. Very little has been said about the positive contributions that religion can make to a multireligious state. Whether construed evaluatively or organizationally, religion can be a positive force in Nigeria's march toward nationhood. The pluriconfessional character of the country need not be a hindrance to the realization of this goal. What might be an impediment is the refusal, at all levels of society, to come to terms with this diversity. In the next chapter, I will explore ways in which the positive contributions of diverse religions can be concretely embodied in Nigeria's public life.

Notes

1. Peter B. Clarke, "Religion and Political Attitude since Independence," in *Religion and Society in Nigeria: Historical and Socio-*

logical Perspectives, ed. Jacob K. Olupona and Toyin Falola (Ibadan: Spectrum Books, 1991), 227.

2. Olupona, "Religious Pluralism and Civil Religion," 42.

3. John Paden, "Religious Tolerance and Conflict Resolution in Nigeria" (paper presented at the Conference on Intolerance and Conflict: Sudan and Nigeria, Washington, D.C., 3–5 October 1991), 14.

4. Federal Government of Nigeria, *Report of the Constitution Drafting Committee containing the Draft Constitution,* (Lagos: Times Publications 1976), 1:xli (hereafter referred to as CDC).

5. Nigeria, *Report of the Political Bureau,* 6.

6. C. S. Whitaker, "Second Beginnings: The New Political Framework," in *Perspectives on the Second Republic in Nigeria,* ed. C. S. Whitaker (Waltham, Mass.: Crossroads Press, 1981), 2–14. Nigeria's principle of federalism has been continually defended by some of the notable students of the country's politics. Sklar suggests that "while the number of states in Nigeria's federation has varied and remains contentious, federalism per se is an article of national faith, the virtually unquestioned premise of national unity. . . . At present nineteen [now thirty] states accommodate a richly textured and wondrously complex tapestry of democratic political life." Sklar, Democracy in Africa," 19.

7. A. H. M. Kirk-Greene, "'A Sense of Belonging': The Nigerian Constitution of 1979 and the Promotion of National Loyalty," *Journal of Commonwealth and Comparative Politics* 28, 3 (1990): 158–72.

8. R. Bruce Douglas, "Public Philosophy and Contemporary Pluralism (or, The Murray Problem Revisited)," *Thought* 64, 255 (1989): 344.

9. Clifford Geertz, "The Politics of Meaning," in *The Interpretation of Cultures* (New York: Basic Books, 1973), 312.

10. Nigeria, *Report of the Political Bureau,* 45.

11. Ibid.

12. CDC, 1:xlii.

13. For a synthetic theory of socialism and democracy christened as "participative democracy" or "socialist/welfarist democracy," see Obafemi Awolowo, *The People's Republic* (Ibadan: Oxford University Press, 1968); Carole Pateman, *Participation and Democratic Theory* (Cambridge: Cambridge University Press, 1970); Douglas Sturm,

"A New Social Covenant: From Democratic Capitalism to Social Democracy," in *Community and Alienation,* 164–86. Recent notable works on the supposed compatibility of capitalism and democracy are: Robert Benne, *The Ethic of Democratic Capitalism* (Philadelphia: The Fortress Press, 1981); Michael Novak, *The Spirit of Democratic Capitalism* (New York: Simon and Schuster, 1982).

14. CDC, 1:xlii.

15. Lippmann, *Essays in the Public Philosophy,* 79.

16. Geertz, "Politics of Meaning," 316.

17. Debo Basorun, *Quotes of a General: Selected Quotes of Major General Ibrahim Babangida* (Lagos: Terry, 1987), 8.

18. Federal Government of Nigeria, preamble to *The Constitution of the Federal Republic of Nigeria* (Lagos: Government Printers, 1989), 11.

19. Rosalind I. J. Hackett and Jacob K. Olupona, "Civil Religion," in *Religion and Society in Nigeria: Historical and Sociological Perspectives,* ed. Jacob K. Olupona and Toyin Falola (Ibadan: Spectrum Books, 1991), 268.

20. Jacob K. Olupona, "Religion, Ideology and the Social Order: Civil Religion in Nigeria," in *Religion and State: The Nigerian Experience,* ed. S. A. Adewale (Ibadan: Orita Publications, 1988), 78–80.

21. Markoff and Regan, "Religion, the State and Political Legitimacy," 170.

22. Clarke, "Religion and Political Attitude since Independence," 218.

23. Olupona, "Religious Pluralism and Civil Religion," 41.

24. Charles Taylor, "The Politics of Recognition," in *Multiculturalism and "The Politics of Recognition,"* ed. Amy Gutmann (Princeton: Princeton University Press, 1993), 25–74; Geertz, "Politics of Meaning," 311–26.

25. Subrata Mitra, "The Limits of Accommodation: Nehru, Religion, and the State in India," *South Asia Research* 9, 2 (1989): 125.

26. Geertz, "Politics of Meaning," 314–15.

27. Ibid., 315.

28. For a critical appraisal of the civil religion thesis, see Michael W. Hughey, *Civil Religion and Moral Order: Theoretical and Historical Dimensions* (Westport, Conn.: Greenwood Press, 1983); Tunde

Lawuyi, "Nigeria in the 1980s," 234–36; George Rupp, "From Civil Religion to Public Faith," in *Commitment and Community* (Minneapolis: Fortress Press, 1989), 83–96.

29. Adebanjo Edema, *Christians and Politics in Nigeria* (Ibadan: Codat Publications, 1988), 14.

30. Dare Babarinsa, "Military Leadership: A Battle with the Genie," *Newswatch*, 8 October 1990, 51.

31. *The Guardian* (Lagos), 5 November 1991.

32. Adebayo Adedeji, "Ensuring a Successful Transition," *West Africa*, 11–17 November 1991, 1878.

33. Most students of Nigeria's politics agree that since the country's independence in 1960, military coups d'état have, at least until recently, been tolerated by the citizens partly because of the promise usually made by the military leaders that their ultimate goal was to create conditions conducive to democratic rule. This promise has been consistent with the fact that most political reform programs for democratizing the polity have been initiated by the military. This much at least is true, notwithstanding the fact that Nigeria's failed attempts at democratic experiment cannot be dissociated from the unwillingness of the same military establishment to voluntarily relinquish power. For a recent analysis of this problem, see Paschal S. K. Uwakwe, "The Military and the Transition to Democracy in Nigeria, 1970-1979" (Seminar paper presented at the School of Oriental and African Studies, University of London, 10 December 1991).

34. Oyeleye Oyediran, ed., *Survey of Nigerian Affairs, 1976–77* (Lagos: Nigerian Institute of International Affairs and Macmillan, 1981), 136.

35. Nigeria, *Report of the Political Bureau*, 190.

36. Ibid., 32.

37. Olusegun Obasanjo, "Nigeria and Sudan: Similarities and Dissimilarities" (paper presented at the U. S. Institute of Peace conference on "Sudan and Nigeria: Religion, Nationalism, and Intolerance," Washington D.C., 5 October 1991), 2.

38. Larry Diamond, "Issues in the Constitutional Design of a Third Nigerian Republic," *African Affairs* 86 (1987): 210.

39. Larry Diamond, "The Accountability Gap in the Transition to

Democracy in Nigeria" (paper presented at the 33rd annual meeting of the African Studies Association, Baltimore, 1–4 November 1990), 1.

40. Adedeji, "Ensuring a Successful Transition," 1878. SAP was a form of economic reform programs prescribed for most African countries in the early 1980s, and closely supervised by the World Bank and the International Monetary Fund. The programs were prompted by the conviction that "African governments are unable to manage economic resources efficiently and that the private sector discipline of making a profit will ensure a more efficient use of resources." The main elements of these reform programs include, inter alia, "the reduction of the size of the African state and its controls over the economy, the establishment of incentive prices for agriculture, the freeing-up of prices and the reduction of state subsidies and public employment rolls, the privatization of many government economic units, the liberalization of trade and exchange controls and the revising of investment codes to encourage private (foreign and domestic) investment." See *Perestroika without Glasnost in Africa,* Conference Report Series 2, 1 (Atlanta: Carter Center; report of the inaugural seminar of the Governance in Africa Program, 17–19 February 1989), 10.

41. See for instance, Lucian W. Pye, "Armies in the Process of Political Modernization," in *Political Development and Social Change,* ed. J. L. Finkle and R. W. Gable, 2d ed. (New York: Wiley, 1971).

42. S. Decalo, *Coups and Military Rule in Africa: Studies in Military Style,* 2d ed. (New Haven: Yale University Press, 1990).

43. R. First, *The Barrel of a Gun* (London: Allen Lane, 1970).

44. Ibid., 440.

45. Nigeria, *Report of the Political Bureau,* 33.

46. Whitaker, "Second Beginnings," 6.

47. CDC, 1:v–xiv.

48. Ibid., 1:v.

49. B. O. Nwabueze, *Nigeria's Presidential Constitution, 1979-1983: The Second Experiment in Constitutional Democracy* (London: Longman 1985), 9–20.

50. CDC, 1:vi.

51. Ibid., 1:v.

52. Ibid., 2:36.

53. Nigeria, *Report of the Political Bureau*, 46–47.

54. Ibid., 47.

55. Ibid., 49.

56. Joseph, *Democracy and Prebendal Politics*, 8.

57. Nigeria, *Report of the Political Bureau*, 50.

58. Dudley, *Introduction to Nigerian Government and Politics*, 132.

59. CDC, 2:35.

60. Diamond, "Constitutional Design of a Third Nigerian Republic," 210.

61. Oyediran, *Survey of Nigerian Affairs, 1976–77*, 125.

62. Ibid.

63. Nigeria, *Report of the Political Bureau*, 3.

64. Whitaker, "Second Beginnings," 7.

65. Ibid.

66. Adedeji, "Ensuring a Successful Transition," 1879.

67. Nigeria, *Report of the Political Bureau*, 4–5.

68. Seymour Martin Lipset, *Political Man: The Social Bases of Politics*, expanded ed. (Baltimore: Johns Hopkins University Press, 1981), 39.

69. Ibid. For a theory of education as a means of conscientization and an instrument of existential liberation, see Paulo Freire, *Pedagogy of the Oppressed* (New York: Continuum, 1988). For a critique of unbridled confidence in the moral and emancipatory potency of education and reason, see Niebuhr, *Moral Man and Immoral Society*, 23–50.

70. Kukah, "Religion and Politics in Northern Nigeria," 1.

71. Diamond, "Accountability Gap in the Transition to Democracy," 12–13.

72. Diamond, "Constitutional Design of a Third Nigerian Republic," 209.

73. Agbaje, "Travails of the Secular State," 292.

74. Umar M. Birai, "Islamic Tajdid and the Political Process in Nigeria," in *Fundamentalisms and the State: Remaking Polities, Economies, and Militance*, The Fundamentalism Project, vol. 3, ed. Martin

E. Marty and R. Scott Appleby (Chicago: University of Chicago Press, 1993), 191.

75. Nigeria, *Report of the Political Bureau,* 183.

76. Ibid., 183-84.

77. Hooper, *Ethics of Discourse,* 159.

78. Arlin M. Adams and Charles J. Emmerich, *A Nation Dedicated to Religious Liberty: The Constitutional Heritage of the Religion Clauses* (Philadelphia: University of Pennsylvania Press, 1990), 37.

79. Kukah, "Religion and Politics in Northern Nigeria," 247.

80. Geertz, "Politics of Meaning," 317.

81. Msgr. Hypolite Adigwe, *Sharī'a, Canon, Common, and Customary Law Courts: Contributions to the Debates in the Constituent Assembly 1988, at Abuja* (privately printed, 1988), 9.

82. Catholic Bishops of Nigeria, "Memorandum from the Catholic Bishops of Nigeria on the Review of the Nigerian 1979 Presidential Constitution," in *Christian/Muslim Relations in Nigeria: The Stand of Catholic Bishops* (Lagos: Catholic Secretariat, n.d.), 9.

83. E. B. Gbonigi, "Religion in a Secular Society" (paper presented at the Second Assembly of the Christian Association of Nigeria, Kaduna, 16-17 November 1988), 2.

84. Ibid., 7.

85. Yusuf Bala Usman, "National Cohesion, National Planning, and the Constitution," in *Issues in the Nigerian Draft Constitution,* ed. Suleimanu Kumo and Abubakar Aliyu (Zaria: Ahmadu Bello University Press, 1977), 49.

86. Ibid.

87. Segun Gbadegesin, "The Philosophical Foundation of Secularism" (paper presented at the 31st Congress of the Historical Society of Nigeria, 18-24 May 1985), 14-18.

88. Sanneh, "Religion, Politics, and National Integration," 157.

89. Justice Sambo, "Draft Constitution Fails to Provide for Morality," *New Nigerian,* 5 January 1977, 7.

90. Anwal AbdulNasir, "Religion and Secularism in the Nigerian Context" (paper presented at the 25th annual Religious Studies Conference, Ibadan, 17-20 September 1991), 2.

91. Justice Sambo, "Morality and the Draft Constitution," in *The Great Debate: Nigerians' Viewpoints on the Draft Constitution 1976-77*, ed. W. I. Ofonagoro (Lagos: Times Publications, 1978), 74.

92. Sanneh, "Religion, Politics, and National Integration," 157.

93. Sambo, "Draft Constitution Fails to Provide for Morality," 7.

94. Ibid., 9.

95. Malam Mukhtar, interview with *Newswatch*, 6 May 1991, 16.

96. Alhaji Aliyu, interview with *This Week*, 6 April 1987, 22.

97. Ibid.

98. Sanneh, "Religion, Politics, and National Integration," 157.

99. John Paden, "Religious Identity and Political Values in Nigeria: The Transformation of the Muslim Community" (paper prepared for the Islam and Nationhood Conference, Yale Center for International and Area Studies, Yale University, 12-14 November 1992).

100. Adams and Emmerich, *Nation Dedicated to Religious Liberty*, 51.

101. Berger, *Sacred Canopy*, 107.

102. Janet Martin Soskice, *Metaphor and Religious Language* (Oxford: Oxford University Press, 1986).

103. K. Wald, *Religion and Politics in the United States* (New York: St. Martin's Press, 1987), 3.

104. Berger, *Sacred Canopy*, 110-11.

105. Johannes B. Metz, *Theology of the World*, trans. William Glen-Doepel (New York: Herder and Herder, 1969), 19, 20.

106. Jacob Olupona, "Religion, Law and Order: State Regulation of Religious Affairs," *Social Compass* 37, 1 (1990): 129.

107. AbdulNasir, "Religion and Secularism in the Nigerian Context," 12.

108. Joint Muslim Advisory Council of Oyo State, "An Appeal to the Christian Association of Nigeria (CAN)," *National Concord*, 25 April 1989, 11.

109. Birai, "Islamic Tajdid and the Political Process," 184.

110. See, for instance, Bruce B. Lawrence, *Defenders of God: The Fundamentalist Revolt against the Modern Age* (San Francisco: Harper and Row, 1989).

III. Birai, "Islamic Tajdid and the Political Process," 184.

112. Peter L. Berger, *A Far Glory: The Quest for Faith in an Age of Credulity* (New York: Free Press, 1992), 29.

113. See, for instance, Matthews A. Ojo, "The Contextual Significance of the Charismatic Movements in Independent Nigeria," *Africa* 58, 2 (1988): 175–92.

114. Ruth Marshall, "Power in the Name of Jesus," *Review of African Political Economy* 52 (1991): 32. Austin Ahanotu makes essentially the same point in "Muslims and Christians in Nigeria," 39.

115. Marshall, "Power in the Name of Jesus," 33.

116. Ibid., 21.

117. Elizabeth Hodgkin, "Islamism and Islamic Research in Africa" (paper prepared for the Islam in Modern Africa Research Project, Center of African Studies, University of London, 1990), 1–2. I thank Prof. Cruise O'Brien of London University for calling my attention to this excellent piece of work. Published in *Islam et sociétés au Sud du Sahara,* vol. 4, 1990, pp. 73–130.

118. Ibid., 2.

119. Lawrence, *Defenders of God,* 200.

120. *Tafsir,* 29 March 1990.

121. Shaykh Gumi, interview with *Quality* (Lagos), October 1987.

122. Birai, "Islamic Tajdid and the Political Process," 196–97.

123. Federal Government of Nigeria, *Report of the Constitution Review Committee Containing the Reviewed Constitution* (CRC) (Lagos, 1988), vi, xx.

124. David Hollenbach, "Religion and Public Life," *Theological Studies* 52, 1 (March 1991): 104.

125. T. B. Maston, *Christianity and World Issues* (New York: Macmillan, 1957), 223.

126. Murray, *Problem of Religious Freedom,* 40–41.

127. Adams and Emmerich, *Nation Dedicated to Religious Liberty,* 58.

128. Ibid., 58–59.

129. W. I. Ofonagoro, *The Great Debate: Nigerians' Viewpoints on the Draft Constitution, 1976–77* (Lagos: Times Publications, 1978); David Laitin, "The Sharia Debate and the Origins of Nigeria's Sec-

ond Republic," *Journal of Modern African Studies* 20, 3 (1982): 411–30, idem, *Hegemony and Culture,* 1–6; Ngwoke, *Religion and Religious Liberty,* 51–117.

130. "Our Case, Our Fears," *African Concord,* 5 February 1990, 36.

131. Joseph Schacht, *The Origins of Muhammadan Jurisprudence* (Oxford: Clarendon Press, 1959), 1.

132. Lambton, *State and Government in Medieval Islam,* 1–20.

133. Birai, "Islamic Tajdid and the Political Process," 193.

134. Kukah, "Religion and Politics in Northern Nigeria," 144.

135. A. O. Obilade, *The Nigerian Legal System* (London: Sweet and Maxwell, 1979), 33–40.

136. Agbaje, "Travails of the Secular State," 298.

137. Birai, "Islamic Tajdid and the Political Process," 191–92.

138. Ibid., 192.

139. *New Nigerian,* 29 September 1986.

140. Birai, "Islamic Tajdid and the Political Process," 191.

141. Ibid., 194.

142. *Christian/Muslim Relations in Nigeria,* 9.

143. Ibid.

144. Adigwe, *Sharīʿa, Canon, Common, and Customary Courts,* 14.

145. L. U. Ejiofor, "Judicial Systems for Nigeria," *Daily Star,* 29 January 1977. For a similar view, see T. A. Aguda, "The Judiciary under the Draft Constitution," in *The Great Debate,* ed. W. I. Ofonagoro (Lagos: Times Publications, 1978), 358–59.

146. Laitin, "Sharīʿa Debate and the Origins of Nigeria's Second Republic," 413–14.

147. Ibid., 414.

148. Kukah, "Religion and Politics in Northern Nigeria," 156; see also Agbaje, "Travails of the Secular State," 297.

149. Dahl, *Preface to Democratic Theory* (1956), 91, 96.

150. Laitin, *Hegemony and Culture,* 1–11; Williams, "State, Religion and Politics in Nigeria," 322–55.

151. Fellowship of the Churches of Christ in Nigeria, *Towards the Right Path for Nigeria* (Jos: TEKAN, 1987), 48–54.

152. A. H. Yadudu, "The Prospects for Sharīʿa in Nigeria," Pres-

ented *Islam in Africa: Proceedings of the Islam in Africa Conference,* 36–58 (Ibadan: Spectrum Books, 1993).

153. Adigwe, *Sharīʿa, Canon, Common, and Customary Courts,* 20.

154. Taylor, "Politics of Recognition," 66.

155. Amy Gutmann, introduction to *Multiculturalism and "The Politics of Recognition,"* ed. Amy Gutmann (Princeton: Princeton University Press, 1992), 7.

156. Taylor, "Politics of Recognition," 25. Italics in original.

157. Ibid., 64. Italics are mine.

158. Ibid., 32.

159. *Daily Times,* 4 May 1989.

160. Ibid.

161. Olupona, "Religion, Law and Order," 130–31.

162. *The Guardian,* 16 February 1989, 18.

163. Ibid.

164. *Sunday Tribune,* 23 April 1990.

165. Nigeria, *Constitution of the Federal Republic of Nigeria* (1989), sec. 3–4.

166. Agbaje, "Travails of the Secular State," 304.

167. Nigeria, *Report of the Political Bureau,* 187.

168. Olupona, "Religion, Law and Order," 135.

Chapter 5

Toward the Reconstruction of Public Life in Nigeria: The Religious Contribution

In this chapter, I first review and further develop the key arguments that have been offered in the previous chapters. Then, I propose some practical ways in which religions in Nigeria might contribute to the ongoing efforts to establish and maintain a civic context in which people of diverse persuasions could live together peaceably. I conclude the chapter by suggesting what I believe would be needed to secure for Nigeria a viable future and a bearable present.

Dialogic Politics Revisited

The phenomenon of religious politics in contemporary Nigeria is the country's most disturbing sociological and moral eyesore. It is certainly the Achilles' heel of Nigeria's political life. It has been the basis of widespread fears and uncertainties regarding the prospects of continued peaceful coexistence among the nation's several confessional communities. Clearly, an important question that has to be raised is how to avoid the two extreme attitudes that tend to mark current patterns of political and religious interaction. There is, on the one hand, an attitude tending toward cultural and religious imperialism that would define the interests and values of one group as the common good. On the other hand, there are those who would want to deny the possibility of a common Nigerian purpose even as citizens acknowledge their differences.

The normative and constructive project of this study represents an effort to find a way between these equally unhappy alternatives. In the earlier chapters, I approached the problem of religious politics in Nigeria by locating it within the larger dilemma of pluralism. I utilized the pluralist concept to expose the triumphalistic and imperialistic tendencies of religious institutions, as well as the hegemonic and authoritarian propensities of the state. This approach was shaped by the conviction that the search for a vision of a public-spirited citizenry must focus on all the layers of society if such a vision is to have any sustaining power. Accordingly, I offered a critique of certain theoretical approaches and religious perspectives that, I believe, ill defined the problem of religious pluralism, politics, and the state in Nigeria.

First among these inadequate positions was the pessimistic thrust of certain religious and ideological (mainly Marxist) extremists who regard pluralism as an evil to be conquered, and who would want to predicate citizenship upon either religious conformity through the establishment of a theocracy or upon pure secularism, possibly through the establishment of a party-state. The second position is reflected in the current official thinking about religion as a purely private, apolitical enterprise, with no public relevance. Although this second position accepts the sociological fact of religious pluralism, it does so at a very high price to religious integrity, in that the continued existence of religion within a benign state would depend on its preparedness to be voiceless in the public affairs of its adherents.

I found the first position inadequate because it envisions a form of political community that is neither feasible nor desirable in Nigeria. Theocracy, based on either a single religious tradition or a composite religious culture, is a sociological impossibility. Not every Nigerian identifies with a confessional community, and those who do are separated by denominational as well as theological differences. Theocracy is also undesirable because it underestimates the saliency of historical and political consciousness, notably the constantly advancing levels of human knowledge and the contemporary accent on respect for human dignity and rights as a matrix for measuring political maturity.

The logic of theocracy is frighteningly simple. When it comes to matters as weighty as eternal salvation and the preservation of the state, error has no rights. There is in a theocratic vision little or no realm of common grace by which the affairs of everyday life may be ordered by people of different convictions. While there may be an understandable reason to push for a greater public rôle of religion as a counterpoise to secularist onslaught, it is not clear that such a role could be responsibly played through a dogmatic, extremist, and authoritarian approach. The solution to the Nigerian pluralist dilemma, according to J. A. Atanda of Ibadan University, does not lie in attempting to enthrone a particular religion as a state religion. To do so "is to force people of other religious persuasions to forsake their religions and embrace the one they do not profess." Not only will such a classicist and theologically integralist approach "be counter-productive," it will also, in clearest terms, "violate one of the fundamental human rights, namely, freedom of religious worship, embedded in the constitution."[1]

Pure secularism—that is, the doctrine of the personal, ideational and public irrelevance of religion—is also inadequate to answer the pluralist question as it has arisen in Nigeria. By endorsing an attitude of irresponsibility toward the ultimate problem of truth, it fails the two criteria of religious tolerance spelled out in chapter 2, namely, "the ability to hold vital convictions which lead to action; and also the capacity to preserve the spirit of forgiveness towards those who offend us by holding to convictions which *seem* untrue to us."[2] In fact, most Nigerians would hesitate to define their personal and public value systems in terms of purely secularist prescriptions. The political solution being sought in the country is not how to drive religion from the public, but rather how to prevent a naive and simplistic religious sentimentality from underwriting public life. Furthermore, for any moral prescriptions to be effective in the country, I argued that a new project rooted in a new doctrine would be required.

Proponents of pure secularism certainly claim that they endorse the principle of religious freedom, but in reality, religion is for them a temporary nuisance that would eventually wither away. Their ideological precursors were the French Deists, and later atheists, who tolerated religious differences until humankind could develop beyond the need for any religion. While they ostensibly preached tolerance, their hope was that freedom of religion would ultimately lead to freedom from religion.

The inadequacy of the current official position on religion lies primarily in its ambiguity. The view of a purely private and domesticated religion is not only inappropriate for the Nigerian context, it is also already being heavily criticized in the Western world, where it originally enjoyed a preeminence of place as an outgrowth of the liberal outlook on human social existence. Whether we are talking about the *umma* in Islam or *Ajogbe* among the Yoruba or *covenant* in Christianity, the orienting concept of human social existence in Nigeria is highly communitarian.[3] The Enlightenment philosophy that undergirds the notion of a privatized religion is based on "a nominalist epistemology which denies that human beings possess a true, common nature and views the individual as an atom completely motivated by self-interest."[4]

As I have shown in chapter 2, John Rawls is a key proponent of the view of a privatized and domesticated religion. He has recommended constraints on religion in public discussion on the grounds that religious morality is too comprehensive, and as such, may be divisive or discourteous to some members of the public who do not share the same morality. Clarke and Olupona point out that successive governments in Nigeria at the federal level have, on several occasions, courted religious support, but for purely cosmetic purposes.[5] For instance, the late General Murtala Muhammed told the Council of Catholic Bishops at their Onitsha meeting in 1975 that, while as religious leaders, they were expected to "use their elevated positions . . . to infuse sound moral principles in the people," they must also "identify themselves with the present tempo of the country."[6] Whether or not that tempo was conducive to fostering just social relations and the promotion of the common good seemed irrelevant to the late military leader. The relationship between religion and the state has been a one-way affair in the country. While the governments are anxious to blunt religious influences in the public, they defy the prophetic-critical thrust of religious morality. Characteristically, Nigerian governments have been unwilling "to be scrutinized and questioned."[7]

In its more sophisticated and philosophical formulations, liberal political theory suggests that since propositions about God's will or God's action can only be attested to by those who share the belief in question, the persuasive force of religious language ends at the boundaries of the sanctuary. Politics, from this perspective, is conceived of as a value-free, neutral, and amoral enterprise governed mainly by the canons of rationality and *techne*.[8] Religion is assigned a very restricted role, limited to being merely a curator of rituals and ceremonies, and at best, a purveyor of an emotional tranquilizer on Fridays and Sundays. Precisely because of the alleged socially divisive, inflammatory, and unverifiable characteristics of religious language, contemporary liberals argue that it "must be limited to a legitimating or hortatory role in the public because that is the only way we can be sure we have a public understanding of what it means."[9]

In truth, this Enlightenment critique of religion, the spirit of which undergirded the constitutions of many countries in the English-speaking world, notably the Bill of Rights of the United States Constitution (1791), must be distinguished from the French Deist-Atheistic approach. Much of what the Enlightenment spirit represents is worth appropriating into the Nigerian context. Originally, what is now regarded as the liberal approach to the question of religion and state grew out of the complex interaction of Enlightenment philosophy and the views of the left-wing Calvinists and sectarian thinkers of the Puritan tradition. Liberalism views freedom of religion positively, as necessary to the development of authentic spiritual life. Freedom from state coercion grants to the individual the opportunity to respond to the divine call of conscience. God alone is the Lord of the conscience. When the state speaks in place of God, it produces, at best, hypocrisy and, at worst, idolatry. Freedom of religion is not a temporary safeguard that will eventually mature into flight from religion, but the basis of a sincere faith. In this vision there is a realm of common grace by which people may govern their earthly affairs even while granting freedom of choice of the way to ultimate salvation.

However, this essentially juridical clarification of the place of religion in relation to the state has been conflated with the larger issue having to do with the relation of faith to politics or society at large. For some contemporary political theorists, the institutional separation between organized religion and the state connotes the severance of religious values from the affairs of society.[10] Unfortunately, this distorted rendition of the question is what is presupposed by the usage of *secularity* and *separation* in contemporary discourse on religion and the state in Nigeria. Quite naturally, and rightly too, the Muslims found the interpretation incongruent with, and offensive to, their religious sensibilities. The interpretation is also at variance with the presuppositions and vision of dialogic politics as developed in this work.

Thus I have challenged all the above paradigms of religion, politics, and the state because of their implicit yet imperious disregard for the goal of a common life. I have sought to enrich the discourse by proposing a concept of political community that I believe avoids the weaknesses of these positions while maximally utilizing their strengths. By drawing upon major theories in religious ethics and political philosophy, I have deployed the concept of "dialogic politics" to affirm that the unity of religion is not a prerequisite for political unity in Nigeria; rather, that the most important sine qua non for having a meaningful and enduring political life in the country would be the citizens' subscription to an underlying political-moral consensus. The chief objective of a dialogic political culture is to discern *a common political ground* among religious people with major perspectival differences by encouraging each side to cultivate a sufficient level of trust as the basis for enjoying the good faith of the others.

So conceived, I argued, first, that political unity and stability are possible in Nigeria without uniformity of religious belief and practice, and without the necessity of any governmental restrictions on any religion. Second, I argued that stable unity, understood as enduring agreement on the citizens' common good at the level of performance, has a greater promise of being strengthened if religious differences are excluded from the areas of concern allotted to government. I have used the term *dialogic politics* to accent a teleological view of politics and a contextualist view of religion. Dialogic politics emphasizes issues that transcend the narrow confines of political institutions and the parochial gratifications of particularist religious sensibilities. It encourages us to ask broader questions of political culture, questions related to the web of beliefs that people have about their political system, the goals and values they hold to sustain it, and the characteristic patterns of political interaction among these inclusive ethical goods.

I approached the problematic of religious pluralism, politics, and the state in Nigeria from this broadly construed normative perspective. In the sense being used here, dialogic politics has three main components: the theoretical, the institutional, and the attitudinal. The theoretical dimension of dialogic politics is found in the public philosophy undergirding it, that is, its initiating impulse. Public philosophy primarily functions as a centripetal force in a pluralistic society; it aims at the achievement of civil unity where none had existed, for "if society is to be at all a rational process, some set of principles must motivate the general participation of all religious groups, despite their dissensions, in the oneness of the community."[11]

In chapters 2 and 4, I traced the genesis of the concept of public philosophy, and embraced its heuristic value for the study of Nigeria's religio-political dilemma, mainly because it counsels the need to have such an orienting concept as a foundation for renewing the meaning of public life in the country. Although I argued that some budding traits of the idea of public philosophy are discernible in Nigeria, I readily admitted the risk involved in this kind of theoretical venture. I noted that public philosophy in Nigeria, to the extent that we may speak of one, has a very limited audience and is still afflicted with certain intellectual limits and lack of directional focus.

Language is one obvious barrier to initiating a common and

an all-inclusive deliberative political effort in Nigeria. There is also the patrimonial Nigerian state, marked by "organic-statist orientations," and aggressively committed to a doctrine of "depoliticisation or departicipation" by alienating most of the society's mediating structures in which people find meaning and fulfillment.[12] Whether experienced individually or in a group, locally or universally, alienation is a condition of existence that many philosophical schools, including those with flawed agendas, have condemned in the strictest terms. Marxism, Existentialism, the well-known Frankfurt School, and Process Philosophy are all agreed that alienation is "an inherently contradictory" and "negative form of belonging." It is "a relationship in which people are caught in a pattern of activity contrary to their own good. It is an institutional pattern in which a people suffers from the pernicious consequences of its own life-activity. It is a social form of Frankenstein's monster, a creation that turns back upon and against its creator."[13] This negative form of belonging is what Segun Gbadegesin perceives to be "the crux of contemporary African realities."[14]

Without any pretensions to extricate religion from the repetitive patterns of political instability and institutional decay in Nigeria, I argued that a far greater challenge currently facing the country is how to broaden the public who will be responsible for the care and articulation of the nation's public philosophy. To be sure, the role of the *studium* in this regard is indispensable. The Nigerian academic communities constitute, together with the religious bodies, powerful mediating sectors that stand between the people and the state, and that must perforce bear "the responsibility of using their power in that high service of justice and the freedom of the people."[15] In addition to these institutions, there are also "organized groups outside the state—of students, trade unions, women, journalists, lawyers and other professionals, producers of all kinds, and yes, even of ethnic kinsmen" which could "provide a check of sorts on the extreme abuse of centralized state power and an obstacle to the consolidation of authoritarian rule."[16]

Besides the urgency to enlarge the number of those involved in the construction of Nigeria's public philosophy, there is the added and more poignant question of the substance or the material content of that philosophy. As a moral category, public philosophy is intended to provide an ethical horizon and a set of value preferences in a religiously pluralistic society. Central among these value preferences is the common good of the nation, "the good of the whole, which is derivative from the interrelations of its component individuals, and also necessary for the existence of each of these individuals."[17] The common good is the normative guiding principle of public life, the moral compass necessary for organizing and predicting the life in common. No society or civilization can endure without this kind of corrective, metaphysical-moral vision. But it is not simply enough to have this guiding vision at the core of society's life—Max L. Stackhouse adds that the vision must also be sufficiently strong and intrinsically reliable. Thus, in order for a civilization to stand, "the metaphysical-moral vision that . . . it hosts must be capable of guiding the ethical and spiritual life as it is lived out in a larger context over the course of time. When the vision is constituted on a narrow basis, or grows cold, or rests on foundations that are untrue or unjust . . . , the civilization begins to lose its inner vitality."[18] Religiously speaking, the concept of the common good is covenantal. It requires mutual accountability not only to one another, but also before God. It places "the moral health of each individual" as well as "the righteousness or waywardness of the whole community" under mutual scrutiny.[19]

In political terms, the prospects of achieving this goal in Nigeria would require "consensus on critical question of national development by the different nationalities that make up the geographical configuration called Nigeria."[20] For this reason, I insisted that the scope of the public philosophy is political, not theological. Its aim is not to achieve agreement on dogmatic questions, but to counsel deliberation on how life in common is to be lived. In effect, I rejected the position that "any communal vision of the good society can only be secured by intolerance for the rights of individuals and their self-determination,"[21] because such a notion is fed by the mistaken assumption that the material content of the common good is to be conceived as an absolute already known, impermeable by the creative juices of historical insights. I emphasized instead the deliberative feature of the common good by designating it as what is minimally achievable at any given time; not something clearly defined, but something to be discovered through communal search.

More significantly, I refused to characterize politics as an amoral activity, one that avoids questions "about how human beings are meant to live and what they require from one another to flourish in a human society."[22] Dialogic politics is guided by the fundamental premise that the key to the reconstruction of public life "is a new attentiveness to the normative dimensions of our ideas about human nature."[23] Properly speaking, political questions belong in this normative category. What Theodor W. Adorno and Max Horkheimer said about the ethical dimension of politics confirms not just the classical understanding (especially Aristotelian) of this enterprise, but also our ordinary sense of the proper goal of human actions. According to them, "politics that does not contain theology [normative vision] within itself, however little considered, may often be shrewd but remains in the end no more than a business."[24] Such an instrumental understanding of politics contains all potential signals of making it a "grim and barbaric" business.[25]

It is also pertinent to the concept of dialogic politics developed here that the dialogue which goes on within the political community made possible by this kind of politics must be structured. Dialogue requires both another human face as well as an environment conducive to exchange. I proposed a democratic framework, marked by tolerance, accommodation, and the spirit of humility, as a "contextual or situational requirement" for actualizing the ideals of dialogic politics.

A political community is not likely to endure if its constituent units pursue only their selfish particular interests, fight all the time, and squeeze out half-satisfactory compromise solutions. The purpose of a common political culture, a part of which must be explicitly expressed in the constitution, would be to provide a consensus on basic premises for any conflict resolution. My interpretation of the various guidelines on religion and the state in the federal constitution of Nigeria regards them as a species of the generic ethical directives for the nation. As a charter of freedom and a plan for political order, the constitution consists of rough agreement on certain basics, such as "the treatment of all individuals as free and equal; the understanding of society as a system of uncoerced cooperation; the right of each individual [and group] to claim a fair share of the fruits of that cooperation; and the duty of all citizens to support and uphold institutions that embody a shared conception of fair principles."[26]

My review of the country's political history reveals that Nigerians have been willing to initiate, but quite unable to respect and maintain, a constitutional tradition within a democratic framework. Whether or not they will be able to recognize what is good for themselves and for the nation as a whole will hinge on their ability to carry on reasoned discourse, and to rely in such discourse on persuasion, not coercion or manipulation. I recognize that there are some circumstances in which people may reluctantly have to rely on the coercive power of law because of human sinfulness and innate frailty. Nevertheless, dialogic politics proposes a continual striving for a discovery of some basis for social unity that is respectful of both individual freedom and cultural integrity.

The frayed relationship between the Nigerian state and the constituting units of the federation requires new linkages, and in the judgment of Crawford Young, "a rewoven fabric must include robust threads of democracy."[27] That being the case, Nigerians need to provide for a political culture that combines autonomy with solidarity, genuine pluralism with a universal emancipatory rationality. They must be courageous and creative enough to use their public institutions of education, religion, and the press to search for some level of agreement on those basic conditions necessary to remain a community.

Most of all, they must make allowance for younger generations to be educated in all those values and meanings that are part of the country's inheritance, if the envisioned civil unity is not to be a merely transient achievement. Francis Deng, a seasoned Sudanese diplomat, has said that "the process of national self-discovery is essentially a function of education."[28] Properly speaking, the ethical goal of civil education is to counterbalance the scandal of social injustice, for among all the social and cultural infrastructure that a society may possess, education—formal and informal—remains the single most important "avenue of escape offered by society to the next generation of its citizens, one way for them to learn how to live useful lives as socially responsible persons."[29]

One lingering question has been how the differing religions in the country might help to encourage the emergence of an appropriate political climate, coupled with the theological virtues of religious humility, within which the state and the religious individuals and communities can find both their limits and freedom. In the previous chapters, I argued that addressing this kind of question is not an illicit thing for religion to do. It is a fact that religious groups constitute an integral part of the public. For that reason, their contributions to the justification of, and deliberation about, political questions and legitimate expressions of their civil obligations and constitutional right. To remove such contributions from the discourse because they are not widely shared unfairly privileges morality not derived from religious considerations. Consequent upon the communitarian accent of dialogic politics, I pressed for a more expansive definition of politics as an activity in which "beliefs about human good play a basic role in public deliberations about, and public justifications of, contested political choices."[30]

In this deliberative and justificatory effort, religion could potentially offer "a vision of final and radical reconciliation, a set of beliefs about how one is or can be bound or connected to the world—to the 'other' and to 'nature'—and above all, to Ultimate Reality in a profoundly intimate and ultimately meaningful way."[31] Since every religious vision comprises moral beliefs about how one should live, every such conception of what it means to be fully human implies acceptance of some basic responsibility for the well-being of others. Religion "without political love quickly becomes sentimental and irrelevant interiority."[32] In fact, all the influential religions in Nigeria are political in this sense. Neither Islam nor Christianity nor traditional religions endorse a "ghetto spirituality," which is a form of religious withdrawal "into a fortress within which all the old norms, doctrinal as well as behavioral, can be maintained."[33] Cognitive negotiation, as opposed to cognitive retrenchment or cognitive surrender, is the defining characteristic of dialogic politics. Such dialogical bargaining helps to strengthen political bonds. It performs an integrative function by transforming sensibilities and by bringing cognitive changes.

I did not pretend to overlook the divisions that religious discourse can bring. These divisions manifest themselves at two different levels in Nigeria. At the level of interreligious relationship, there is what J. A. Atanda calls "horizontal intolerance," that is, the intolerance by adherents of one religion against the members of other religions. Islam and Christianity are more susceptible to this kind of intolerance than are traditional religions. In addition, within each religious community, there is another form of intolerance, "vertical intolerance," such as is found among many Christian denominations or Muslim brotherhoods.[34] Vertical intolerance is the animosity harbored by one group against the other groups within the same religion. Both forms of intolerance can impede and frustrate the ideals of dialogic politics. It is in realization of this fact that I characterized dialogic politics as fallibilist, because it embraces self-critical rationality, and pluralist, because it respects divergent ways of life as a source of deepening moral insight. These aspects, plus compassion, I believe, would lead to political tolerance, not to autocracy; in that no one would be inclined to coerce the state for purely selfish purposes nor will the state allow itself to be so used. Dialogic politics is informed by the theological realism that recognizes that "the vanities of the other group or person, from which we suffer, is [sic] not different in kind, though possibly in degree, from similar vanities in our life. It also includes a religious sense of the mystery and greatness of the other life, which we violate if we seek to comprehend it too simply from our own standpoint."[35]

In the next major section of this chapter, I will deploy the concept of "mediating structures" to suggest two other important ways in which religions in Nigeria could contribute positively to the reconstruction and renewal of the nation. One is through their prophetic-critical functions, and the other through their social-welfarist involvements.

Religions as Mediating Structures

In Nigeria, an accurate census has been a historical rarity. As a result, there are no reliable data about the numbers of religious adherents in the country. However, over 80 million of an estimated 105 million Nigerians belong to the nation's two dominant religions, namely, Islam and Christianity, while more than half of the rest of the population associate themselves with the indigenous religions.[36] Religious presence in Nigeria is thus a very formidable phenomenon. What is more unsettling, as Dr. O. A. Olukunle of the University of Ibadan has pointed out, is the disjunction between this high religiosity and a very arid moral life of the people. In his usual melancholic prognostication about Nigeria, he believed "the future is not particularly bright for religious dispositions in this country, not because there are not enough copies of the Bible and the Koran and not because there are not enough religious leaders to preach but precisely because the grounds have been prepared to make religion (not God) a lame duck."[37]

While Olukunle's prophecy may be dismissed by some people as the rattle of an unrepentant Marxist, a religious insider's observation may serve to confirm the point that the ethical impact of religions in Nigeria has been infinitesimal. Adebanjo Edema, pastor of a Nigerian Pentecostal church, said in a paper presented to the Nigerian Fellowship of Graduate Christians, that the greatest malady that has infested the country is not really the absence of religious people in public service but the failure of those who have served to mediate the ethical meaning of their respective traditions to society writ large. In a tone reminiscent of the Old Testament prophets, he told his audience that "the indifference or short-sightedness of most Christians about national affairs [has] brought . . . the nation to her knees. . . . The Christians who once participated in politics made little or no impact on our culture. Many were easily carried down the lane of moral bankruptcy, having listened to and imitated those who have no regards for morals."[38] Mutatis mutandis, what Edema said about the Christians is equally applicable to the Muslims, and certainly, to all Nigerian religious adherents who are concerned about making a positive public difference.

One way by which religious people and communities could mediate an ethical meaning to the Nigerian society is by conceiving of themselves as "mediating structures." Peter Berger and Richard Neuhaus define mediating structures as "those institutions standing between the individual in his private life and the large institutions of public life."[39] Examples are the neighborhood, family, church, and voluntary associations. Mediating structures are those "little platoons [which] we belong to in society," and constitute "the first principle of public affections."[40] Alexis de Tocqueville describes the science of mediating structures or independent associations as "the mother of science; the progress of all the rest depends upon the progress it has made."[41]

The concept of mediating structures is no doubt fraught with definitional imprecision. In many accounts of the concept, not only are the boundaries not clearly defined, the contours constantly shift and the landmarks change. By rejecting the commonplace description of mediating structures as nonprofit and nongovernmental, Franklin Gamwell prefers the term "independent associations," which, to him, "are the most important associations in the social order."[42] In the literature of political science, the concept of mediating structures has been somehow identified with the idea of "middle structures" existing in both the governmental and the private sector. Johannes Althusius was said to be the first to use the concept of "middle structures" to describe "the lower tiers of government, such as the provinces (or states) and the local governments, along with the family and other associations not under the direction of the central political order."[43] What now pass for "voluntary associations" in contemporary discourse are just a component of Althusius's idea of middle organizations.

James Luther Adams appropriates Althusius's insight to

render "democratic society" or state as "an association of associations."[44] This is a more expansive definition of associational
life, and certainly extends the scope of the concept beyond the
early Tocquevillian approach or some contemporary discussions
of the concept of mediating structures that tend to bracket out
the governmental sector and large multinational corporations
from this category. In this chapter I shall be using *mediating
structures* against the backdrop of the definition offered by
Berger and Neuhaus. It is noteworthy that James Luther Adams
himself believes that these structures, in the way they are
construed here, "function as wedges" that prevent "overween-
ing powers from presenting a united front against criticism."[45]

The ethical understanding of mediating structures is that
they are indispensable to the moral reconstruction of public
life. The modern world, according to Berger and Neuhaus, is
characterized by the crisis of "meaning, fulfillment, and personal identity."[46] This crisis is of a kind that no government
can singularly alleviate it by imposing on life one comprehensive order of meaning. Antonio Gramsci once said that "society
is a system of sectors which are partly autonomous, analytically
distinct, but mutually influential."[47] Moreover, given the fact
that "human needs are multiple and complex, diverse forms of
social organizations are required to address them."[48]

Gramsci specifically pressed for an appreciation of the potentially reformist contributions of religion to public life. He
rejected certain anti-intellectual and antireligious implications
of the Marxist dictum that it was not consciousness that determined existence, but existence that determined consciousness. He stressed the creative role of those who, like the
Protestant Reformers or the *philosophes* of the French revolution, were clearly thinkers, but were "organically" related to
decisive groups of society.[49] Thus, the potential for political
and cultural reform increases as mediating structures are able
"to pose alternative visions of a better future, to provide citi-

zen training, to foster community rebuilding, and to work for constructive public policy change."[50]

In the last two decades, African scholarship has been marked by a significant appreciation for the potential role of mediating structures to initiate political innovations on the continent.[51] At the core of the arguments in this direction is that "the empowerment of groups in civil society and the enhancement of their capacity to serve as building blocks of the new order" is a fundamental requirement if Africa wants "to forge its own political renaissance."[52] This desired new political culture must be democratic in orientation, and the mediating structures, otherwise referred to in the literature as voluntary or independent associations, can advance it by helping to "give voice to popular demands" as well as encouraging the pluralization of "the institutional environment."[53]

Religious communities should be able to take a lead in this venture, but they will only succeed in doing so if they are willing to "accept and value diversity of membership in an increasingly pluralistic society . . . , restrain crusading habits of repressive moralism or tendencies to exclude people who are different," and "act in solidarity with the powerless to challenge unjust institutional practices and empower movements for change."[54] Two possible areas stand out as ethical matrices for assessing the effectiveness and relevance of religious contributions to public life, and these relate to the prophetic-critical responsibility of religions and certain concrete embodiment of that responsibility.

The Prophetic-Critical Functions of Religions

Bryan Hehir, an American Catholic theological ethicist, suggested that the success of the participation of religious bodies in the formation of public policy will depend partly on the availability of a strong intellectual leadership and of institutional vehicles of dissemination.[55] These two requirements have been met in Nigeria, not by separate denominational bodies, but mainly through the activities of ecumenically formed bodies within Islam as well as within Christianity.

As early as 1929, the Christian Council of Nigeria (CCN) was formed to provide a single theological-ethical voice for the mainstream Protestant churches in the country at both the national and international levels.[56] But in postindependence Nigeria, the most unified voice for the Christian community in the country has been aired through the Christian Association of Nigeria (CAN), formed on 27 August 1976. The members of CAN include the Catholic Church, all members of the CCN, and other Christian churches that do not belong to the CCN. The objectives of CAN include the promotion of "a common understanding among all the Christians in the country" and the creation of "good fellowship of all Christians on the social level that will help [them] to the better practice of their faith and the good of the country." These two goals are however subordinate to the more militant and political aspiration to stand together for the purpose of "projecting Christian ethics [onto the larger society] and also defending the rights of the Church."[57]

The equivalent ecumenical body founded by the Muslims in 1974 is the Nigerian Supreme Council for Islamic Affairs (NSCIA), in whose charter are listed more than twenty aims and objectives. The most significant of these objectives include

> catering to and protecting the interests of Islam throughout Nigeria; serving as a channel of contact with the Government of Nigeria on Islamic affairs; fostering brotherhood and cooperation among Muslims in Nigeria and other parts of the world . . . ; encouraging the establishment of institutions of learning wherein Islamic religion and culture as well as the Arabic language and other subjects of general education shall be taught; encouraging

legitimate economic activities of all Muslims . . . ; and engaging in any lawful activities in fulfillment and furtherance of the foregoing aims and objectives.[58]

Most studies of the activities of religious bodies (mostly Christian churches) during the Nigerian civil war (1967-1970) have emphasized their relief and philanthropic roles.[59] But by far their greatest contribution was their interpretation of the events of that period that made it possible first to anticipate the war and later to discard the prophecies of those who thought by then that Nigeria might never be able to reunite. Two years before the war, the Student Christian Movement of Nigeria (SCM) had warned at its Uyo meeting in December 1965 that "God's judgment is inescapable where man violates the laws of the moral universe and of his own nature as ordained by God."[60] The pervasive lifestyles of the period contained all portentous signals for an imminent catastrophe. Justice was not only being "turned upside down, those in power [were also] acquiring wealth by questionable means; masses of our people [were being] oppressed; hooliganism and thuggery [were] licenced and maintained at the expenses of tax payers; Federal and Regional elections [were] conducted in the most questionable way; [and] truth [was being] distorted or evaded." In no uncertain terms, the SCM declared that the evil could no longer be postponed.[61]

I have cited this incident to illustrate how religious perspectives can help to raise a seemingly mundane affair to the level of fundamental ethical principles, thereby jettisoning the idea that human behavior is subject to no other laws besides those defined and colored by the interests and aspirations of society —which, more often than not, could be very myopic. The SCM tried to accent the point that Nigerians needed to recognize that they do have a fundamental ability and responsibility to bond into a self-disciplining political community. The distinction between "facts" and "value," between what is empirically observable and what is normative, has remained one of the cardinal issues in philosophical and theological ethics.[62] In his own contribution to this debate, Reinhold Niebuhr argues that "while egoism is 'natural' in the sense that it is universal, it is not natural in the sense that it does not conform to man's nature who transcends himself indeterminedly and can only have God rather than self for his end." To counterpoise the culture of narcissistic hedonism, Niebuhr argues that "love [by which he meant solidarity for the pursuit of the common good] rather than self-love is the law of [human] existence in the sense that man can only be healthy and his communities at peace if man is drawn out of himself and saved from the self-defeating consequences of self-love."[63]

Unfortunately, this kind of prophetic fervor has been declining since the 1970s in the religions of Nigeria. Religious life in the country, to the extent that we can speak of it, is now marked more by "sentimental self-flagellation" than by "substantive social consciousness." This is so because, like so much of the nation's life, "it suffers from social amnesia," a disease that "prevents systemic social analysis of power, wealth, and influence in society from taking hold" among the people.[64]

Contrary to popular expectations, the national ecumenical religious bodies mentioned above have failed to contribute to the shaping of national public life and to assist in the formation of a coherent moral framework within a pluralistic social order. They have not articulated a macromorality that is intelligible beyond their immediate religious provenances. Instead, they have succumbed to the ethos of politicizing religion that is pervasive in the entire nation.[65]

Surely, there are real differences among the various religious groups in Nigeria; however, it is reasonable to suppose that when these differences are seen from the perspective of dialogic politics, they do not appear entirely insurmountable. Cultural differences need not entail ethical irreconcilability. Thus, through a continuous interchange of ideas, religions in Nigeria could help to provide a new macromoral insight that is conducive to national interests and at the same time respectful of those specific religious identities that nourish the spirituality of their diverse members. This is a task that every religious community should feel impelled to undertake, and something like a "federated theological basis" is not particularly necessary to accomplish it. Muslims, Christians, and members of other religious bodies possess abundant theological-ethical resources that can help to illumine problems of value and choice in society.

Similarly, a religious takeover of the state is not required to mediate effectively this ethical meaning to the society. As I have shown through the "indirect-effect" theories of Ibn Khaldūn and Murray, religious impact is most effective and responsible, especially in a pluralistic context, when the different religions limit themselves to influencing the spirit and the ethos, the moral sensitivities, and the value systems of the national community as well as preparing their members spiritually and socially for responsible public service.

Within Islam, Christianity, and the indigenous religions, "there are liberative streams, revolutionary urges, and prophetic voices."[66] An apt example is the Yoruba religion, which, according to Akinsola Akiwowo, is not a codified system of beliefs but a way of life. The central ethical norm in this faith-tradition is "the Orunmilaist perspective," grounded in humanist philosophy, according to which human beings are understood as carriers of spiritual values. Notable among the values that human beings are expected to facilitate and actualize in their societies include "knowledge that is complete, and a state of happiness that never diminishes. A state of harmonious existence in which man has overcome all his fears, such as fears of the hostility of enemies or of the attacks of snakes or other ferocious beasts. A state of existence in which there are no fears of death, illness, losses, court cases, witches, wizards, or Esu; a state of existence in which all fears of want and poverty are nil."[67]

Similarly, the two monotheistic religions stand at a point in history when they must genuinely affirm the relevance of faith in "a God who both supports and transcends the community of faith and its self-understanding."[68] The cosmic character of God as understood in these traditions should serve as a theological-ethical impetus for their adherents in Nigeria to encourage the emergence of "those types of public spaces in which individuals can come together and debate; can encounter each other in the formation, clarification, and testing of opinions; where judgment, deliberation, and *phronesis* can flourish; where individuals become aware of the creative power that springs up among them; where there is a tangible experience of overcoming the privatization, subjectivization, and the narcissistic tendencies so pervasive in our daily lives."[69]

The contributions of the various religious groups to, and their participation in, public dialogue must however be imbued with the theological virtue of religious humility. Their involvement must be viewed "less as a voice of expertise and more . . . as one human voice among others," directed to the very public in which their own lives are involved.[70] They should regard themselves as participants in a drama that involves numerous other actors, and realize that neither the Christian *ecclesia* nor the Muslim *umma* is the director of this drama, but God— "the God who created the worlds of politics, law, science, economics, and culture just as surely as God created the [religious communities] and gave [them] a mission."[71] Inasmuch as Muslims and Christians may see the "free expression clause" in the federal constitution as an opportunity to make a public difference, they ought also to see the nonadoption of religion clause as an occasion for responsibility. This responsibility includes, inter alia, developing a new vocabulary of communication that could facilitate "the complementarity of religious fidelity and public civility."[72]

While each religious discussant might enter public debate on his or her theological terms, there should be a simultaneous recognition of the fact that the source of the social bond and fabric cannot be located in the tenets of any particular religious tradition, for God's presence and God's truth are not exclusively confined to any single religion and its institutions. Because dialogic politics takes historical consciousness seriously, it stipulates that no one of pluralism's many goods ought to be absolutized or allowed to dominate others; rather, "the place of each must be recognized and respected in the framework of social existence."[73] Accordingly, efforts to shape public affairs that have not been tested by the rigors of intelligent public argument that presupposes the good will of one's neighbors risk degenerating into ideology and self-deception.

It is mistaken to claim that cultures and religions are ultimately incommensurable, for among the forced options in our contemporary world that cannot be ignored without incurring even greater harm or dangers are interreligious conversations. Paul Knitter submits:

> To believe that we are all ultimately trapped within our own cultural-religious confines with at the most the ability to shout across our borders but never to really engage in conversation, can lead to a type of cultural solipsism in which one is protected from criticisms and suspicions of others; or it can bring one to a new form of fidelism by which one has no grounds to criticize one's own cultural-linguistic system, or to a potential ethical toothlessness brought about by the lack of any basis on which to validly and coherently resist what appears to be intolerable in other cultural-linguistic systems.[74]

The practical import of the argument being offered here is that a particular religious community can often not attain its political goal. An integral part of dialogic politics is what Robin W. Lovin describes as "mutual help in material in need and mutual criticism in moral terms."[75] A particular proposal may be scrutinized, and perhaps rejected, if the strategies adopted for its mediation or its aims (or both) are found to be unsuitable to the common good. But this kind of criticism does not mean a disdain for the integrity of that religion's vision of life and the depth of its adherents' commitment.

One dimension of the religious pluralist dilemma in Nigeria is how to justify the official recognition of certain aspects of religious requirements, (e.g., the place of Islamic *sharī‘a* in the country's judicial system. While the Muslims remain intransigent in their affirmation of the superiority of the *sharī‘a* to the system of common law, the Christians are also unyielding in their objection to establishing a religious law. One promising way of redefining this problem in a way that may please both sides is the approach proposed by the late Ustadh Mahmoud Mohamed Taha of Sudan.

Adopting a hermeneutical method that is congruent with the definition of *historical consciousness* offered in chapter 2, he explained that there are two overlapping messages in Islam: "an eternal and universal one of complete justice and equality for all human beings without distinction as to race, creed, or gender, and a transitional message of relative justice among believers in terms of the quality of their belief."[76] Mahmoud proceeded from this basic premise to declare the *sharī‘a* as the transitional message, "which by now has served its purpose . . . [and] must be superseded by the eternal and universal message, the practical implementation of which has, thus far, been precluded by the realities of human existence."[77] In a tone reminiscent of Ibn Khaldūn, Mahmoud argued that "whereas the public law of *sharī‘a* was appropriate for the previous stages of human society, it is no longer appropriate and must make way for another version of the public law of Islam."[78]

In his reflection upon the approach of Mahmoud (who was unfortunately executed by the Sudanese government of Nimeiri for holding a heretical view), Abdullahi A. An-Naʾim, himself a Sudanese Muslim and an internationally renowned legal scholar, saw it as "a viable Islamic alternative."[79] On the one hand, it does not dismiss the public relevance of Islam as a religion, and at the same time it "confront[s] the proponents of *sharīʿa* with the inadequacy of their model because it will never permit national integration, which is the essential prerequisite for political stability, national security, and social economic development."[80]

Although Nigeria and Sudan may be radically dissimilar in the way that power is distributed among the key ethnic groups, they are comparable in a number of other ways. They are both multiethnic and multireligious, and in both countries there is a strong advocacy for the establishment of religion as a state religion. It was suggested in the previous chapter that the current official policy on the place of the *sharīʿa* in the Nigerian constitution be construed as a compromise solution that avoids the two extreme positions represented by Christian and Muslim advocates. Both sides would need to become agents of mature dialogue by subordinating their narrow interests to the civil well-being of all.

It is a fact that both Islam and Christianity emphasize the finitude of human knowledge through their different doctrines of sin, and that fact should serve as a major corrective of the distortions of judgment to which all humans are prone. The doctrine provides a credible moral basis for holding suspect "any notion that in a pluralistic society just one religion has the only answer to all the problems of human life at all times, for all peoples, and in all cultures." Plurality of religions, Samartha argues further, "introduces an element of choice when faced with the profound perplexities of life to which people respond differently in different cultures. Alternative visions of life offer different possibilities of meaning and direction to human life. Moreover, in a pluralistic situation the possibilities of mutual criticism and mutual enrichment are greater than in a monoreligious situation."[81]

Whether or not any of these possibilities will occur will depend on two contingencies. First, it will depend on whether the state will be alert to its duty and responsibility by providing creative space for dialogue in order that a climate of profound tolerance might grow in the life of the nation. No matter how genuine the intentions of people of various persuasions may be, without an appropriate political context (such as rigorous adherence to constitutional protections) that encourages intercommunal cooperation, such efforts will surely be impeded and frustrated. Military dictatorship, civilian-bureaucratic autocrats, and some greedy religious leaders still constitute an ominous reality in Nigeria. Therefore every effort must be made to debunk the myth underpinning the perpetuation of these dynastic demagogues.

The second condition on which the realization of dialogic politics in Nigeria would depend is the tenacity and credibility of religiously inspired moral vision. Given the historical contributions of Islam and Christianity to Nigerian civilization, one hopes that their adherents will be courageous enough to correct the popular misconception that morality is merely a personal matter, and that the development of public policy is a purely secular or political endeavor, or merely economic or technological in scope. Thus, quite apart from their common monotheistic provenance, Muslims and Christians also have a common task to remind society that there are important moral and religious dimensions to each of the problems facing the country, and that those dimensions be taken into consideration in the development of public policy.

The contemporary Nigerian realities, as accurately described by Segun Gbadegesin, are manifested at three distinct levels of

social existence—economic, social, and political. At the economic level, there are "poverty and hunger, low productivity in
the midst of wealth and natural abundance, and economic exploitation of individuals and nations."[82] On the social plane is
found "a cabal of hardened criminals."[83] The political level does
not fare better. Political violence, election rigging, and political
intolerance are rules rather than exceptions in Nigeria. In
Gbadegesin's words, "'democratically' elected leaders detest opposition while dictators hate criticisms. Leaders seem now to be
the only patriots as critics are declared saboteurs and are liable
to indefinite incarceration." A clear proof of this situation was
the promulgation of a decree, signed into law on 4 May 1993, by
the Babangida government according to which "a person who
levies a war against Nigeria in order to intimidate or overawe
the president and commander-in-chief of the armed forces or
the governor of a state is guilty of treason and liable on conviction to the death sentence."[84]

From the religious ethical standpoint, these realities reflect
"a spiritual crisis [which is] located at the heart of the temporal order."[85] They are symptoms of what Cornel West characterizes as "an existential emptiness" that religion cannot and
should not ignore.[86] In contrast to accommodationist forms of
religion, which usually aid and abet the socioeconomic and
structural-political conditions that produce this existential absurdity, a prophetic-critical religious spirituality "highlights
systemic social analysis under which tragic persons struggle."[87]
By critically retrieving the prophetic potential of their respective religions, Nigerian communities of faith could provide
moral leadership in the common bid to uproot the underlying
causes of the country's present problems. Muslims, Christians,
and traditionalists can all prove to be religiously productive
and socially relevant if they attempt "to project a vision and
inspire a praxis which fundamentally transforms the prevailing status quo in light of the best of [their traditions] and the

flawed yet significant achievements of the present order."[88] Concrete areas of society's life in which the moral resources of these religions can be registered include education and other social-welfare services.

Religions and Social-Welfare Services in Nigeria

Several studies have shown the important role of religious institutions in the fields of health and education in Nigeria.[89] To be sure, schools and hospitals were initially used by their proprietors for proselytizing and missionary purposes.[90] But they also provided at least a modicum of spiritual and symbolic cohesion for the social order. In precolonial northern Nigeria, for instance, the dominant Qur'anic education "underpinned and legitimated the Islamic state system established at the time of the Muslim reform movement at the beginning of the nineteenth century." It was also "the main supplier of clerks, administrators, advisers, physicians, judges and scribes."[91]

In chapter 3 I highlighted the civilizing and economic fruits of the Christian missions' schools, as well as the attendant disparity in the developmental pace between the southern and northern regions of the country. The colonial amalgamation of several nationalities into one country, the differential geographical distribution of religious patterns in the country, and the divergent philosophies of education held by Christians and Muslims introduced an element of competition, rivalry, and mutual accusation into the social-welfare activities of voluntary religious bodies in the country. This situation, plus the increasing assumption of the Nigerian state as "a distributor of resources,"[92] led to the government takeover of hospitals and schools established by religious institutions in 1977, an action regarded by the late E. Bolaji Idowu, patriarch of the Methodist Church of Nigeria, as a signal indication of "the weakness of the Church in Nigeria." He warned that the action would have detrimental effects on the country in the long run as it involves, in certain areas, "a wanton destruction of history and therefore an attack on our cultural roots." Citing C. S. Lewis with approval, Idowu feared that education that is divorced from religion would produce "'men without chests': that is, men [and women] who have their heads garnished with intellectual matters but are totally drained of moral and spiritual emotions."[93] Like Idowu, many other knowledgeable observers expressed concern about the grave dangers with which the idea was fraught from its inception insofar as it implied, in effect, the transfer of the management of schools to the Ministries of Education at the district, state, and federal levels.[94] These "Government ministries," according to Justice Esin, "are not ideal places for the day-to-day management of schools. They are too remote, too unwieldy, and too addicted to sluggish administrative routines and procedures."[95] But the government justified its action on the grounds that many in the population were already expressing displeasure with the existing system, which allowed private agencies to maintain control of the schools when the state provided most of the funds.

Unfortunately, albeit expected, the statist, centralized, and controlled nature of the Nigerian economy hampered the ability of religious institutions to defy the government order, as many of them lacked the financial resources with which to remain competitive in the provision of educational and health services.[96] The only exceptions were the Catholic and Baptist churches, both of whom were able to work out an agreement with the government to retain some forms of ecclesial influence in their respective hospitals; the other churches virtually acquiesced to the government directives, especially on health matters.[97] The result has been a total collapse of the country's health care system, a situation so deplorable that it became, though ironically, the justifying reason for the military ouster of the civilian government on 31 December 1983. In his address to the nation shortly after the coup, Babangida expressed the obvious truth: that the conditions of the nation's hospitals were worse than conditions in consulting clinics, and he promised that the military would speedily rectify this situation. Regrettably, however, these conditions have hardly improved since then.

While it may be difficult for most of the religious institutions in the country to run their hospitals if the government now decides to return them, given the current harsh economic realities facing the country, the nation can still benefit immensely from a reconsidered policy that allows the participation of religious institutions in the supervision of these hospitals. At a practical level, religious representatives can serve on several committees (e.g., ethics committees) having responsibility to deliberate about ways in which the quality of health care systems can be improved. The quandaries of health, death, and survival are issues that ought not to be limited to either the state managers or the medical and nursing professionals. Because of the concern of religion for whole persons and their larger cultural circumstances, issues that seem trivial to the profit-oriented and career-conscious professionals may be cast in deeper existential light by religious ethics. Allocation of resources to the hospitals, the work ethic of the health delivery professionals, access of the poor and the disadvantaged to adequate health care, and the content of the medical and nursing schools' curricula are issues that can be greatly enriched by religious perspectives.

Likewise, the disarray that now marks Nigerian institutions of learning may not be unconnected with lack of clarity in official policy on education and the ostracization of religious-moral values in schools.[98] As I will argue below, the way in which the religious authorities have reacted to the issue of education and religion has aided the perpetuation of a moral stalemate on the most important and vital organ of the nation's life. The frequency with which normal learning processes are being interrupted in Nigeria is a clear evidence of the deterioration in the quality of the nation's educational system.

The constitutional provision permitting "religious instruction" in schools hides more than it says. For instance, section 37, subsections 2 and 3, of the federal constitution of 1989 stipulates that "no person attending any place of education shall be required to receive religious instruction . . . if such instruction . . . relates to a religion other than his own, or a religion not approved by his parent or guardian; [and that] no religious community or denomination shall be prevented from providing instruction for pupils of that community or denomination in any place of education maintained wholly by that community or denomination." The ambiguity of this provision revolves around the definition of "religious instruction." According to the Draft Constitution of 1979, religious instruction means "instruction relating to the advancement of the practice of any religion but does not include the teaching of religious studies or of religion as a discipline."[99]

From that definition, it can be inferred that religious instruction is limited to the seminary and Qur'anic education or Sunday school classes. One would expect this kind of religious instruction as a logical consequence of religious freedom in general, which is also provided for in the constitution. Despite this apparent circumscribed permission of religious instruction in the constitution, virtually every Nigerian university has a department of religious studies, and Christian or Islamic knowledge (or both) are taught in primary and secondary schools across the nation. The majority of those who teach these subjects have degrees either in religious studies or in the theological sciences of Islam or Christianity. Therefore, the fears of most religious leaders that the government takeover of schools would lead to the eradication of religious sciences in schools appear unfounded.

What has been lacking so far in the "religion and education" debate is a clear definition of what the goals of education should be, and how religion can best assist in achieving them. It is also important to examine the prospects and the integrative potential of the public school system in a religiously pluralistic society. Contributions from the religious authorities have been marked by blatant rhetoric and morally arid concerns for retaining the symbolic vestiges of religious institutions—such as giving religious names to schools, swelling the number of confessional teachers in the schools, prayers at school, and so forth.[100] Although these are by no means irrelevant issues, they are subordinate to the larger question of how religions in Nigeria might contribute to the achievement of *paideia* in the country's institutions of learning.

Against the backdrop of the idea of political life developed in this book, it is further submitted that through "a close cooperation and a continuous dialogue among the various religious groups and sects"[101] in the country, religious visions can contribute to "a kind of formation that involves not only schooling but also those patterns of social life that build character and inculcate virtue."[102] The most important task in Nigeria at this juncture of its history is how to mine both "national and religious histories and to search the practices of contemporary communities for elements of the paideia that is required to form new visions of the commonweal, those 'collective convictions about the shape of things to come' that can 'unleash incredible strength.'"[103]

It is vitally important for the adherents and authorities of each religion in the country to articulate their role and objectives in a pluralistic setting. The quest for the kind of education that is oriented to public values, to those purposes that a community or society holds in common, may require an internal critique or renewal within every religious body. This intrareligious pedagogic metanoia may take the forms of theological reorientation, reform of religious education of the younger generation, drastic revision of syllabi for the study of religions in Qur'anic schools, theological colleges, and seminaries, and developing links with other religious communities, so that all religions may make genuine contributions to the value basis of the nation and the growth of public morality.

When this creative and critical perspective is extended to the larger society, education, whether in religious or in liberal or scientific subjects, ceases to be merely a means to becoming a good Muslim or Christian, scientist or engineer, but one that also assists a person to cultivate "the civic self—the art of acting in concert with others for the common good."[104] As Nigerians search for how to forge a consensus about how they should live together, they must also devise the means by which such a consensus, if and when found, can be continually tested and reformed. Religious institutions which occupy an important place at the baseline of society cannot and should not be left out or behind in this critical and innovative search. Writing about another society, Wesley Ariarajah suggested that perhaps

> the time has come to "institutionalize" the reconciling potential of religion as well. Inter-religious councils, multi-religious fellowships of religious leaders, peace education, studies in peaceful methods of conflict-resolution, education for justice and peace, exposure to each other's prayer and spiritual practices, etc., may have to be the new "institutions" that supplement the institutions that brought education, healing and service to communities. Peace does not come about by wishing it; we have to be peace-makers. One has to work for and build peace, and strive to preserve it.[105]

All of this does not imply that religious groups are always going to be able to agree on all issues perceived to be in the interest of everybody. Conflict of views is a fact that history will not let us deny. Even if Muslims, Christians, and other religionists are able to agree on the importance of making a genuinely public difference by refusing to permit a secularist domestication of their religions, they may still disagree on the mode and the extent to which religion should shape public policy. For instance, there is a substantial agreement between the Christians and the so-called secularists that juridical questions are distinguishable from those of religious morality. In contrast, Muslims see religion, law, and ethics as "extensively intertwined in a common Sharīʿa or Sharʿ, 'the road leading to water' (or the source of life)."[106]

These perspectival differences between the adherents of the two leading religions in particular will affect the ways in which many domestic and foreign policy issues are resolved. To what extent, for example, should religious considerations be allowed to define the content of public education? How can the state achieve a coherent and effective foreign policy when there are some confessionalists who see their loyalty in transnational terms? Should the government continue to be actively involved in the pilgrimage affairs at the expense of other nonreligious taxpayers? These are sample questions that illustrate the enormity of the strains involved in handling interreligious affairs in the country.

Besides these practical difficulties, there is the more poignant ethical problem associated with what Niebuhr calls the sin of pride, to which all human beings and groups are prone. All humans "are persistently inclined," he argues, "to regard themselves more highly and are more assiduously concerned with their own interests than any 'objective' view of their importance would warrant."[107] These prideful illusions are stronger in the religious realm than in other spheres of life. Religious intolerance persists in the country, not because there are too many religious virtuosos but precisely because religious contestants hide their more particular mundane interests behind religious absolutes. This moral-anthropological fact is pregnant with trouble, especially in the absence of a public consensus by which to "harness, equilibrate and deflect, as well as sublimate and suppress, self-interest."[108] Thus, despite the attractiveness of the ideals of dialogic politics, many forces are arrayed against the prospects of its fruition, not only in Nigeria, but in other culturally fragmented societies as well.

Another impediment standing in the way of forging a common political ground in Nigeria is the unstable and unpredictable nature of what I have referred to as the "contextual or situational requirements" of dialogic politics. Quite apart from the hegemonic pretensions of the state which have been discussed extensively, there is also the factor of real or perceived inequity in the manner in which socioeconomic benefits are distributed in the country. The politicization of communal ties will continue unabated, and the prospects of forging a political bond frustrated, as long as some regions, or some ethnic communities, or some members of religious groups continue to be treated as second-class citizens in the country.[109] When people perceive a real threat to their continued survival, asking them to engage in a dialogue of any sort might sound like a dispensable luxury.

There are thus theological, ethical, economic, and political difficulties besetting the prospects of political advancement in Nigeria. Despite these monumental problems, dialogic politics offers one promising way of achieving peaceful conflict resolution, political tolerance, and cultural negotiation in the country. One step toward the amelioration of these obstructive factors is to acknowledge that they do exist. Only then can people learn to substitute fear and paranoia for hope and trust, both in their patterns of sociation and in the destiny of the nation. Murray's advice, given about three decades ago, is still relevant to the situation of many religiously pluralistic societies that genuinely aspire to forge a common political, as opposed to doctrinal, ground among themselves. He urged any such society to be wary about "project[ing] into the future of the Republic the nightmares, real or fancied, of the past."[110]

Notes

1. J. A. Atanda, "Paradoxes and Problems of Religion and Secularism in Nigeria: Suggestions for Solutions," in *Nigeria since Independence: The First Twenty-Five Years*, vol. 9, *Religion*, ed. J. A. Atanda, Garba Ashiwaju, and Yaya Abubakar (Ibadan: Heinemann, 1989), 189.

2. Reinhold Niebuhr, *The Nature and Destiny of Man*, vol. 2, Human Destiny (New York: Scribner's, 1943), 219. The italics are mine.

3. See, for instance, Akinsola Akiwowo, *Ajobi and Ajogbe: Variations on the Theme of Sociation*, Inaugural Lecture Series, no. 46 (Ile-Ife, Nigeria: University of Ife Press, 1983); John S. Mbiti, *African Religions and Philosophy* (London: Heinemann, 1969).

4. William R. Luckey, "The Contribution of John Courtney Murray, S.J.: A Catholic Perspective," in *John Courtney Murray and the American Civil Conversation*, ed. Robert P. Hunt and Kenneth L. Grasso (Grand Rapids, Mich.: Eerdmans, 1992), 37.

5. Peter B. Clarke, *West Africa and Christianity: A Study of Religious Development from the 15th to the 20th Century* (London: Edward Arnold, 1986), 227–43;Olupona, "Religion, Law and Order," 127–35; idem, "New Religious Movements and the Nigerian Social Order," in *New Religious Movements and Society in Nigeria*, ed. Gudrun Ludwar-Ene, Bayreuth African Studies Series, no. 17 (Bayreuth: Eckhard Breitinger, 1991), 31–52.

6. Murtala Ramat Muhammed, "What Role for the Church?" (Goodwill message delivered to the National Episcopal Conference of Nigeria, Onitsha, 9–14 September 1975), eventually published in *Survey of Nigerian Affairs 1975*, ed. O. Oyediran (Ibadan: Oxford University Press, 1980), 151.

7. Diamond, "Nigeria," 56.

8. Perry, "Neutral Politics," in *Love and Power,* 8–28.

9. Robin W. Lovin, "Social Contract or a Public Covenant?," in *Religion and American Public Life: Interpretations and Explorations,* ed. Robin W. Lovin (New York: Paulist Press, 1986), 133.

10. Robert Audi, "The Separation of Church and State and the Obligations of Citizenship," *Philosophy and Public Affairs* 18, 3 (1989): 259–96.

11. Murray, *We Hold These Truths,* 10.

12. Thomas M. Callaghy, "Politics and Vision in Africa: The Interplay of Domination, Equality and Liberty," in *Political Domination in Africa: Reflections on the Limits of Power,* ed. Patrick Chabal (Cambridge: Cambridge University Press, 1986), 32.

13. Sturm, *Community and Alienation,* 23, 22.

14. Gbadegesin, *African Philosophy,* 141.

15. Murray, *We Hold These Truths,* 124.

16. Larry Diamond, "Beyond Autocracy: Prospects for Democracy in Nigeria," in *Beyond Autocracy in Africa,* working paper, inaugural seminar of the Governance in Africa Program, Carter Center of Emory University, Atlanta, 17–18 February 1989, 26.

17. Sturm, *Community and Alienation,* 26–27.

18. Max L. Stackhouse, "Public Theology and the Future of Democratic Society," in *The Church's Public Role: Retrospect and Prospect,* ed. Dieter T. Hessel (Grand Rapids, Mich.: Eerdmans, 1993), 74.

19. Lovin, "Social Contract or a Public Covenant?" 135.

20. Okey Ekeocha, "The Crisis of Federalism," *African Guardian,* 13 April 1992, 25.

21. Mooney, *Boundaries Dimly Perceived,* x.

22. Lovin, "Social Contract or a Public Covenant?" 141.

23. Ibid.

24. Cited in Perry, *Love and Power,* 2.

25. Ibid.

26. William A. Galston, "Pluralism and Social Unity," *Ethics 99,* 4 (July 1989), 711.

27. Crawford Young, "Beyond Patrimonial Autocracy: The African Challenge," in *Beyond Autocracy in Africa,* working paper, in-

augural seminar of the Governance in Africa Program Carter Center of Emory University, Atlanta, 17-18 February 1989, 22.

28. Francis Deng, "A Three-Dimensional Approach to the Conflict in the Sudan," in *Religion and National Integration in Africa: Islam, Christianity, and Politics in the Sudan and Nigeria,* ed. John O. Hunwick (Evanston, Ill.: Northwestern University Press, 1992), 43.

29. Mooney, *Boundaries Dimly Perceived,* xii.

30. Perry, *Love and Power,* 43.

31. Ibid., 77.

32. Ibid., 2.

33. Berger, *Far Glory,* 43.

34. Atanda, "Religion and Secularism in Nigeria" (1989), 188-89.

35. Reinhold Niebuhr, *The Irony of American History* (New York: Scribner's, 1952), 139.

36. James O'Connell, "Nigeria," in *Religion in Politics: A World Guide,* ed. Stuart Mews (Essex: Longman, 1989), 196.

37. O. A. Olukunle, "The Impact of Religion on Nigerian Society: The Future Perspective" (paper presented at the 25th annual Religious Studies Conference, Ibadan, 17-20 September 1991), 2.

38. Edema, *Christians and Politics in Nigeria,* vii.

39. Peter L. Berger and Richard John Neuhaus, *To Empower People: The Role of Mediating Structures in Public Policy* (Washington, D.C.: American Enterprise Institute for Public Policy Research, 1977), 2.

40. Ibid.

41. Ibid.

42. Franklin I. Gamwell, *Beyond Preference: Liberal Theories of Independent Associations* (Chicago: University of Chicago Press, 1984), 5.

43. James Luther Adams, "Mediating Structures and the Separation of Powers," in *Democracy and Mediating Structures: A Theological Inquiry,* ed. Michael Novak (Washington, D.C.: American Enterprise Institute for Public Policy Research, 1980), 2.

44. Ibid., 3.

45. Ibid., 4.

46. Berger and Neuhaus, *To Empower People*, 2.

47. Cited in Max L. Stackhouse, "Religion, Society, and the Independent Sector: Key Elements of a General Theory," in *Religion, the Independent Sector, and American Culture,* ed., Conrad Cherry and Rowland A. Sherrill (Atlanta: Scholars Press, 1992), 12.

48. Michael Bratton, "Enabling the Voluntary Sector in Africa: The Policy Context," in *African Governance in the 1990s: Objectives, Resources and Constraints,* working paper, 2d annual seminar of the African Governance Program, Carter Center of Emory University, Atlanta, 23-25 March 1990, 105.

49. Antonio Gramsci's *Opera* were published in Turin in six volumes between 1947 and 1954, although many of them were written in jail under the Fascists, in the 1930s and 40s. Translations of his *Modern Prince* was published in London, and of his *Open Marxism* in New York in 1957. The term *sectors* does not appear as an analytical category in the dictionaries and encyclopedias of the social sciences before that time.

50. Dieter T. Hessel, "Making a Public Difference after the Eclipse," in *The Church's Public Role: Retrospect and Prospect,* ed. Dieter T. Hessel (Grand Rapids, Mich.: Eerdmans, 1993), 3.

51. Before the recent upsurge of Africanists' interest in this process, the idea was first introduced in the early 1960s by Immanuel Wallerstein in "Voluntary Associations," in *Political Parties and National Integration in Tropical Africa,* ed. James S. Coleman and Carl G. Rosberg (Berkeley: University of California Press, 1964), 318-39. One of the most articulate contemporary exponents of the concept in the field of African studies is Jean-François Bayart. Some of the working papers delivered at the seminars of the African Governance Program have similarly espoused the idea of mediating structures.

52. *Perestroika without Glasnost in Africa,* 7. The views were attributed to Michael Bratton.

53. Bratton, "Enabling the Voluntary Sector," 104.

54. Hessel, "Public Difference after the Eclipse," 6.

55. J. Bryan Hehir, "The Catholic Bishops and the Nuclear Debate: A Case Study of the Independent Sector," in *Religion, The Independent Sector, and American Culture,* ed. Conrad Cherry and Rowland A. Sherrill (Atlanta: Scholars Press, 1992), 98-112.

56. C. O. Oshun, "Ecumenism: An Approach to Peaceful Co-Existence," in *Religion, Peace, and Unity in Nigeria,* ed. Sam Babs Mala and Z. I. Oseni (Ibadan: Nigerian Association for the Study of Religions, 1984), 121.

57. A. O. Makozi and O. J. A. Ojo, eds., *History of the Roman Catholic Church in Nigeria* (Ibadan: Macmillan, 1982), 93.

58. For the complete list, see *Constitution of the Nigerian Supreme Council for Islamic Affairs* (Kano: Rasco Press, n.d.), 2-3. The constitution was adopted on 24 September 1985.

59. See, for instance, M. M. Familusi, *Methodism in Nigeria, 1842–1992* (Ibadan: NPS Educational Publishers, 1992), 68-87; M. Y. Nabofa, "Christianity in Nigeria: Its Role in Nati n- uilding," in *Nigeria since Independence: The First Twenty-Five Years,* vol. IX, *Religion,* ed. J. A. Atanda, Garba Ashiwaju, and Yaya Abubakar (Ibadan: Heinemann, 1989), 104-6; Walls, "Religion and the Press in 'the Enclave,'" 207-15.

60. Christian Council of Nigeria, *Justice and Peace* (Ibadan: Daystar Press, 1971), 6.

61. Ibid.

62. This debate finds its locus classicus in Philippa Foot, *Virtues and Vices and Other Essays in Moral Philosophy* (Berkeley: University of California Press, 1978); G. E. Moore, *Principia Ethica* (1902; reprint, Buffalo: Prometheus Books, 1988); C. L. Stevenson, *Facts and Values: Studies in Ethical Analysis* (New Haven: Yale University Press, 1963).

63. Niebuhr, *Christian Realism and Political Problems,* 129-30.

64. West, *Prophetic Fragments,* x.

65. Clarke, "Religion and Political Attitude," 224.

66. S. J. Samartha, One Christ, Many Religions: Toward a Revised Christology (Maryknoll, N.Y.: Orbis Books, 1991), 56.

67. Translation: "Amotan ohun gbogbo, ayo nigba gbogbo, wiwa laisi eru, tabi ominu ota, ija ejo, tabi eranko buburu miran, laisi iberu iku, arun, ejo, ofo, oso, aje, tabi esu, Laisi eru ifarapa, omi, ina, ewe-oro tabi iwo, laisi iberu aini tabi osi." Esu is a Yoruba god with both good and evil qualities. All Yoruba believe it is important to sacrifice to him. See Akiwowo, *Ajobi and Ajogbe,* 11-12.

68. Lovin, "Religion and American Public Life," 21.

69. Richard J. Bernstein, "The Meaning of Public Life," in *Reli-*

gion and American Public Life: Interpretations and Explorations, ed. Robin W. Lovin (New York: Paulist Press, 1986), 46.

70. Conrad Cherry and Rowland A. Sherrill, introduction to *Religion, The Independent Sector, and American Culture*, ed. Conrad Cherry and Rowland Sherrill (Atlanta: Scholars Press, 1992), 6.

71. Hollenbach, *Justice, Peace, and Human Rights*, 13.

72. Ibid., 14.

73. Mooney, *Boundaries Dimly Perceived*, 26.

74. Paul F. Knitter, "Common Ground or Common Response? Seeking Foundations for Interreligious Discourse," *Studies in Interreligious Dialogue* 2, 2 (1992): 114.

75. Lovin, "Social Contract or a Public Covenant?" 135.

76. Abdullahi Ahmed An-Na'im, "Islam and National Integration in the Sudan," in *Religion and National Integration in Africa: Islam, Christianity, and Politics in the Sudan and Nigeria*, ed. John O. Hunwick (Evanston, Ill.: Northwestern University Press, 1992), 32.

77. Ibid.

78. Ibid., 33.

79. Ibid.

80. Ibid., 33-34.

81. Samartha, *One Christ, Many Religions*, 47.

82. Gbadegesin, *African Philosophy*, 138

83. Ibid., 140.

84. *Newswatch*, 24 May 1993, 14.

85. Murray, *Pattern for Peace*, 11.

86. West, *Prophetic Fragments*, ix.

87. Ibid., x.

88. Ibid., xi.

89. For a comprehensive list of the relevant literature, see Gerrie ter Haar, "Religious Education in Africa: Traditional, Islamic, and Christian," *Exchange XVII*, 17, 50 (September 1988), 7-86.

90. Sanneh, *West African Christianity*, 127-67.

91. Peter B. Clarke, "The Religious Factor in the Developmental Process in Nigeria: A Socio-Historical Analysis," *Genève-Afrique* 17, 1 (1979): 51.

92. P. Brass, "Ethnic Groups and the State," in *Ethnic Groups and the State*, ed. P. Brass (Totowa, N.J.: Barnes and Noble, 1985), 29.

93. E. Bolaji Idowu, foreword to *Government Policy on Education at both the Federal and State Levels Has Left a Lot to Be Desired,* by Justice O. A. Esin (Lagos: Methodist Literature Department, 1980), 1, 2.

94. Federal Government of Nigeria, *National Policy on Education* (Lagos: Government Printers, 1977), sec. 2, nos. 86–87.

95. Esin, *Government Policy on Education,* 8.

96. E. Ikenga-Metuh, "Religious Education in State-Controlled Schools in Nigeria," in *Religion, Peace, and Unity in Nigeria,* ed. Sam Babs Mala and Z. I. Oseni (Ibadan: Nigerian Association for the Study of Religions, 1984), 136–52.

97. For problems of logistics within the Methodist Church, see Familusi, *Methodism in Nigeria.*

98. M. I. Mozia, "Religion and Morality in Nigeria: An Overview," in *Nigeria since Independence: The First Twenty-Five Years,* vol. 9, *Religion,* ed. J. A. Atanda, Garba Ashiwaju, and Yaya Abubakar (Ibadan: Heinemann, 1989), 172–73.

99. CDC, 1:22.

100. Peter B. Clarke and Ian Linden, *Islam in Modern Nigeria: A Study of a Muslim Community in a Post-Independence State 1960–1983* (Mainz: Grüneworld; Munich: Kaiser, 1984), 145–61.

101. Ikenga-Metuh, "Religious Education in State-Controlled Schools," 147.

102. Barbara G. Wheeler, "A Forum on Paideia," introduction to *Caring for the Commonweal: Education for Religious and Public Life,* ed. Parker J. Palmer, Barbara G. Wheeler, and James W. Fowler (Macon, Ga.: Mercer University Press, 1990), 2.

103. Ibid.

104. William F. May, "Public Happiness and Higher Education," in *Caring for the Commonweal: Education for Religious and Public Life,* ed. Parker J. Palmer, Barbara G. Wheeler, and James W. Fowler (Macon, Ga.: Mercer University Press, 1990), 244.

105. S. Wesley Ariarajah, *Current Dialogue* 3(1987): 3.

106. Carney, "Some Aspects of Islamic Ethics," 161.

107. Niebuhr, *Irony of American History,* 7.

108. Niebuhr, "Dark Light on Human Nature," 7.

109. Robert Melson and Howard Wolpe, "Modernization and the

Politics of Communalism: A Theoretical Perspective," in *Nigeria: Modernization and the Politics of Communalism,* ed. Robert Melson and Howard Wolpe (East Lansing: Michigan State University Press, 1971), 1–42.

110. Murray, *We Hold These Truths,* 34.

Conclusion

The relationship between religion and the state, even in a culturally homogenous context, is certainly a complicated one. Pluralism of theological and ideological confessions makes the situation more precarious by inducing religious practitioners to engage in competitive, and sometimes demonizing, strategies for the sole purpose of monopolizing the human and material perquisites of faith-based enterprises. In a socially and politically volatile context, religious plurality transforms neighbors and fellow citizens into potential and/or actual enemies; levels of mutual suspicion are constantly raised, rules of social intercourse become less predictable, and public debate is either nonexistent or dominated by cacophonous voices. My central aim in this work has been to show how to mitigate political conflicts occasioned by religious differences. Toward this end, I have raised two programmatic questions, the first having to do with the kind of political framework that would more fully encourage just relationships between the state and the different religious bodies. The second question focuses on the kind of political attitudes that would most encourage a sense of mutual acceptance within which the diverse religious allegiances can find both their freedom and their limits. It is my hope that these questions have been judiciously and charitably answered.

My explicit theoretical aim is to challenge the conceptual dichotomy between religion and secular life, or between private and public life. I accomplished this by drawing together the interests and approaches of various disciplines, thereby showing the need to transcend the climate of intellectual sectarianism that currently characterizes the study of religion and politics in

Nigeria. Religious studies scholars have largely concentrated on the ritual, missiological, and exotic manifestations of faith systems in the country, while political theorists and scientists continue to perpetuate the secularizing reductivism of viewing religion as archaic and anachronistic. The result is a double disjunction of elements that need to be interpreted in their interplay. Intellectual sectarianism, often a function of disciplinary boundaries or institutional biases, exists to the detriment of all groups. The nature of the present work requires that we find a new approach that diverges from the reigning methodological fad. Because I have zeroed in on "pluralism" as the thematic problem in the study, and proposed dialogic politics as both a desirable mode and goal of intergroup relations, it has become an obvious methodological necessity to use pluri-theoretical approach for charting the path toward the attainment of this goal. Substantively, the central thesis of the book is that in order for Nigeria's diverse religious population to establish and maintain a civil harmony, it is neither necessary to strip the state of religious values, nor to make it the guardian of holy shrines, but only to endow it with robust civility "that will allow citizens of all religious faiths, or none, to engage one another in continuing democratic discourse."[1]

Another implicit, yet far reaching, significance of this study is its global focus. Religious nationalism, culture wars, civil protests, and an ever-widening trend of national and international terrorism are samples of volatile events that are more likely to appear as headlines during the broadcast of world news than the more mundane such as childbirth or the economic growth index. Thus, many dimensions of the problem discussed in the book—such as identity, power, order, domination, freedom, justice, consensus, and conflict—are present in varying degrees in different parts of the world today. Seen in this light, the lessons learned in areas of religious conflict are at the same time lessons worth learning in relation to more stable situations where inequality, racism, sexism, and class division also abound, even though the political and economic infrastructures in these situations still hold. The discourse on religion and the state in Nigeria, given the demographic, ethnic, social, economic, and political contradictions within the country, constitutes an important global focus with implications well beyond its own borders. The issues involved have significance for the wider international community, at the center of which is the political and ethical imperative to balance civil unity with religious integrity. Thus, this is not a study of a problem peculiar to Nigeria; it is a critical engagement with a common crisis.

Tensions and conflict will always remain a part of any human society. Yet while conflict can be creative, as some people argue, endemic civil strife along the lines of cultural cleavage is surely not a path to either peace or prosperity. The test of civility is how conflicts are managed and contained in ways that do not rock the boat of the commonweal. Religious diversity in Nigeria can no longer be seen as a colonial slander. It is a sociological reality, an integral part of daily experience. Coming to terms with this fact, at all levels of society, rather than refusing it, is the first practical step to be taken in creating a civil environment. This is a task that requires the cooperation of the state and adherents of all religions in the country.

The government can encourage accommodationist behavior if it acts with an awareness of the implications of its decisions for communal relations and with the intention of promoting reconciliation among groups. It must always demonstrate the foresight to anticipate religious issues so as to be able to study and resolve them in advance. Politicians and administrators must go beyond being managers of the present to be more imaginative molders of the future. A democratic political system is more likely to bring forth such consummate political managers than a more authoritarian regime.

The present constitutional arrangement that separates the institutions of religion from those of the state must be considered an unbreachable contract by the state. I have argued throughout the book that this arrangement is not to be construed as requiring the abolition of religions in the state. Rather, it makes a minimalist prescription: that none of the religions should be made a state religion. Accordingly, no president or other highly placed functionaries of government may use their offices severally or jointly to overtly or covertly promote their individual religions at the expense of other religions.

Religious adherents and groups also need to make conscious attempts to cultivate a tolerant attitude towards each other, thereby helping to create and sustain a civil environment. Only when people are willing to tolerate each other's existence, the existence of their houses of worship, and the rights of every religious group to proselytize can they experience social peace and, perhaps, material progress as well. The importance of the habit of live and let live goes beyond the lure of moral prudence; it is a theological affirmation of God's presence in every being and every association organized in His name. To treat the issue of peace too cavalierly in relation to the mission of religious traditions is to strip peace of its moral credence. Especially in the Nigerian context, an atmosphere characterized by innumerable violent and repressive edicts, a civil, peace-seeking, and peace-loving religious citizenry is one sure defense, among many, against the tyrannical impulses of the state.

This of course does not mean that religious people must accept the impulse of public quiescence. As I have already explained, quiescence may take two forms, either private resignation or radical subjectivism. Both forms are potentially dangerous to the commonweal. When religious faith is public, it reaffirms the existence of ideals and standards that are independent of personal subjectivity, ideals and standards that are publicly known and must be publicly reckoned with. When totally personalized, privatized, and domesticated, religious faith cannot perform that critical function of being a guard against either political anarchy or political tyranny.

The radical subjectivists or pure secularists who claim that it is ultimately parasitic and uninteresting to talk about the issues of truth and the common good are equally mistaken. To argue that there is no meaning to life except that which the individual chooses to bestow upon it, that there is no justice except that which exists in the realization of particular individual interests, that virtue is entirely personal and perspectival, is to deny that there is a public realm to which we all belong.

Finally, we must acknowledge the painful fact that there is no single solution to the problem of the relation between religion and public life. Communities of faith in Nigeria must recognize that they cannot escape the inevitable ambiguity of the concreteness of their own life and that of the nation which belongs to all. Sentimental idealists must also learn how to temper zealous patriotism with a humble recognition that the achievement of national integration is a gradual process in which intergroup relations move along a continuum from continual conflict to more frequent cooperation. National integration cannot be attained once and for all; it requires constant dedication and watchfulness. Above all, it requires an enlightened civic consciousness. It requires the contributions, insights, and perspectives of different people and different universes of meaning. The probing diagnosis of the American pluralist dilemma made by Ronald F. Thiemann is appropriate for concluding this work:

> Our society desperately needs people who will bring a commitment to justice into the public sphere, people who have both the intelligence and the patience to bring together a vision of righteousness with the careful analysis of public policy. We have enough

prophets who fire their moral broadsides against the evils of our society; we have enough policy-makers who determine our future through efficiency studies and cost-effective analysis. What we lack are those who combine prophetic vision with careful analysis; and until we cultivate and nurture such persons, our public life will remain diffuse and spiritless.[2]

Notes

1. Perry, *Love and Power,* 45.
2. Thiemann, *Constructing a Public Theology,* 41–42.

Bibliography

A. Books

Abbott, Walter M., and Joseph Gallagher, eds. *The Documents of Vatican II*. New York: America Press, 1966.

Achebe, Chinua. *Things Fall Apart*. London: Heinemann, 1958.

Adams, Arlin M., and Charles J. Emmerich. *A Nation Dedicated to Religious Liberty: The Constitutional Heritage of the Religion Clauses*. Philadelphia: University of Pennsylvania Press, 1990.

Adeleye, R. A. *Power and Diplomacy in Northern Nigeria 1804–1906: The Sokoto Caliphate and Its Enemies*. New York: Humanities Press, 1971.

Adigwe, Hypolite. *Sharia, Canon, Common, and Customary Law Courts: Contributions to the Debates in the Constituent Assembly 1988, at Abuja*. Privately printed, 1988.

Agbaje, Adigun A. B. *The Nigerian Press, Hegemony, and the Social Construction of Legitimacy 1960–1983*. Lewiston, N.Y.: Edwin Mellen Press, 1992.

Ajayi, J. F. Ade. *Christian Missions in Nigeria, 1841–1891: The Making of a Modern Elite*. London: Longmans, 1965.

———. *The Problems of National Integration in Nigeria: A Historical Perspective*. Distinguished Lecture Series, no. 11. Ibadan: Nigerian Institute of Social and Economic Research, 1984.

Ajayi, J. F. Ade, and R. S. Smith. *Yoruba Warfare in the Nineteenth Century*. Cambridge: Cambridge University Press, 1964.

Akiwowo, Akinsola. *Ajobi and Ajogbe: Variations on the Theme of Sociation*. Inaugural Lecture Series, no. 46. Ile-Ife, Nigeria: University of Ife Press, 1983.

Almond, Gabriel A., and Sidney Verba. *The Civic Culture: Political Attitudes and Democracy in Five Nations, An Analytic Study.* Boston: Little, Brown, 1963.

Amucheazi, E. C. *Church and Politics in Eastern Nigeria, 1945–1966: A Study in Pressure Group Politics.* Lagos: Macmillan, 1986.

Awolowo, Obafemi. *Awo: The Autobiography of Chief Obafemi Awolowo.* Cambridge: Cambridge University Press, 1960.

———. *The People's Republic.* Ibadan: Oxford University Press, 1968.

Ayandele, E. A. *The Missionary Impact on Modern Nigeria, 1842–1914: A Political and Social Analysis.* London: Longmans, 1966.

———. *Nigerian Historical Studies.* London: Frank Cass, 1979.

Babangida, Ibrahim. *Quotes of a General: Selected Quotes of Major General Ibrahim Babangida.* Edited by Debo Basorun. Lagos: Terry, 1987.

Barth, Karl. *The Christian Life.* Grand Rapids, Mich.: Eerdmans, 1981.

Bellah, Robert N. *Beyond Belief: Essays on Religion in a Post-Traditional World.* New York: Harper and Row, 1970.

Bellah, Robert N., William M. Sullivan, Ann Swidler, and Steven M. Tipton, *Habits of the Heart: Individualism and Commitment in American Life.* Berkeley: University of California Press, 1985.

Benne, Robert. *The Ethic of Democratic Capitalism: A Moral Reassessment.* Philadelphia: Fortress Press, 1981.

Berger, Peter L. *A Far Glory: The Quest for Faith in an Age of Credulity.* New York: Free Press, 1992.

———. *The Sacred Canopy: Elements of a Sociological Theory of Religion.* Garden City, N.Y.: Doubleday, 1969.

Berger, Peter L., and Richard John Neuhaus. *To Empower People: The Role of Mediating Structures in Public Policy.* Washington, D.C.: American Enterprise Institute for Public Policy Research, 1977.

Brass, Paul, ed. *Ethnic Groups and the State.* Totowa, N.J.: Barnes and Noble, 1985.

Catholic Bishops of Nigeria. *Christian/Muslim Relations in Nigeria: The Stand of the Catholic Bishops.* Lagos: Catholic Secretariat, n.d.

Cherry, Conrad, and Rowland A. Sherill, eds. *Religion, the Independent Sector, and American Culture.* Atlanta: Scholars Press, 1992.

Christian Council of Nigeria. *Justice and Peace.* Speeches and reports presented at the 15th General Assembly of the Christian Council of Nigeria, 11–18 December 1970. Ibadan: Daystar Press, 1971.

Clarke, Peter B. *West Africa and Islam: A Study of Religious Development from the Eighth to the Twentieth Century.* London: Edward Arnold, 1982.

———. *West Africa and Christianity: A Study of Religious Development from the Fifteenth to the Twentieth Century.* London: Edward Arnold, 1986.

Clarke, Peter B., and Ian Linden. *Islam in Modern Nigeria: A Study of a Muslim Community in a Post-Independence State, 1960–1983.* Mainz: Grünewald; Munich: Kaiser, 1984.

Cohen, Abner. *Custom and Politics in Urban Africa: A Study of Hausa Migrants in Yoruba Towns.* Manchester: Manchester University Press, 1969.

———. *Two-Dimensional Man: An Essay on the Anthropology of Power and Symbolism in Complex Society.* London: Routledge and Kegan Paul, 1974.

Coleman, James S. *Nigeria: Background to Nationalism.* Berkeley: University of California Press, 1958.

Crampton, E. P. T. *Christianity in Northern Nigeria.* London: Geoffrey Chapman, 1979.

Crowder, Michael. *The Story of Nigeria.* 2d ed. London: Faber and Faber, 1966.

Cruise O'Brien, Donal B. *Saints and Politicians: Essays in the Organization of a Senegalese Peasant Society.* African Studies Series, no. 15. London: Cambridge University Press, 1975.

Cuddihy, John Murray. *No Offense: Civil Religion and Protestant Taste.* New York: Seabury Press, 1978.

————. *The Ordeal of Civility: Freud, Marx, Lévi-Strauss, and the Jewish Struggle with Modernity.* Boston: Beacon Press, 1987.

Curran, Charles E. *American Catholic Social Ethics: Twentieth-Century Approaches.* Notre Dame, Ind.: University of Notre Dame Press, 1982.

Dahl, Robert A. *Dilemmas of Pluralist Democracy: Autonomy vs. Control.* New Haven: Yale University Press, 1982.

————. *Modern Political Analysis.* Englewood Cliffs, N.J.: Prentice-Hall, 1963.

————. *A Preface to Democratic Theory.* Chicago: University of Chicago Press, 1956.

Davies, H. O. *Nigeria: Prospects for Democracy.* London: Weidenfeld and Nicolson, 1961.

Decalo, Samuel. *Coups and Army Rule in Africa: Studies in Military Style.* 2d ed. New Haven: Yale University Press, 1990.

Dignitatis Humanae. Washington, D.C.: National Catholic Welfare Conference, 1956.

Dudley, Billy. *Instability and Political Order: Politics and Crisis in Nigeria.* Ibadan: Ibadan University Press, 1973.

————. *An Introduction to Nigerian Government and Politics.* Bloomington: Indiana University Press, 1982.

————. *Parties and Politics in Northern Nigeria.* London: Frank Cass, 1968.

Durkheim, Emile. *The Elementary Forms of the Religious Life.* New York: Free Press, 1915.

Echewa, T. Obinkaram. *I Saw the Sky Catch Fire.* New York: Plume, 1993.

Edema, Adebanjo. *Christians and Politics in Nigeria.* Ibadan: Codat Publications, 1988.

Ekechi, F. K. *Missionary Enterprise and Rivalry in Igboland, 1857–1914.* Cass Library of African Studies. London: Frank Cass, 1972.

Ekeh, Peter. *Colonialism and Social Structure.* Inaugural Lecture Series. Ibadan: University of Ibadan Press, 1983.

Elder, Charles D., and Roger W. Cobb. *The Political Uses of Symbols.* New York: Longman, 1988.

Emory University, Governance in Africa Program. *Perestroika without Glasnost in Africa.* Conference Report Series, vol. 2, no. 1. Atlanta: The Carter Center of Emory University, 1989.

Enloe, Cynthia. *Ethnic Conflict and Political Development.* Boston: Little, Brown, 1973.

Esin, Justice O. A. *Government Policy on Education at Both the Federal and State Levels Has Left a Lot to Be Desired.* Lagos: Methodist Literature Department, 1980.

Eze, Osita C. *Human Rights in Africa: Some Selected Problems.* Lagos: Nigerian Institute of International Affairs, 1984.

Fadipe, N. A. *The Sociology of the Yoruba.* Ibadan: Ibadan University Press, 1970.

Fafunwa, A. Babs. *History of Education in Nigeria.* London: Allen and Unwin, 1974.

Familusi, M. M. *Methodism in Nigeria, 1842–1992.* Ibadan: NPS Educational Publishers, 1992.

Feinberg, Joel. *Social Philosophy.* Englewood Cliffs, N.J.: Prentice-Hall, 1973.

Figgis, J. N. *Churches in the Modern State.* London: Longmans, Green, 1913.

Finer, Samuel Edward. *Comparative Government.* Harmondsworth: Penguin Books, 1970.

First, Ruth. *The Barrel of a Gun: Political Power in Africa and the Coup d'Etat.* London: Allen Lane, 1970.

Foot, Philippa. *Virtues and Vices and Other Essays in Moral Philosophy.* Berkeley: University of California Press, 1978.

Freire, Paulo. *Pedagogy of the Oppressed.* New York: Continuum, 1988.

Furnivall, J. S. *Colonial Policy and Practice: A Comparative Study of Burma and Netherlands India.* Cambridge: Cambridge University Press, 1948.

Gamwell, Franklin I. *Beyond Preference: Liberal Theories of Independent Associations.* Chicago: University of Chicago Press, 1984.

Gbadamosi, T. G. O. *The Growth of Islam among the Yoruba, 1841–1908.* Ibadan History Series. Atlantic Highlands, N.J.: Humanities Press, 1978.

Gbadegesin, Segun. *African Philosophy: Traditional Yoruba Philosophy and Contemporary African Realities.* New York: Peter Lang, 1991.

————, ed. *The Politicization of Society during Nigeria's Second Republic, 1979–83.* Lewiston, N.Y.: Edwin Mellen Press, 1991.

Geertz, Clifford. *The Interpretation of Cultures: Selected Essays.* New York: Basic Books, 1973.

Graf, William D. *The Nigerian State: Political Economy, State Class, and Political System in the Post-Colonial Era.* London: James Currey, 1988.

Greenawalt, Kent. *Religious Convictions and Political Choice.* New York: Oxford University Press, 1988.

Hackett, Rosalind I. J., ed. *New Religious Movements in Nigeria.* Lewiston, N.Y.: Edwin Mellen Press, 1987.

Hallowell, John H. *The Moral Foundation of Democracy.* Chicago: University of Chicago Press, 1954.

Hamilton, Alexander, James Madison, and John Jay. *The Federalist Papers.* Introduction by Clinton Rossiter. New York: New American Library, 1961.

Hampshire, Stuart. *Two Theories of Morality.* Oxford: Oxford University Press, 1977.

Hennelly, Alfred T., and John Langan, eds. *Human Rights in the Americas: The Struggle for Consensus.* Washington, D.C.: Georgetown University Press, 1982.

Hessel, Dieter T., ed. *The Church's Public Role: Retrospect and Prospect.* Grand Rapids, Mich.: Eerdmans, 1993.

Hiskett, Mervyn. *A History of Hausa Islamic Verse.* London: University of London, School of Oriental and African Studies, 1975.

————. *The Sword of Truth: The Life and Times of the Shehu Usuman dan Fodio.* New York: Oxford University Press, 1973.

Hobbes, Thomas. *Leviathan*. Edited, with an introduction, by C. B. Macpherson. Harmondsworth: Penguin Books, 1968.

Hocking, William Ernest. *The Coming World Civilization*. New York: Harper and Row, 1956.

Hodgkin, Thomas. *Nigerian Perspectives: An Historical Anthology*. West African History Series. London: Oxford University Press, 1960.

Hollenbach, David. *Justice, Peace, and Human Rights: American Catholic Social Ethics in a Pluralistic Context*. New York: Crossroad, 1988.

Hooper, J. Leon. *The Ethics of Discourse: The Social Philosophy of John Courtney Murray*. Washington, D.C.: Georgetown University Press, 1986.

Hughey, Michael W. *Civil Religion and Moral Order: Theoretical and Historical Dimensions*. Westport, Conn.: Greenwood Press, 1983.

Hunter, James Davison. *Culture Wars: The Struggle to Define America*. New York: Basic Books, 1991.

Huntington, Samuel P. *Political Order in Changing Societies*. New Haven: Yale University Press, 1968.

Hunwick, John O., ed. *Religion and National Integration in Africa: Islam, Christianity, and Politics in the Sudan and Nigeria*. Evanston, Ill.: Northwestern University Press, 1992.

Idowu, E. Bolaji. *African Traditional Religion: A Definition*. London: SCM, 1973.

———. *God in Nigerian Belief*. Lagos: Federal Ministry of Information, 1963.

———. *Towards an Indigenous Church*. Oxford: Oxford University Press, 1965.

James, William. *Essays in Radical Empiricism: A Pluralistic Universe*. 2 vols. in one. New York: Longmans, Green, 1958.

Johnson, Samuel. *The History of the Yorubas, from the Earliest Times to the Beginning of the British Protectorate*. Lagos: CMS Bookshops, 1921.

Joseph, Richard A. *Democracy and Prebendal Politics in Nigeria:*

The Rise and Fall of the Second Republic. Cambridge: Cambridge University Press, 1987.

Kalu, O. U., ed. *The History of Christianity in West Africa*. London: Longman, 1980.

Khaldūn, Ibn. *The Muqaddimah: An Introduction to History*. 3 vols., Translated by Franz Rosenthal. London: Routledge and Kegan Paul, 1958.

Kirk-Greene, A. H. M. *Crisis and Conflict in Nigeria: A Documentary Sourcebook*. 2 vols. London: Oxford University Press, 1971.

Kuper, Leo, and M. G. Smith, eds. *Pluralism in Africa*. Berkeley: University of California Press, 1971.

Laitin, David. *Hegemony and Culture: Politics and Religious Change among the Yoruba*. Chicago: University of Chicago Press, 1986.

Lambton, Ann K. S. *State and Government in Medieval Islam: An Introduction to the Study of Islamic Political Theory: The Jurists*. London Oriental Series, vol. 36. Oxford: Oxford University Press, 1981.

Laski, H. J. *Authority in the Modern State*. New Haven: Yale University Press, 1919.

Lasswell, Harold. *Politics: Who Gets What, When, How*. New York: Meridian Books, 1958.

Last, Murray. *The Sokoto Caliphate*. London: Longman, 1967.

Lawrence, Bruce B. *Defenders of God: The Fundamentalist Revolt against the Modern Age*. San Francisco: Harper and Row, 1989.

Lippman, Walter. *Essays in the Public Philosophy*. Boston: Little, Brown, 1955.

Lipset, Seymour M. *Political Man: The Social Bases of Politics*. Expanded ed. Baltimore: Johns Hopkins University Press, 1981.

Locke, John. "A Letter Concerning Toleration" in Focus, edited by John Horton and Susan Mendus. London: Routledge, 1991.

Lonergan, Bernard. *Insight: A Study of Human Understanding*. New York: Philosophical Library, 1958.

Lovin, Robin W., ed. *Religion and American Public Life: Interpretations and Explorations*. New York: Paulist Press, 1986.

Lugard, F. J. D. *Political Memoranda: Revision of Instructions to Political Officers on Subjects Chiefly Political and Administrative, 1913–1918.* 3d ed. London: Frank Cass, 1970.

Mackintosh, John P., ed. *Nigerian Government and Politics.* London: Allen and Unwin, 1966.

Makozi, A. O., and O. J. A. Ojo, eds. *History of the Catholic Church in Nigeria.* Ibadan: Macmillan, 1982.

Mala, Sam Babs, and Z. I. Oseni, eds. *Religion, Peace, and Unity in Nigeria.* Ibadan: Nigerian Association for the Study of Religions, 1984.

Maritain, Jacques. *Man and the State.* Chicago: University of Chicago Press, 1951.

Martin, David. *The Breaking of the Image: A Sociology of Christian Theory and Practice.* Oxford: Blackwell, 1980.

———. *A General Theory of Secularization.* New York: Harper and Row, 1978.

Marx, Karl. *Selected Works.* Moscow: Progress, 1982.

Marx, Karl, Friedrich Engels, and V. I. Lenin. *On Historical Materialism: A Collection.* Moscow: Progress, 1976.

Maston, T. B. *Christianity and World Issues.* New York: Macmillan, 1957.

May, William F. *The Physician's Covenant: Images of the Healer in Medical Ethics.* Philadelphia: Westminster Press, 1983.

Mbiti, John. *African Religions and Philosophy.* London: Heinemann, 1969.

McLellan, David. *The Thought of Karl Marx: An Introduction.* 2d ed. London: Macmillan, 1980.

Metz, Johannes B. *Theology of the World.* Translated by William Glen-Doepel. New York: Herder and Herder, 1969.

Mews, Stuart, ed. *Religion in Politics: A World Guide.* Harlow, Essex: Longman, 1989.

Mill, John Stuart. *Collected Works of John Stuart Mill,* edited by J. M. Robson. Vol. 19. Considerations on Representative Government. Toronto: University of Toronto Press, 1977.

————. *Essays on Politics and Culture.* Edited by Gertrude Himmelfarb. Garden City, N.Y.: Doubleday, 1962.

————. *John Stuart Mill: A Selection of His Works.* Edited by J. M. Robson. New York: Odyssey Press, 1966.

Mol, Hans. *Identity and the Sacred: A Sketch for a New Social-Scientific Theory of Religion.* Oxford: Basil Blackwell, 1976.

Mooney, Christopher F. *Boundaries Dimly Perceived: Law, Religion, Education, and the Common Good.* Notre Dame, Ind.: University of Notre Dame Press, 1990.

Moore, G. E. *Principia Ethica.* 1902. Reprint, Buffalo: Prometheus Books, 1988.

Mouw, Richard, and Sander Griffioen. *Pluralisms and Horizons: An Essay in Christian Public Philosophy.* Grand Rapids, Mich.: Eerdmans, 1993.

Mudimbe, V. Y. *The Invention of Africa: Gnosis, Philosophy, and the Order of Knowledge.* Bloomington: Indiana University Press, 1988.

Muffet, D. J. M. *Let Truth Be Told.* Zaria: Hudahuda, 1982.

Murray, John Courtney. *The Pattern for Peace and the Papal Peace Program.* Pamphlet of the Catholic Association for International Peace. Washington, D.C.: Paulist Press, 1944.

————. *The Problem of Religious Freedom.* Westminster, Md.: Newman Press, 1965.

————. *We Hold These Truths: Catholic Reflections on the American Proposition.* New York: Sheed and Ward, 1960; New York: Doubleday, Image Books, 1964.

Neuhaus, Richard John. *The Naked Public Square: Religion and Democracy in America.* 2d ed. Grand Rapids, Mich.: Eerdmans, 1984.

Ngwoke, Ikem B. C. *Religion and Religious Liberty in Nigerian Law: From the Colonial Days to 1983.* Rome: Pontificia Universita Lateranense, 1984.

Nicholls, David. *The Pluralist State.* London: Macmillan, 1975.

————. *Three Varieties of Pluralism.* London: Macmillan, 1974.

Niebuhr H. Richard. *Christ and Culture*. New York: Harper and Row, 1951.

Niebuhr, Reinhold. *Beyond Tragedy: Essays on the Christian Interpretation of History*. New York: Scribner's, 1937.

——. *The Children of Light and the Children of Darkness: A Vindication of Democracy and a Critique of Its Traditional Defense*. New York: Scribner's, 1944; Scribner Library Edition, 1960.

——. *Christian Realism and Political Problems*. New York: Scribner's, 1953; Fairfield, N.J.: Augustus M. Kelley, 1977.

——. *The Contribution of Religion to Cultural Unity*. Hazen Pamphlets, no. 13 (1945).

——. *The Irony of American History*. New York: Scribner's, 1952.

——. *Love and Justice: Selections from the Shorter Writings of Reinhold Niebuhr*. Edited by D. B. Robertson. Louisville, Westminster/John Knox Press, 1957.

——. *Moral Man and Immoral Society: A Study in Ethics and Politics*. New York: Scribner's, 1932; Scribner Library Edition, 1960.

——. *The Nature and Destiny of Man: A Christian Interpretation*, Vol. 1, *Human Nature*. Vol. 2, *Human Destiny*. New York: Scribner's, 1941-1943; Scribner Library Edition, 1964.

——. *Reinhold Niebuhr on Politics: His Political Philosophy and Its Application to Our Age as Expressed in His Writings*. Edited by Harry R. Davis and Robert C. Good. New York: Scribner's, 1960.

Nigerian Supreme Council for Islamic Affairs. *Constitution of the Nigerian Supreme Council for Islamic Affairs*. Kano, Nigeria: Rasco Press, n.d.

Nisbet, Robert. *The Social Philosophers: Community and Conflict in Western Thought*. New York: Crowell, 1973.

Noll, Mark A., ed. *Religion and American Politics: From the Colonial Period to the 1980s*. New York: Oxford University Press, 1990.

Novak, Michael. *The Spirit of Democratic Capitalism*. New York: Simon and Schuster, 1982.

Nwabueze, B. O. *Nigeria's Presidential Constitution, 1979–1983: The Second Experiment in Constitutional Democracy.* London: Longman, 1985.

Obilade, A. O. *The Nigerian Legal System.* London: Sweet and Maxwell, 1979.

Ofonagoro, W. I., Abiola Ojo, and Adele Jinadu, eds. *The Great Debate: Nigerians' Viewpoints on the Draft Constitution, 1976–77.* Lagos: Times Publication, 1978.

Olupona, Jacob K. *Kingship, Religion, and Rituals in a Nigerian Community: A Phenomenological Study of Ondo Yoruba Festivals.* Stockholm: Almqvist and Wiksell International, 1991.

Olupona, Jacob K., and Toyin Falola, eds. *Religion and Society in Nigeria: Historical and Sociological Perspectives.* Ibadan: Spectrum Books, 1991

Oyeleye, Oyediran, ed. *Survey of Nigerian Affairs, 1975.* Ibadan: University Press, 1980.

———. *Survey of Nigerian Affairs, 1976–77.* Lagos: Nigerian Institute of International Affairs and Macmillan, 1981.

Paden, John N. *Ahmadu Bello, Sardauna of Sokoto: Values and Leadership in Nigeria.* London: Hodder and Stoughton, 1986.

———. *Religion and Political Culture in Kano.* Berkeley: University of California Press, 1973.

Palmer, Parker J., Barbara G. Wheeler, and James W. Fowler, eds. *Caring for the Commonweal: Education for Religious and Public Life.* Macon, Ga.: Mercer University Press, 1990.

Pateman, Carole. *Participation and Democratic Theory.* Cambridge: Cambridge University Press, 1970.

Peel, J. D. Y. *Ijeshas and Nigerians: The Incorporation of a Yoruba Kingdom, 1890s–1970s.* Cambridge: Cambridge University Press, 1983.

Pelotte, Donald E. *John Courtney Murray: Theologian in Conflict.* New York: Paulist Press, 1976.

Perry, Michael J. *Love and Power: The Role of Religion and Morality in American Politics.* New York: Oxford University Press, 1991.

Pfeffer, Leo. *God, Caesar, and the Constitution: The Court as Referee of Church-State Confrontation.* Boston: Beacon Press, 1975.

Post, Kenneth, and Michael Vickers. *Structure and Conflict in Nigeria, 1960–1966.* London: Heinemann, 1973.

Pye, Lucian W. *Aspects of Political Development: An Analytic Study.* Boston: Little, Brown, 1966.

Pye, Lucian, and Sidney Verba, eds. *Political Culture and Political Development.* Princeton: Princeton University Press, 1965.

Rabushka, Alvin, and Kenneth A. Shepsle. *Politics in Plural Societies: A Theory of Democratic Instability.* Columbus, Ohio: Charles E. Merrill, 1972.

Robbins, Thomas, and Roland Robertson, eds. *Church-State Relations: Tensions and Transitions.* New Brunswick, N.J.: Transaction Books, 1987.

Robertson, D. B., ed. *Love and Justice: Selections from the Shorter Writings of Reinhold Niebuhr.* Louisville: Westminster/John Knox Press, 1957.

Rosenthal, Erwin I. J. *Political Thought in Medieval Islam: An Introductory Outline.* Cambridge: Cambridge University Press, 1958; Westport, Conn.: Greenwood Press, 1985.

Rupp, George. *Commitment and Community.* Minneapolis: Fortress Press, 1989.

Samartha, S. J. *One Christ, Many Religions: Toward a Revised Christology.* Maryknoll, N.Y.: Orbis Books, 1991.

Sanneh, Lamin. *Encountering the West: Christinaity and the Global Cultural Process: The African Dimension.* Maryknoll, N.Y.: Orbis Books, 1993.

———. *West African Christianity: The Religious Impact.* Maryknoll, N.Y.: Orbis Books, 1983.

Schacht, Joseph. *The Origins of Muhammadan Jurisprudence.* Oxford: Clarendon Press, 1959.

Schattschneider, E. E. *Party Government.* New York: Holt, Rinehart and Winston, 1942.

Shue, Henry. *Basic Rights: Subsistence, Affluence, and U.S. Foreign Policy.* Princeton: Princeton University Press, 1980.

Sklar, Richard L. *Nigerian Political Parties: Power in an Emergent African Nation.* Princeton: Princeton University Press, 1963.

Soskice, Janet Martin. *Metaphor and Religious Language.* Oxford: Clarendon Press, 1985.

Stackhouse, Max L. *Creeds, Society, and Human Rights: A Study in Three Cultures.* Grand Rapids, Mich.: Eerdmans, 1984.

Stevenson, C. L. *Facts and Values: Studies in Ethical Analysis.* New Haven: Yale University Press, 1963.

Sturm, Douglas. *Community and Alienation: Essays on Process, Thought, and Public Life.* Notre Dame, Ind.: University of Notre Dame Press, 1988.

Taylor, Charles. *Multiculturalism and "The Politics of Recognition": An Essay.* Edited by Amy Gutmann. Princeton: Princeton University Press, 1992.

TEKAN. *Towards the Right Path for Nigeria.* Jos, TEKAN, 1987.

Thiemann, Ronald F. *Constructing a Public Theology: The Church in a Pluralistic Culture.* Louisville: Westminster/John Knox Press, 1991.

Thompson, Kenneth. *Beliefs and Ideology.* London: Tavistock, 1986.

Tocqueville, Alexis de. *Democracy in America.* 2 vols. New York: Schocken Books, 1961.

Troeltsch, Ernst. *Religion in History.* Translated by James Luther Adams and Walter F. Bense. Minneapolis: Fortress Press, 1991.

Turner, Victor. *Dramas, Fields, and Metaphors: Symbolic Action in Human Society.* Ithaca: Cornell University Press, 1974.

Usman, Y. B. *The Manipulation of Religion in Nigeria, 1977–1987.* Kaduna, Nigeria: Vanguard, 1987.

Wald, Kenneth. *Religion and Politics in the United States.* New York: St. Martin's Press, 1987.

Walzer, Michael. *Spheres of Justice: A Defense of Pluralism and Equality.* New York: Basic Books, 1983.

West, Cornel. *Prophetic Fragments: Illuminations of the Crisis in American Religion and Culture.* Grand Rapids, Mich.: Eerdmans, 1988.

Whitaker, C. S. *The Politics of Tradition: Continuity and Change in Northern Nigeria, 1946-1966.* Princeton: Princeton University Press, 1970.

Wilson, Bryan. *Religion in Sociological Perspective.* Oxford: Oxford University Press, 1982.

Wolterstorff, Nicholas. *Until Justice and Peace Embrace.* Grand Rapids, Mich.: Eerdmans, 1983.

Young, Crawford. *Ideology and Development in Africa.* New Haven: Yale University Press, 1982.

————. *The Politics of Cultural Pluralism.* Madison: University of Wisconsin Press, 1976.

————, ed. *The Rising Tide of Cultural Pluralism: The Nation-State at Bay?* Madison: University of Wisconsin Press, 1993.

B. Published Articles

Adams, James Luther. "Mediating Structures and the Separation of Powers." In *Democracy and Mediating Structures: A Theological Inquiry,* edited by Michael Novak, 1-33. Washington, D.C.: American Enterprise for Public Policy Research, 1980.

Adedeji, Adebayo. "Ensuring a Successful Transition." *West Africa* (11-17 November 1991): 1878-79.

Adediran, Biodun. "The Origins of Nigerian Peoples." In *Nigerian History and Culture,* edited by Richard Olaniyan, 10-19. Harlow, England: Longman, 1985.

Afigbo, A. E. "Christian Missions and Secular Authorities in South-Eastern Nigeria from Colonial Times." In *The History of Christianity in West Africa,* edited by O. U. Kalu, 187-99. London: Longman, 1980.

————. "The Missions, the State, and Education in South-Eastern Nigeria, 1956-1971." In *Christianity in Independent Africa,* edited by Edward Fashole-Luke et al., 176-92. Bloomington: Indiana University Press, 1978.

Agbaje, Adigun. "Travails of the Secular State: Religion, Politics, and the Outlook on Nigeria's Third Republic." *Journal of Commonwealth and Comparative Politics* 28, 3 (1990): 288–308.

Agbese, Dan. "The Long Shadow." *Newswatch,* 6 May 1991.

Aguda, T. A. "The Judiciary under the Draft Constitution." In *The Great Debate: Nigerians' Viewpoints on the Draft Constitution, 1976–77,* edited by W. I. Ofonagoro, Abiola Ojo and Adele Jinadu, 358–59. Lagos: Times Publications, 1978.

Ahanotu, Austin. "Muslims and Christians in Nigeria: A Contemporary Political Discourse." In *Religion, State, and Society in Contemporary Africa: Nigeria, Sudan, South Africa, Zaire, and Mozambique,* edited by Austin M. Ahanotu, 11–69. New York: Peter Lang, 1992.

Ajayi, J. F. Ade. "Colonialism: An Episode in African History." In *Colonialism in Africa,* edited by L. H. Gann and P. Duignan, 1:497–508. Cambridge: Cambridge University Press, 1969.

Akinrinade, Olusola, and M. A. Ojo. "Religion and Politics in Contemporary Nigeria: A Study of the 1986 OIC Crisis." *Journal of Asian and African Studies* 4, 1 (Fall 1992): 44–59.

Akinyemi, A. Bolaji. "Religion and Foreign Affairs: Press Attitudes towards the Nigerian Civil War." *Jerusalem Journal of International Relations* 4, 3 (1980): 56–81.

Allen, Joseph L. "Power and Political Community." *Annual of the Society of Christian Ethics* (1993): 3–20.

Aluko, Olajide. "Nigeria's Foreign Policy." In *Nigerian History and Culture,* edited by Richard Olaniyan, 211–19. Harlow, England: Longman, 1985.

An-Na'im, Abdullahi Ahmed. "Islam and National Integration in the Sudan." In *Religion and National Integration in Africa: Islam, Christianity, and Politics in the Sudan and Nigeria,* edited by John O. Hunwick, 1–38. Evanston, Ill.: Northwestern University Press, 1992.

———. "Qur'an, Sharī'a, and Human Rights: Foundations, Deficiencies and Prospects." In *The Ethics of World Religions and Human*

Rights, edited by Hans Küng and Jürgen Moltmann, 6-69. Concilium 1990/2. London: SCM Press, 1990.

Atanda, J. A. "Paradoxes and Problems of Religion and Secularism in Nigeria: Suggestions for Solutions." In *Nigeria since Independence: The First Twenty-Five Years.* Vol. 9, *Religion,* edited by J. A. Atanda, Garba Ashiwaju, and Yaya Abubakar, 184-94. Ibadan: Heinemann, 1989.

Audi, Robert. "The Separation of Church and State and the Obligations of Citizenship." *Philosophy and Public Affairs* 18, 3 (1989): 259-96.

Ayandele, E. A. "The Missionary Factor in Northern Nigeria 1870-1918." In *The History of Christianity in West Africa,* edited by O. U. Kalu, 133-57. London: Longman, 1980.

Babangida, Ibrahim. "Agitation for New States Is Healthy." *Guardian,* 28 August, 1991.

Babarinsa, Dare. "Military Leadership: A Battle with the Genie." *Newswatch,* 8 October 1990.

Balogun, S. A. "Islam in Nigeria: Its Historical Development." In *Nigeria since Independence: The First Twenty-Five Years.* Vol. 9, *Religion,* edited by J. A. Atanda, Garba Ashiwaju, and Yaya Abubakar, 54-70. Ibadan: Heinemann, 1989.

Bayart, Jean-François. "Civil Society in Africa." In *Political Domination in Africa: Reflections on the Limits of Power,* edited by Patrick Chabal, 109-25. Cambridge: Cambridge University Press, 1986.

Benavides, Gustavo, "Religious Articulation of Power." In *Religion and Political Power,* edited by Gustavo Benavides and M. W. Daly, 1-15. Albany: State University of New York Press, 1989.

Bernstein, Richard J. "The Meaning of Public Life." In *Religion and American Public Life: Interpretations and Explorations,* edited by Robin W. Lovin, 29-52. New York: Paulist Press, 1986.

Bienen, Henry. "Religion, Legitimacy, and Conflict in Nigeria." *Annals of the American Academy of Political and Social Science* 483 (1986): 50-60.

Birai, Umar M. "Islamic Tajdid and the Political Process in Nigeria." In *Fundamentalisms and the State: Remaking Polities, Econo-*

mies, and Militance. The Fundamentalism Project. Vol. 3, edited by Martin E. Marty and R. Scott Appleby, 184–203. Chicago: University of Chicago Press, 1993.

Breitling, Rupert. "The Concept of Pluralism." In *Three Faces of Pluralism: Political, Ethnic, and Religious,* edited by Stanislaw Ehrlich and Graham Wootton, 1–19. Farnborough, England: Gower, 1980.

Bratton, Michael. "Civil Society in Africa." In *Beyond Autocracy in Africa.* Working papers for the inaugural seminar of the Governance in Africa Program, 29–34. Carter Center of Emory University, Atlanta, 17–18 February 1989.

———. "Enabling the Voluntary Sector in Africa: The Policy Context." In *African Governance in the 1990s: Objectives, Resources and Constraints.* Working papers from the 2d annual seminar of the African Governance Program, 104–13. Carter Center of Emory University, Atlanta, 23–25 March 1990.

Brenner, Louis. "The Jihad Debate between Sokoto and Borno: An Historical Analysis of Islamic Political Discourse in Nigeria." In *People and Empires in African History: Essays in Memory of Michael Crowder,* edited by J. F. Ade Ajayi and J. D. Y. Peel, 21–43. London: Longman, 1992.

———. "Muhammad al-Amin al-Kanimi and Religion and Politics in Bornu." In *Studies in West African Islamic History.* Vol 1., *The Cultivators of Islam,* edited by John Ralph Willis, 160–76. London: Frank Cass, 1979.

Bukarambe, Bukar. "Nigeria and the Arab World." In *Nigeria's External Relations: The First Twenty-Five Years,* edited by G. O. Olusanya and R. A. Akindele, 420–35. Ibadan: University Press, 1986.

Callaghy, Thomas M. "Politics and Vision in Africa: The Interplay of Domination, Equality, and Liberty." In *Political Domination in Africa: Reflections on the Limits of Power,* edited by Patrick Chabal, 30–51. Cambridge: Cambridge University Press, 1986.

Carney, Frederick S. "Outline of a Natural Law Procedure for Christian Ethics." *Journal of Religion* 47, 1 (January 1967): 26–37.

————. "Some Aspects of Islamic Ethics." *Journal of Religion* 63, 2 (April 1983): 159-74.

Chabal, Patrick. "Introduction: Thinking about Politics in Africa." In *Political Domination in Africa: Reflections on the Limits of Power,* edited by Patrick Chabal, 1-16. Cambridge: Cambridge University Press, 1986.

Clarke, Peter B. "Islam, Development and African Identity: The Case of West Africa." In *Religion, Development, and African Identity,* edited by Kirsten Holst Petersen, 127-46. Uppsala: Scandinavian Institute of African Studies, 1987.

————. "Religion and Political Attitude since Independence." In *Religion and Society in Nigeria: Historical and Sociological Perspectives,* edited by Jacob K. Olupona and Toyin Falola, 216-29. Ibadan: Spectrum Books, 1991.

————. "The Religious Factor in the Developmentmental Process in Nigeria: A Socio-Historical Analysis." *Genève-Afrique* 17,1 (1979): 45-64.

Crampton, E. P. T. "Christianity in Northern Nigeria." In *Christianity in West Africa: The Nigerian Story,* edited by Ogbu Kalu, 1-237. Ibadan: Daystar Press, 1978.

Dahl, Robert A. "Pluralism Revisited." In *Three Faces of Pluralism: Political, Ethnic, and Religious,* edited by Stanislaw Ehrlich and Graham Wootton, 20-33. Farnborough, England: Gower, 1980.

Danmole, H. O. "The Religious Factor in Nigerian Politics: Awolowo and the Muslims, 1957-1983." In *Obafemi Awolowo: The End of an Era?,* edited by Olasope O. Oyelaran, Toyin Falola, Mokwugo Okoye, and Adewale Thompson, 874-98. Ile-Ife, Nigeria: Obafemi Awolowo University Press, 1988.

Dare, Leo. "Political Change in Nigeria." In *Social Change in Nigeria,* edited by Simi Afonja and Tola Olu Pearce, 71-91. White Plains: Longman, 1986.

Demerath, N. J., and Rhys H. Williams. "A Mythical Past and Uncertain Future." In *Church-State Relations: Tensions and Transitions,* edited by Thomas Robbins and Roland Robertson, 77-90. New Brunswick, N.J.: Transaction Books, 1987.

Deng, Francis. "Let's Define Arab and African in Terms That Will Shed Light on the Common Ground." *Middle East Report* 21, 5 (September/October 1991): 31-33, 38.

———. "A Three-Dimensional Approach to the Conflict in the Sudan." In *Religion and National Integration in Africa: Islam, Christianity, and Politics in Sudan and Nigeria,* edited by John O. Hunwick, 39-62. Evanston, Ill.: Northwestern University Press, 1992.

Diamond, Larry. "Beyond Autocracy: Prospects for Democracy in Nigeria." In *Beyond Autocracy in Africa.* Working papers for the inaugural seminar of the Governance in Africa Program, 25-28. Carter Center of Emory University, Atlanta, 17–18 February 1989.

———. "Class Formation in the Swollen African State." *Journal of Modern African Studies* 25, 4 (1987): 567-96.

———. "Issues in the Constitutional Design of a Third Nigerian Republic." *African Affairs* 86 (1987): 209-26.

———. "Nigeria: Pluralism, Statism, and the Struggle for Democracy." In *Politics in Developing Countries: Comparing Experiences with Democracy,* edited by Larry Diamond, Juan J. Linz, and Seymour Martin Lipset, 351-410. Boulder: Lynne Rienner, 1990.

Douglas, R. Bruce. "Public Philosophy and Contemporary Pluralism (or, The Murray Problem Revisited)." *Thought* 64, 255 (December 1989): 344-61.

Ejiofor, L. U. "Judicial Systems for Nigeria." *Daily Star,* 29 January 1977.

Ekeh, Peter. "Colonialism and the Two Publics in Africa: A Theoretical Statement." *Comparative Studies in Society and History* 17, 1 (1975): 91-112.

Ekoko, A. E., and L. A. Amadi. "Religion and Stability in Nigeria." In *Nigeria Since Independence: The First Twenty-Five Years.* Vol. 9, *Religion,* edited by J. A. Atanda, Garba Ashiwaju, and Yaya Abubakar, 110-33. Ibadan: Heinemann, 1989.

Galston, William A. "Pluralism and Social Unity." *Ethics* 99, 4 (July 1989): 711-26.

Gambari, Ibrahim. "British Colonial Administration." In *Nigerian History and Culture,* edited by Richard Olaniyan, 159-75. Essex: Longman, 1985.

——. "The Role of Religion in National Life: Reflections on Recent Experiences in Nigeria." In *Religion and National Integration in Africa,* edited by John O. Hunwick, 85-100. Evanston, Ill.: Northwestern University Press, 1992.

Garaudy, Roger. "Human Rights and Islam: Foundation, Tradition, Violation." In *The Ethics of World Religions and Human Rights,* edited by Hans Küng and Jürgen Moltmann, 46-60. Concilium 1990/2. London: SCM Press, 1990.

Haar, Gerrie ter. "Religious Education in Africa: Traditional, Islamic, and Christian." *Exchange* XVII, 17, 50 (September 1988): 1-88.

Hackett, Rosalind I. J., and Jacob K. Olupona. "Civil Religion." In *Religion and Society in Nigeria: Historical and Sociological Perspectives,* edited by Jacob K. Olupona and Toyin Falola, 265-81. Ibadan: Spectrum Books, 1991.

Hehir, J. Bryan. "The Catholic Bishops and the Nuclear Debate: A Case Study of the Independent Sector." In *Religion, the Independent Sector, and American Culture,* edited by Conrad Cherry and Rowland A. Sherrill, 98-112. Atlanta: Scholars Press, 1992.

Herberg, William. "Religious Group Conflict in America." In *Religion and Social Conflict,* edited by Robert Lee and Martin E. Marty, 127-42. New York: Oxford University Press, 1964.

Hessel, Dieter T. "Making a Public Difference after the Eclipse." In *The Church's Public Role: Retrospect and Prospect,* edited by Dieter T. Hessel, 1-20. Grand Rapids, Mich.: Eerdmans, 1993.

Hiskett, Mervyn. "Islam in Hausa Political Verse Propaganda from 1946 to Northern Nigerian Independence." In *Christian and Islamic Contributions towards Establishing Independent States in Africa, South of the Sahara,* edited by J. D. Y. Peel. Papers and proceedings of the Africa Colloquium, Bonn Bad Godesberg, 2-4 May 1979, 100-114. Stuttgart: Institut für Auslandsbeziehungen, 1979.

Hoffman, Stanley. "Reaching for the Most Difficult: Human Rights as a Foreign Policy Goal." *Daedalus* 112 (1983): 19-49.

Hollenbach, David, S.J. Foreword to *The Ethics of Discourse: The Social Philosophy of John Courtney Murray,* by J. Leon Hooper. Washington, D.C.: Georgetown University Press, 1986.

————. "Religion and Public Life." *Theological Studies* 52, 1 (March 1991): 87-106.

Horton, Robin. "African Conversion." *Africa* 41 (1971): 85-108.

Ibrahim, Jibrin. "The Politics of Religion in Nigeria: The Parameters of the 1987 Crisis in Kaduna State." *Review of African Political Economy* 45/46 (1989): 65-82.

Idowu, E. Bolaji. Foreword to *Government Policy on Education at Both the Federal and State Levels Has Left a Lot to Be Desired,* by Justice O. A. Esin. Lagos: Methodist Literature Department, 1980.

Ikenga-Metuh, E. "Religious Education in State-Controlled Schools in Nigeria." In *Religion, Peace, and Unity in Nigeria,* edited by Sam Babs Mala and Z. I. Oseni, 136-52. Ibadan: Nigerian Association for the Study of Religions, 1984.

Ilega, D. I. "Religion and 'Godless' Nationalism in Colonial Nigeria: The Case of the God's Kingdom Society and the NCNC." *Journal of Religion in Africa,* 18, 2 (1988): 163-82.

Iroh, Eddie. "Winning at All Costs." *Newswatch,* 30 November, 1992.

Jeyifo, Biodun. "For Chinua Achebe: The Resilience and the Predicament of Obierika." In *Chinua Achebe: A Celebration,* edited by Kirsten Holst Petersen and Anna Rutherford, 51-70. Oxford: Heinemann, 1990.

Joseph, R. A. "National Objectives and Public Accountability: An Analysis of the Draft Constitution." In *Issues in the Nigerian Draft Constitution,* edited by Suleimanu Kumo and Abubakar Aliyu, 1-12. Report of the confernce held at the Institute of Administration, Ahmadu Bello University, 21-24 March 1977. Zaria: Ahmadu Bello University Press, 1977.

Kalu, Ogbu U. "Christianity and Colonial Society." In *The History of*

Christianity in West Africa, edited by Ogbu U. Kalu, 182-86. London: Longman, 1980.

————. "Religions in Nigeria: An Overview." In *Nigeria since Independence: The First Twenty-Five Years.* Vol. 9, *Religion,* edited by J. A. Atanda, Garba Ashiwaju, and Yaya Abubakar, 11-24. Ibadan: Heinemann, 1989.

Kirk-Greene, A. H. M. "'A Sense of Belonging': The Nigerian Constitution of 1979 and the Promotion of National Loyalty." *Journal of Commonwealth and Comparative Politics* 28, 3 (1990): 158-72.

————. "Ethnic Engineering and the Federal Character of Nigeria: Boon of Contentment or Base of Contention?" *Ethnic and Racial Studies* 6, 4 (1983): 457-76.

Knitter, Paul F. "Common Ground or Common Response? Seeking Foundations for Interreligious Discourse." *Studies in Interreligious Dialogue* 2, 2 (1992): 111-22.

Laitin, David D. "Religion, Political Culture, and the Weberian Tradition." *World Politics* 30, 4 (July 1978): 563-92.

————. "The Sharia Debate and the Origins of Nigeria's Second Republic." *Journal of Modern African Studies* 20, 3 (1982): 411-30.

Laski, H. J. "The Pluralistic State." *Philosophical Review* 28 (1919): 562-75.

Last, D. M. "Some Economic Aspects of Conversion in Hausaland (Nigeria)." In *Conversion to Islam,* edited by Nehemia Levtzion, 247-65. New York: Holmes and Meier, 1979.

Lawuyi, Tunde. "Nigeria in the 1980s: Religion and National Integration." In *Religion and Society in Nigeria: Historical and Sociological Perspectives,* edited by Jacob K. Olupona and Toyin Falola, 230-43. Ibadan: Spectrum Books, 1991.

Lipset, Seymour M. "Social Conflict, Legitimacy, and Democracy." In *Legitimacy and the State,* edited by William Connolly, 88-103. New York: New York University Press, 1984.

Locke, John. "A Letter Concerning Toleration." In *Focus,* edited by John Horton and Susan Mendus, 12-56. London: Routledge, 1991.

Lonsdale, John. "States and Social Processes in Africa: A Historiographical Survey." *Africa Studies Review* 24, 2/3 (1981): 139-224.

Lovin, Robin W. "Perry, Naturalism, and Religion in Public." *Tulane Law Review* 63 (1989): 1517–39.

———. "Religion and American Public Life: Three Relationships." In *Religion and American Public Life: Interpretations and Explorations,* edited by Robin W. Lovin, 7–28. New York: Paulist Press, 1986.

———. "Social Contract or a Public Covenant?" In *Religion and American Public Life: Interpretations and Explorations,* edited by Robin W. Lovin, 132–45. New York: Paulist Press, 1986.

Lubeck, Paul. "Islamic Protest under Semi-Industrial Capitalism: 'Yan Tatsine' Explained." *Africa* 55, 4 (1985): 369–89.

Luckey, William R. "The Contribution of John Courtney Murray, S.J.: A Catholic Perspective." In *John Courtney Murray and the American Civil Conversation,* edited by Robert P. Hunt and Kenneth L. Grasso, 19–43. Grand Rapids, Mich.: Eerdmans, 1992.

Mala, Sam Babs. "Religious Pluralism in Nigeria: The Way Out and Factors Favoring It." In *Religion, Peace, and Unity in Nigeria,* edited by Sam Babs Mala and Z. I. Oseni, 242–63. Ibadan: Nigerian Association for the Study of Religions, 1984.

Markoff, John, and Daniel Regan. "Religion, the State, and Political Legitimacy in the World's Constitutions." In *Church-State Relations: Tensions and Transitions,* edited by Thomas Robbins and Roland Robertson, 161–82. New Brunswick, N.J.: Transaction Books, 1987.

Marshall, Ruth. "Power in the Name of Jesus." *Review of African Political Economy* 52 (1991): 21–37.

Martin, David. "The Secularization Thesis and the Decline of Particular Religions." In *Der Untergang von Religionen,* edited by Hartmut Zinser, 309–19. Berlin: Dietrich Reimer Verlag, 1986.

Marty, Martin E. Foreword to *Religion and American Public Life: Interpretations and Explorartions,* edited by Robin W. Lovin. New York: Paulist Press, 1986.

May, William F. "Public Happiness and Higher Education." In *Caring for the Commonweal: Education for Religious and Public*

Life, edited by Parker J. Palmer, Barbara G. Wheeler, and James W. Fowler, 227-50. Macon, Ga.: Mercer University Press, 1990.

Mazrui, Ali A. "Pluralism and National Integration." In *Pluralism in Africa,* edited by Leo Kuper and M. G. Smith, 333-49. Berkeley: University of California Press, 1971.

Melson, Robert, and Howard Wolpe. "Modernization and the Politics of Communalism: A Theoretical Perspective." In *Nigeria: Modernization and the Politics of Communalism,* edited by Robert Melson and Howard Wolpe, 1-42. East Lansing: Michigan State University Press, 1971.

Mitchell, Basil. Introduction to *Law and Justice. Christian Law Review* 82/83 (1984): 87.

Mitra, Subrata. "The Limits of Accommodation: Nehru, Religion, and the State in India." *South Asian Research* 9, 2 (November 1989): 107-27.

Morton-Williams, Peter. "The Fulani Penetration into Nupe and Yoruba in the Nineteenth Century." In *History and Social Anthropology,* edited by I. M. Lewis, 1-24. London: Tavistock Press, 1968.

Mozia, M. I. "Religion and Morality in Nigeria: An Overview." In *Nigeria since Independence: The First Twenty-Five Years.* Vol. 9, *Religion,* edited by J. A. Atanda, Garba Ashiwaju, and Yaya Abubakar, 168-83. Ibadan: Heinemann, 1989.

Murray, John Courtney. "The Church and Totalitarian Democracy." *Theological Studies* 13 (December 1952): 525-63.

———. "Contemporary Orientations of Catholic Thought on Church and State in the Light of History." *Theological Studies* 10 (June 1949): 177-234.

———. "The Declaration on Religious Freedom: A Moment in its Legislative History." In *Religious Liberty: An End and A Beginning,* edited by John Courtney Murray, 15-44. New York: Macmillan, 1966.

———. "Free Speech in Its Relation to Self-Government." *Georgetown Law Journal* 37 (May 1949): 654-62.

————. "Government Repression of Heresy." *Proceedings of the Third Annual Convention of the Catholic Theological Society of America* (1948): 26-98.

————. "The Issue of Church and State at Vatican II." *Theological Studies* 27 (December 1966): 580-606.

————. "Leo XIII on Church and State: The General Structure of the Controversy." *Theological Studies* 14 (March 1953): 1-30.

————. "Leo XIII: Separation of Church and State." *Theological Studies* 14 (June 1953): 145-214.

————. "Leo XIII: Two Concepts of Government: Government and the Order of Culture." *Theological Studies* 15 (March 1954): 1-33.

————. "The Problem of 'The Religion of the State.'" *American Ecclesiastical Review* 124 (May 1951): 327-52.

————. "Religious Freedom." In *The Documents of Vatican II,* edited by Walter M. Abbott and Joseph Gallagher, 672-700. New York: American Press, 1966.

————. Review of *Free Speech in Its Relation to Self-Government,* by Alexander Meikeljohn (New York: Harper, 1948). *Georgetown Law Journal* 37 (May 1949): 654-62.

Nabofa, M. Y. "Christianity in Nigeria: Its Role in Nation-Building." In *Nigeria since Independence: The First Twenty-Five Years.* Vol. 9, *Religion,* edited by J. A. Atanda, Garba Ashiwaju, and Yaya Abubakar, 98-109. Ibadan: Heinemann, 1989.

Niebuhr, Reinhold. "A Dark Light on Human Nature." *Messenger* 13 (27 April 1948).

O'Connell, James. "Nigeria." In *Religion and Politics: A World Guide,* edited by Stuart Mews. Harlow, England: Longman, 1989.

Ohadike, Don. "Muslim-Christian Conflict and Political Instability in Nigeria." In *Religion and National Integration in Africa,* edited by John O. Hunwick, 101-24. Evanston, Ill.: Northwestern University Press, 1992.

Ojo, Matthews A. "The Contextual Significance of the Charismatic Movements in Independent Nigeria." *Africa* 58, 2 (1988): 175-92.

Olupona, Jacob K. "Beyond Ethnicity: Civil Religion in Nigeria." In

Church Divinity Monograph Series, edited by John H. Morgan, 131-44. Notre Dame, Ind.: Foundations, 1982.

————. "New Religious Movements and the Nigerian Social Order." In *New Religious Movements and Society in Nigeria,* edited by Gudrun Ludwar-Ene, 31-50. Bayreuth African Studies Series, no. 17. Bayreuth: Eckhard Breitinger, 1991.

————. "Religion and Politics in the Second Republic." In *Nigeria's Second Republic: Presidentialism, Politics, and Administration in a Developing State,* edited by Victor Ayeni and Kayode Soreme-kun, 121-34. Lagos: Times Publications, 1988.

————. "Religion, Ideology, and the Social Order: Civil Religion in Nigeria" In *Religion and State: The Nigerian Experience,* edited by S. A. Adewale, 77-95. Ibadan: Orita Publications, 1988.

————. "Religion, Law and Order: State Regulation of Religious Affairs." *Social Compass* 37, 1 (1990): 127-35.

————. "Religious Pluralism and Civil Religion in Africa." *Dialogue and Alliance* 2, 4 (1988/89): 41-48.

Omoruyi, Omo. "Representation in Federal (Plural) Systems: A Comparative View." In *Readings on Federalism,* edited by A. B. Akinyemi, P. D. Cole, and Walter Ofonagoro, 372-80. Lagos: Nigerian Institute of International Affairs, 1979.

Onaiyekan, John. "Recent History of Religions in Nigeria." In *The Economic and Social Development of Nigeria.* Proceedings of the National Conference on Nigeria since Independence. Vol. 2. Edited by M. O. Kayode and Y. B. Usman, 360-68. Zaria: Panel on Nigeria Since Independence Project, 1983.

Opeloye, Muhib O. "Religious Factor in Nigerian Politics: Implications for Christian-Muslim Relations in Nigeria." *Journal of Institute of Muslim Minority Affairs* 10, 2 (1989): 351-60.

Oshun, C. O. "Ecumenism: An Approach to Peaceful Co-Existence." In *Religion, Peace, and Unity in Nigeria,* edited by Sam Babs Mala and Z. I. Oseni, 107-23. Ibadan: Nigerian Association for the Study of Religions, 1984.

Oyeshola, D. A. "Religious Obstacles to Development in Africa." *Orita,* 23, 1 (1991): 37-48.

Peel, J. D. Y. "The Cultural Work of Yoruba Ethnogenesis." In *History and Ethnicity,* edited by Elizabeth Tonkin, Maryon McDonald, and Malcolm Chapman, 198-215. London: Routledge, 1989.

Pye, Lucian W. "Armies in the Process of Political Modernization." In *Political Development and Social Change,* edited by J. L. Finkle and R. W. Gable. 2d ed. New York: Wiley, 1971.

Ranger, Terence. "The Invention of Tradition in Colonial Africa." In *The Invention of Tradition,* edited by Eric Hobsbawn and Terence Ranger, 211-62. Cambridge: Cambridge University Press, 1983.

Rawls, John. "The Idea of an Overlapping Consensus." *Oxford Journal of Legal Studies* 7 (1987): 1-25.

————. "Justice as Fairness: Political Not Metaphysical." *Philosophy and Public Affairs* 14 (1985): 223-51.

Robertson, Roland. "Church-State Relations in Comparative Perspective." In *Church-State Relations: Tensions and Transitions,* edited by Thomas Robbins and Roland Robertson, 153-60. New Brunswick, N.J.: Transaction Books, 1987.

————. "Considerations from within the American Context on the Significance of Church-State Tension." *Sociological Analysis* 42 (Fall 1981): 193-208.

Salamone, F. A. "Becoming Hausa: Ethnic Identity Change and Its Implications for the Study of Ethnic Pluralism and Stratification." *Africa* 45, 4 (1975): 410-24.

————. "Ethnic Identities and Religion." In *Religion and Society in Nigeria: Historical and Sociological Perspectives,* edited by Jacob K. Olupona and Toyin Falola, 45-65. Ibadan: Spectrum Books, 1991.

Sambo, Justice. "Draft Constitution Fails to Provide for Morality." *New Nigerian,* 5 January 1977.

————. "Morality and the Draft Constitution." In *The Great Debate: Nigerians Viewpoints on the Draft Constitution, 1976-77,* edited by W. I. Ofonagoro. Lagos: Times Publicatons, 1978.

Sampson, Cynthia. "'To Make Real the Bond between Us All': Quaker Conciliation during the Nigerian Civil War." In *Religion, the Missing Dimension of Statecraft,* edited by Douglas Johnston and

Cynthia Sampson, 88-118. New York: Oxford University Press, 1994.

Sanneh, Lamin. "Religion and Politics: Third World Perspectives on a Comparative Religious Theme." *Daedalus* 120, 3 (1991).

———. "Religion, Politics, and National Integration: A Comparative African Perspective." In *Religion and National Integration,* edited by John O. Hunwick, 151-68. Evanston, Ill.: Northwestern University Press, 1992.

Sklar, Richard L. "Democracy in Africa." In *Political Domination in Africa: Reflections on the Limits of Power,* edited by Patrick Chabal, 17-29. Cambridge: Cambridge University Press, 1986.

Smith, M. G. "Institutional and Political Conditions of Pluralism." In *Pluralism in Africa,* edited by Leo Kuper and M. G. Smith, 27-65. Berkeley: University of California Press, 1971.

Stackhouse, Max L. "Public Theology and the Future of Democratic Society." In *The Church's Public Role: Retrospect and Prospect,* edited by Dieter T. Hessel, 63-83. Grand Rapids, Mich.: Eerdmans, 1993.

———. "Religion, Society, and the Independent Sector: Key Elements of a General Theory." In *Religion, the Independent Sector, and American Culture,* edited by Conrad Cherry and Rowland A. Sherill, 11-29. Atlanta: Scholars Press, 1992.

Taylor, Charles. "The Politics of Recognition." In *Multiculturalism and "The Politics of Recognition,"* edited by Amy Gutmann, 25-71. Princeton: Princeton University Press, 1993.

Ubah, C. N. "Islamic Culture and Nigerian Society." In *Traditional and Modern Culture,* edited by Edith Ihekweazu, 225-42. Readings in African Humanities. Enugu, Nigeria: Fourth Dimension, 1985.

Usman, Yusuf Bala. "National Cohesion, National Planning, and the Constitution." In *Issues in the Nigerian Draft Constitution,* edited by Suleimanu Kumo and Abubakar Aliyu, 45-56. Zaria: Ahmadu Bello University Press, 1977.

Wallerstein, Immanuel. "Voluntary Associations." In *Political Parties and National Integration in Tropical Africa,* edited by James S. Coleman and Carl G. Rosberg, 318–39. Berkeley: University of California Press, 1964.

Walls, A. F. "Religion and the Press in 'the Enclave' in the Nigerian Civil War." In *Christianity in Independent Africa,* edited by Edward Fashole-Luke et al., 207–15. Bloomington: Indiana University Press, 1978.

Westerlund, David. "Secularism, Civil Religion or Islam: Islamic Revivalism and the National Question in Nigeria." In *Religion, State, and Society in Contemporary Africa: Nigeria, Sudan, South Africa, Zaire and Mozambique,* edited by Austin Ahanotu, 71–101. New York: Peter Lang, 1992.

Wheeler, Barbara G. "A Forum on Paideia." Introduction to *Caring for the Commonweal: Eduction for Religious and Public Life,* edited by Parker J. Palmer, Barbara G. Wheeler, and James W. Fowler, 1–8. Macon, Ga.: Mercer University Press, 1990.

Whitaker, C. S. "Second Beginnings: The New Political Framework." In *Perspectives on the Second Republic in Nigeria,* edited by C. S. Whitaker, 2–14. Waltham, Mass.: Crossroads, 1981.

Williams, Bayo. "The Paradox of a Nation." *Newswatch* (3 October, 1985): 5–10.

Wilson, John F. "The Public as a Problem." In *Caring for the Commonweal: Education for Religious and Public Life,* edited by Parker J. Palmer, Barbara G. Wheeler, and James W. Fowler, 9–22. Macon, Ga.: Mercer University Press, 1990.

Wiseberg, Laurie W. "Christian Churches and the Nigerian Civil War." *Journal of African Studies* 2, 13 (1975): 297–331.

Young, Crawford. "Beyond Patrimonial Autocracy: The African Challenge." In *Beyond Autocracy in Africa.* Working Papers for the Inaugural Seminar of the Governance in Africa Program, 22–24. Carter Center of Emory University: Atlanta, 17–18 February 1989.

Ziegler, Aloysius K. "Pope Gelasius I and His Teachings on the Relation of Church and State." *Catholic Historical Review* 27 (1942): 412–37.

C. Unpublished Articles

AbdulNasir, Anwal. "Religion and Secularism in the Nigerian Context." Paper presented at the Twenty-Fifth Annual Religious Studies Conference, Ibadan, 17–20 September 1991.

Bratton, Michael. "Enabling the Voluntary Sector in Africa: The Policy Context." In African Governance in the 1990s: Objectives, Resources and Constraints, working paper, 2d annual seminar of the African Governance Program, Carter Center of Emory University, Atlanta, 23–25 March 1990, 105.

Brenner, Louis. "Representations of Power and Powerlessness among West African Muslims." Paper presented to the Colloque Religion et Histoire en Afrique au Sud du Sahara, Paris, 15–17 May 1991.

Diamond, Larry. "The Accountability Gap in the Transition to Democracy in Nigeria." Paper presented at the 33rd annual meeting of the African Studies Association, Baltimore, 1–4 November 1990.

Gbadegesin, Segun. "The Philosophical Foundation of Secularism." Paper presented at the 31st congress of the Historical Society of Nigeria, 18–24 May 1985.

Gbonigi, E. B. "Religion in a Secular Society." Address delivered at the 2d assembly of the Christian Association of Nigeria, Kaduna, 16–17 November 1988.

Hodgkin, Elizabeth. "Islamism and Islamic Research in Africa." Paper prepared for the "Islam in Modern Africa Research Project," Center for African Studies, University of London, 1990.

Ibrahim, Jibrin. "Some Considerations on Religion and Political Turbulence in Nigeria: Muslims, Christians, "Pagans," "Fundamentalists," and All That. . . . Paper presented at the "Social Movements" Seminar, Institute of Social Studies, The Hague, 16 October 1989. Subsequently published as: "Religion and Political Turbulence in Nigeria," *Journal of Modern African Studies* 29, 1 (1991): 115–136.

Kukah, Matthew Hassan. "Religion and Politics in Northern Nigeria since 1960." Ph. D. thesis, University of London, 1989.

Martin, David. "The Limits of Ecumenism." London School of Economics. Mimeographed.

———. "Preliminary Excursus on Centre and Periphery." Southern Methodist University. Mimeographed.

———. "Religious Passion and Civil Tumult: A Sociological Background." Address delivered at the "First Liberty" Summit, Southern Methodist University, Dallas, 25 June 1988.

Muffet, D. J. M. "The Coups D'etat in Nigeria, 1966: A Study in Elite Dynamics." Ph.D. dissertation, University of Pittsburgh, 1971.

Obasanjo, Olusegun. "Nigeria and Sudan: Similarities and Dissimilarities." Paper presented at the U.S. Institute of Peace conference on "Sudan and Nigeria: Religion, Nationalism, and Intolerance," Washington, D.C., 5 October 1991.

Olukunle, O. A. "The Impact of Religion on Nigerian Society: The Future Perspective." Paper presented at the 25th annual Religious Studies Conference, Ibadan, 17-20 September 1991.

Paden, John N. "Religious Identity and Political Values in Nigeria: The Transformation of the Muslim Community." Paper prepared for the Islam and Nationhood Conference, Yale Center for International and Area Studies, Yale University, 12-14 November 1992.

———. "Religious Tolerance and Conflict Resolution in Nigeria." Paper presented at the Conference on Intolerance and Conflict: Sudan and Nigeria, Washington, D.C., 3-5 October 1991.

Reichmuth, Stefan. "The Development of Islamic Learning in Ilorin, Nigeria, and Its Interaction with 'Western' Forms of Education." Paper presented at the conference on "Islamic Identities in Africa," London, 18-20 April 1991.

Sodiq, Yushau. "Muslim-Christian Relations in Nigeria: Causes of Tensions." Paper presented at the 10th annual meeting of the American Council for the Study of Islamic Society, Washington, D.C., 5-6 March 1993.

Thomas, Abraham Vazhayil. "The Role of the Christian Community in a Secular State: India as a Case Study." Th.D. dissertation, Boston University, 1969.

Uwakwe, Paschal S. K. "The Military and the Transition to Democracy in Nigeria, 1970-1979." Seminar paper presented at the School of Oriental and African Studies, University of London, 10 December 1991.

Williams, Patricia A. "The State, Religion, and Politics in Nigeria." Ph.D. thesis, University of Ibadan, Nigeria, 1988.

Yadudu, A. H. "The Prospects for Sharī'a in Nigeria." Paper presented at the conference on "Islam in Africa," Abuja, 24 November 1989.

D. Government Publications

Federal Government of Nigeria, *The Constitution of the Federal Republic of Nigeria.* Lagos: Times Publications, 1979.

———. *The Constitution of the Federal Republic of Nigeria.* Lagos: Government Printers, 1989.

———. *National Policy on Education.* Lagos: Government Printers, 1977.

———. *The Report of the Commission Appointed to Enquire into the Fears of the Minorities and the Means of Allaying Them.* London: Her Majesty's Stationery Office, 1958.

———. *Report of the Constitution Drafting Committee Containing the Draft Constitution.* 2 vols. Lagos: Times Publications, 1976.

———. *Report of the Constitution Review Committee Containing the Reviewed Constitution* [CRC]. Lagos: Government Printers, 1988.

———. *The Report of the Political Bureau.* Abuja: Directorate for Public Enlightenment and Social Mobilization, 1987.

Western Region Government. Western House of Assembly Debates: Official Report. Ibadan, 1958.

E. Newspapers and Magazines

African Concord (Lagos).

African Guardian (Lagos).

Citizen (Kaduna).

National Concord (Lagos).

Daily and Sunday Times (Lagos)

Daily Star (Enugu).

The Guardian (Lagos).

New Nigerian (Kaduna).

Newswatch (Lagos).

The Punch (Ibadan).

Quality (Lagos)

Tafsir

Daily and Sunday Tribunes (Ibadan).

West Africa (London).

West African Pilot (Lagos).

Author Index

Subject Index

DATE DUE

			Printed in USA

HIGHSMITH #45230